Rewarding Teams

Rewarding Teams

Lessons from the Trenches

Glenn Parker, Jerry McAdams, and David Zielinski

Jossey-Bass Publishers
San Francisco

Jossey-Bass books and products are available through most bookstores. To contact Jossey-Bass directly, call (888) 378-2537, fax to (800) 605-2665, or visit our website at www.josseybass.com.

Substantial discounts on bulk quantities of Jossey-Bass books are available to corporations, professional associations, and other organizations. For details and discount information, contact the special sales department at Jossey-Bass.

 Manufactured in the United States of America on Lyons Falls Turin Book. This paper is acid-free and 100 percent totally chlorine-free.

Library of Congress Cataloging-in-Publication Data

Parker, Glenn M., 1938–
Rewarding teams: lessons from the trenches / Glenn Parker, Jerry McAdams, and David Zielinski.— 1st ed.
        p. cm. — (The Jossey-Bass business & management series)
Includes bibliographical references and index.
ISBN 0–7879–4809–8
1. Incentives in industry. 2. Incentive awards. 3. Teams in the workplace. I. McAdams, Jerry. II. Zielinski, David. III. Title. IV. Series.
HF5549.5.I5 P376   2000   99–050601
658.3'142—dc21

FIRST EDITION
HC Printing 10 9 8 7 6 5 4 3 2 1

The Jossey-Bass
Business & Management Series

To Judy, my favorite team player
—G. P.

To Jane, Ryan, and Mitchell
—J.L.M.

To my ever-supportive parents,
Jim and Carol Zielinski,
and my inspirational wife, Barbara
—D. Z.

CONTENTS

PREFACE

T he bookshelves of American businesses spill over with works on how to build, train, coach, and sustain teams, and on the nature of virtual teams, self-directed teams, global teams, and dysfunctional teams. That's not surprising; the potential of efficient teamwork is boundless. But creating good teams is a vexing challenge, especially in the United States. How can you get employees in the world's most individualistic culture to sacrifice and pull together for the common good?

To the abundance of books on teamwork, however, we add one more. And for good reason: how to best reward and recognize the work of business teams— of whatever kind—is still neglected territory.

Certainly there are good books for compensation professionals (see the Bibliography: McAdams, 1996; Belcher, 1995; Lawler, 1990; Wilson, 1999) on the technical aspects of designing incentive plans for teams, and handbooks that offer creative laundry lists of recognition ideas for individual contributors. But there are few sources for people on the firing line looking for practical advice coupled with real-life examples of how to design reward and recognition systems for teams, not individuals.

This book provides practical advice and detailed examples of effective organizational unit (group) incentives, project team incentives, and recognition plans. It is for managers in organizations that have made a commitment to a collaborative culture and who want to create effective reward systems for teams. The "team of the month" award won't do: you need incentives that are fair, motivational, and properly linked to desired behaviors and results and that reflect the unique aspects of your business and its structure, systems, and culture.

We suspect that many leaders in business, government, and nonprofits want real-world advice on such issues as these:

- Determining what works, what doesn't, and why, according to those who have used various reward plans
- Rewarding individual excellence on teams
- Making recognition plans work
- Deciding when and how to use cash rather than noncash awards
- Dealing with team members who don't pull their weight but still receive team incentives or recognition
- Understanding the organization's payoff from good team reward plans
- Knowing how to combine plans, such as recognition and organizational unit incentives, for maximum impact
- Ensuring that everyone in the plan understands it
- Knowing how the design process differs between large and small organizations
- Using incentive plans to build business literacy in the workforce

At the heart of this book are case studies of reward plans in companies large and small, in many industries, and of many cultures. For every Chase Manhattan or Rockwell, we have included a Markem Corp. or a nonprofit such as the Texas Guaranteed Student Loan Corporation.

Whenever organizations try to make teamwork the norm, many supporters become frustrated because the usual reward-and-recognition programs don't support it. In this book, the fictional BIZCOM Corporation and its managers show how frustration about teams can turn into success. BIZCOM's trials and tribulations are based on the authors' years of experience working with organizations.

The numerous sidebars, graphs, and the like that you will see are simply parenthetical discussions that draw out lessons learned and offer advice in using reward and recognition tactics to spur teams to new heights.

WHO SHOULD READ THIS BOOK?

To put it simply: executives and managers looking to implement a strategy that has teamwork and collaboration as a central tenet; team champions, sponsors, and leaders who need to understand the critical role and implications of team rewards and recognition; human resource professionals called upon to advise teams on the options and issues associated with rewards and recognition; and compensation experts who are asked to add to their expertise and understanding to new team reward and recognition plans.

- If you are an executive or manager, this book explains how to create a successful team-based organization. It describes the key role of reward and recognition systems in supporting the transition to effective teams, gives cases and examples you can adapt to your company's environment, and explains how management must reinforce rewards and recognition for teams so as to achieve strategic goals.

- If you're a team champion, sponsor, or leader, you'll come to understand that even well-intentioned efforts to build and nurture effective teams may fail without meaningful reward and recognition practices. You'll learn what it means to "hit the wall" and, most importantly, how to get beyond it.

- If you're a human resources professional, you may have seen promising teams become derailed even when the track seemed clear and well maintained. Even with your successful coaching, facilitation, and training efforts, you've seen some of the best teams bog down or fail to reach their potential. This book should help you understand how critical it is in team-based cultures to link rewards and recognition to other organizational systems. We provide examples and advice to use as a framework for driving needed changes in your rewards and recognition systems.

- If you're a compensation professional or consultant, the case examples and accompanying analyses may be useful. The "warts-and-all" approach helps highlight and bring to life the challenges of designing and implementing team systems in the often messy real world.

HOW THIS BOOK CAME TO BE WRITTEN

The three authors bring distinct but overlapping skill sets to this book. Glenn Parker's books and surveys on teams and teamwork are a staple in the field. Jerry McAdams has led much of the research on reward and recognition systems in North America. Dave Zielinski has covered the human resources, organizational development, and business management fields as a journalist for more than ten years.

The book is primarily based on the friendship of Parker and McAdams, which began when they appeared separately at human resources conferences around the country but compared notes over dinner. The friendship eventually became a professional collaboration. As the team revolution took hold in the early 1990s, McAdams focused more and more on the reinforcement of teams, and Parker on the connection between team development and team rewards.

Enter Zielinski. He used his knowledge of human resources and organizational development, and his uncanny ability to translate technicalities into readable text, to create this book.

OVERVIEW OF CONTENTS

Chapter One describes BIZCOM, a fictitious company that wants to use a team approach to address a critical business problem. It delineates the natural history of teams and includes a discussion of team and organizational development issues such as vision, sponsorship, membership, stakeholders, launches, training, coaching, management style, and organizational support.

In Chapter Two, BIZCOM's leadership takes a hard look at environmental barriers to team success and develops a road map for creating a team-based organization. Building reward and recognition systems for teams is explored at length, including detailed explanations of how best to use group incentives, team recognition plans, and project team incentives.

Chapters Three through Five detail more than two dozen case studies of recognition plans, project incentives, and organizational unit incentives that encourage and reward team performance. Each explores why the organization launched one or more teamwork reward plans, how the plans work, what units or teams the plans cover, obstacles encountered in design or implementation, lessons learned, and how each plan is measured for success.

Chapter Six brings it all together. It summarizes the cases and advises you on how to apply your new knowledge to your unique work environment. And we take a last look at BIZCOM for some final lessons.

ACKNOWLEDGMENTS

We thank Susan Williams of Jossey-Bass for her immeasurable patience, flexibility, and support. She did everything we asked—and then some—to help us complete this project. Likewise, Byron Schneider provided useful feedback and ongoing support.

We thank Mike Lockwood of Maritz Performance Improvement Corp. for helping to unearth case study leads and Cynthia Voss of Watson Wyatt Worldwide for both following up and keeping our spirits up.

The research team from CARS contributed greatly to this book. Susan Murphy, Ph.D., Elizabeth Hawk and Amy Halliburton of Sibson and Company, Kimerle Watterson of Watson Wyatt Worldwide, and the Gantz Wiley organization all deserve our thanks. Those in the blinded case studies gave their insight and honest opinions willingly, regardless of the outcomes.

Rewarding Teams: Lessons from the Trenches would not have been possible without the cooperation of the many, many people who provided information and insight for the case studies. Each is mentioned in the case studies. All were generous with their time, thoughts, and ideas.

THE AUTHORS

G *lenn Parker*, an author and consultant, works with organizations to create and sustain high-performing teams, effective team players, and team-based systems. His clients include major industrial, pharmaceutical, health care, telecommunication, retail, and governmental organizations. In great demand as a speaker at corporate meetings and national conferences, Parker is author of numerous books and instruments. His best-selling *Team Players and Teamwork* (Jossey-Bass, 1990) has been published in several languages and was selected as one of the ten best business books of 1990.

Jerry McAdams served as National Practice Leader of Reward and Recognition Systems for Watson Wyatt Worldwide, and is located in St. Louis. He is also codirector of the nonprofit Consortium for Alternative Reward Strategy Research (CARS) and was previously vice president of Maritz, Inc., in St. Louis. He is a consultant to a number of leading sales and marketing, health care, financial, industrial, and service firms on the design, implementation, and evaluation of compensation, reward, and recognition plans. McAdams is the author of many publications, including *The Reward Plan Advantage: A Manager's Guide to Improving Business Performance Through People* (Jossey-Bass, 1996); *Organizational Performance and Rewards* (CARS, 1995), and *People, Performance, and Pay* (APQC, 1988).

David Zielinski is a freelance journalist based in Minneapolis who has covered the human resources, organizational development, and business management fields for the past twelve years. He is the former managing editor of the

Lakewood Publications newsletter group and is a frequent contributor to national and Twin Cities–based business magazines and newsletters.

Rewarding Teams

CHAPTER ONE

The Natural History of a Work Team

*S*usan Vitale, vice president of operations at BIZCOM, gazes out her office *window for a few moments at the idyllic corporate campus that is the day-time home of 1,200 employees. The rolling hills, beautiful trees, small pond, and jogging trails were designed to stimulate creative thinking. The facility is home to a variety of scientific, technical, marketing, and administrative employees focused on the development and marketing of new products.*

The physical environment simulates an academic research center, so it should appeal to employees who were recruited from universities. Behind the beauty, however, is a hard-nosed business goal: beat the competition at every turn.

Susan has overall responsibility for product development, marketing, and related functions. She has just returned from a conference where she heard several presentations on the value of team approaches to product development, process improvement, and customer service. As she looks out at a few joggers on the campus, she wonders about establishing a team to analyze the product development process.

Everyone seems to agree that the company's current approach takes too long and is cumbersome. If, as Susan believes, the time to market can be reduced and the process streamlined, the company will eventually benefit from increased market share and reduced costs. The business folks will love the idea, she thinks, but the scientific types may be unhappy. How can she position change such that the scientists see it as making better use of their talents and the senior managers view it as connected to the bottom line? Susan is also concerned about a corporate culture that is highly individualistic and competitive; teamwork and cross-organizational collaboration are rare, and team-based reward and recognition practices are rarer still.

Teams: the approach that just won't go away. Got a quality problem? Form a team. Reengineering the organization? You need teams. Customers want better service? Try a team approach. Developing a new product? Put a team together.

As the challenges facing business have grown more complex, the goals and roles of teams have become more varied. There are cross-functional teams, self-directed teams, ad hoc project teams, process improvement teams, management teams, and many other kinds. Teams have moved from the manufacturing floor to the office, the cockpit, the movie set, and the board room.

As the movement toward teams has grown, so has knowledge about how to form, train, develop, and facilitate them. How best to reward and recognize them is the last frontier in the teams movement, as Susan Vitale will soon find out. This book uses the fictional Susan and her fictional organization, BIZCOM, to demonstrate the barriers to developing a true team-based organization that rewards and recognizes good team members. The story of the BIZCOM case is a composite of the authors' experiences in working with a wide variety of organizations. The boxes offer advice and ideas for organizations facing similar challenges.

CREATING A TEAM

Most teams are created because someone thinks that using a collaborative approach will improve some aspect of the business. He or she has a "vision" of a better way and thinks that a team is the best way to get there.

A vision is a statement of where you want to be: your "druthers," hopes, and dreams—a place you've never been but have imagined. Even hard-nosed business goals start with a vision. It may exist only as a construct in someone's mind and may never be written into a proposal, but it is the motivating force. Some team efforts, however, start with a visioning process that is much like a team-building exercise.

The vision is often turned into something more concrete, such as an overarching goal for a project. This is the "ideation" stage. The leader ("sponsor" or "champion") has an idea that is his or her (or the team's) vision of a new way to do business. Then what? The next few steps are critical.

Too often, the leader, with the best of intentions, provides too much direction for the team. This often limits the team's flexibility and freedom such that its goal becomes satisfying the leader or following rigid team guidelines.

Sometimes leaders, whether they create visions or present high-level views of the problem or opportunity to the team, hand it off to others for sponsorship. Sometimes the leader and sponsor are one and the same.

Either way, at this stage the vision or overarching goal should state, in general terms, what is expected from the team, but not how it should be accomplished. Thus it should broadly define senior management's desires, allow the sponsor or team sufficient latitude to add scope and depth to the goal, and enable the team to create a plan to get it done. For examples of a team visioning activity and an overarching goal, see the following boxes:

TEAM VISIONING ACTIVITY

The leadership team gathers in a quiet room for about two hours. The leader or facilitator explains the purpose of the meeting is to create a shared vision of the organization. The participants are each given a sheet of flip chart paper and some large felt-tip markers. The leader asks them to imagine it is two years from now.

"You are in a helicopter looking down on your workplace. What would you like to see? What would please you? In what ways is it better or improved over the way it is now? Draw a picture of that vision."

The visions are posted on the wall, and participants view the exhibition. The leader facilitates a discussion directed toward creating a consensus vision of the new workplace. That shared vision is created on a new sheet of paper. The components of the vision are listed. The next steps are developing a plan for "getting from here to there."

SAMPLE OVERARCHING TEAM GOAL

"To improve the overall cash flow and customer satisfaction by reducing the cycle time of the BIZCOM product"

Susan Vitale decides to establish a team to address the consumer product development process. Her goal is to reduce the time it takes to move "from concept to carton." Because she learned about teams at the conference she attended, she chooses to try the concept with one team as a pilot. She will be overall champion of the effort, but asks John Chin to be the team's sponsor. John manages one of the science areas, has the respect of the scientific community, and possesses an MBA. He understands the connection between good science and good business.

Although Susan decides to start with one project team to establish the process and test the limits of the current culture, her vision includes a shift of the overall organizational culture at the site to a team-based operation.

Susan has lunch with John and presents the goal and his proposed role as the sponsor. She explains that he will have to outline the project to key department heads and explain that they will need to identify potential team members from relevant departments, work with the team to establish objectives and a project plan, and help the team in various ways such as clearing barriers and obtaining resources. John signs on as the team's sponsor.

Then they talk about potential team leaders. John proposes Judy Stiller-Cohen. "She's been with the company for only two years," John says, "but she's a respected scientist with good collaboration skills." Susan knows Judy from the Diversity Task Force and quickly agrees. John will talk with Judy about the assignment.

BUILDING THE TEAM

The vision leads to an overarching goal. The goal is handed off to the sponsor. The sponsor begins the team-forming process. Who should be selected as team leader? The sponsor should select someone with both a working knowledge of the technical issues and the ability to manage a diverse and perhaps geographically dispersed group of people. Too often, only technical experts with time on their hands are chosen to head teams. Forgotten are the interpersonal and conflict management skills usually needed to succeed as a team leader, especially when the team includes people from a variety of functions. The following box describes some of the characteristics that good team leaders must possess.

LEADERSHIP CHARACTERISTICS FOR PROJECT TEAMS

A working knowledge of the technical issues being addressed by the team

Experience and skills in managing group process issues

An ability to work with little, no, or unclear authority

A willingness and the relevant skills to develop ongoing relationships with key stakeholders in other parts of the organization

The know-how to help the team establish a mission and set goals and objectives

The knowledge and assertiveness to obtain the necessary resources for the team

The ability to protect the team from undue and counterproductive outside interference

A willingness to change and adapt as conditions change and the needs of the team evolve

A sense of humor—effective leaders take the work but not themselves seriously

---

John Chin finds Judy Stiller-Cohen in the lab. He outlines the team project and describes Susan Vitale's vision and her interest in pilot-testing a team approach to process improvement. Judy is interested but expresses some concerns. "My boss won't like me being pulled off my current project," she says.

"No problem," says John. "The team is part-time, and I'll clear it with your boss." But Judy also wonders about the support some senior scientists will give to the project team. "They don't like anything that even hints at cutting corners in the development process," she says.

"I understand that," says John. "Susan and I will try to make sure they all realize the importance of the team. Even so, you'll probably have to address the issue with the team itself early on. But you're a respected scientist, so you can explain to people that good science and good business are not mutually exclusive."

Judy and John agree to meet again to discuss her role in more detail. As she leaves, Judy thinks to herself: "I like the idea of being a team leader, but is this really going to help my career? Around here, most people still think that the best ideas come from working on your own. This is not a team-oriented organization."

Where possible, John handles most meetings with other stakeholders informally. He catches one in the cafeteria, another in the company gym, and two others by just walking around their offices. Some travel often, so he uses the corporate calendering software to make appointments with them. Most meetings go well, although everyone is concerned about the time their people will have to spend on the team project. John assures them that team responsibilities will take no more than 20 percent of their time.

One department head, Ravi Chowdhury, is not happy. "I can't give away one day a week of my best people," he says. But John suspects it's not the time but the purpose of the team that Ravi opposes. "Hey," he tells Ravi. "I don't necessarily need your best scientist. I just need a good one who can play well with others."

"Okay, then," says Ravi. "How about Gary Gates?"

John knows that Gary is young and hasn't yet proven himself, but he has a strong academic background and played on a championship lacrosse team in college. "Sounds like a good choice," he says. John then goes on to explain the support that Gary will need if he becomes a team member. As he leaves Ravi's office, he wonders if Ravi might actually reflect the thinking of a number of other stakeholders who are just too "political" to openly state their objections.

Judy and John discussed the prospective team members identified by the department heads. They are concerned about two things. They were thinking the team might have seven or eight members, but more have been recommended. Beyond that, they wonder if some of the people recommended are too busy to fully contribute or are too new and thus will learn more than they contribute. They decide to create a core team of eight, with an additional four adjunct members who will be asked to carry out specific tasks or attend review meetings. John and Judy agree there is no need to offend department heads now by telling them they don't want some of their people.

Too often, teams are launched with little or no preparation. There is a widespread belief that if you just put people together in a room teamwork will simply happen. Typically, a memo goes out indicating that a team is being formed to look at a problem or business opportunity, and individuals are directed to show up at the first meeting. Or department heads are simply asked to contribute a person to the team.

However, key stakeholders—department heads, support groups, vendors, customers—all need to be brought into the process early on. At this point the sponsor should review the objectives, timeline, importance, and resource needs of the project. They should focus on the type of person who will represent the department on the team and on the support that person will need from his or her department manager. Discussion between the sponsor and the department head should focus on the following factors:

- The time the potential team member would need to devote to the project (full-time or part-time? If part-time, what percentage of his or her time?)
- The priority of the project in comparison with other department responsibilities
- How the team member's performance will be reviewed and measured
- That person's work experience and skill set
- His or her personal style in working in teams
- Other required resources, such as labs, facilitation resources, support personnel, and budget

So far, the natural history of a team includes articulating a vision, selecting a team sponsor, orienting key stakeholders, and choosing the team leader and team members. Now let's consider actually forming a team.

TEAM LAUNCH: TAKEOFF

It's not as hard to launch a team as it is to launch a Jupiter probe, but the kick-off session that inaugurates a team is vital. The launch meeting is the culmination of lots of planning and preparation. When possible, the team leader should meet with each team member in person and in advance. For members who are located elsewhere, a phone conversation will suffice. Either way, these brief discussions should focus on the purpose of the team, management's vision, the skills and experience of the member, the style of the leader, and the concerns and questions of the members about their role on the team. These should give the leader some idea of the team's strengths and weaknesses.

When the team first gets together, all members as well as the sponsor should attend along with, if possible, the senior management champion. Some teams invite key stakeholders such as department managers and representatives of support groups. Some also invite internal customers.

The purpose of the meeting is to present the sponsor or champion's vision. The discussion should explain management's expectations for the team and its level of empowerment or authority. After the launch meeting, the team should prepare objectives and a plan that is aligned with the vision. Once the sponsor and the team agree on the objectives and plan (and, in some cases, a budget), the team should be empowered to do whatever it takes to achieve them.

Enough time should be set aside at the launch to address concerns and questions members have about the team and their role as members. If these pop up later, it can cripple the team's progress. See the following box for questions and concerns that should be addressed:

CONCERNS AND QUESTIONS ACTIVITY

This activity gives team members an opportunity to voice concerns and receive answers to questions they have about the team's goals and their roles. It takes between forty-five minutes and one hour.

1. The sponsor presents a brief overview of his or her vision for the team as well as any expectations of the team. The level of empowerment of the team should also be included in the presentation.

2. Distribute a three-by-five-inch card to each team member. Ask that they write one concern or question about what the sponsor just said or anything else they need to know (including any rumors they want clarified) about the work of the team. The sponsor will respond to all concerns and questions. Tell people not to sign their name on the card. If necessary, tell them that following the session all the cards will be thrown away.

3. Collect the cards and shuffle them. Then have the sponsor read and answer them one at a time.

4. When all the cards have been read and addressed, ask if there are remaining concerns or questions.

John wants to move quickly, before the grapevine gets into high gear. He schedules the team launch meeting for the first time that most players, including several department managers, are available. Meanwhile, Judy talks with each of the twelve people selected for the team informally and briefly—by phone with those who are on the road.

Many are concerned about the time they'll have to spend on the team and the conflict between current responsibilities and work on the team. Most look to Judy for guidance and appreciate the opportunity to meet with her prior to the team meeting. For some, this is the first time they've spoken with her beyond saying "hi" around the building or at corporate meetings. During the meetings Judy explains the adjunct role to the four people she and John identified for them. They seem okay with it; two are somewhat relieved because they have other deadlines coming up. Although they don't say so directly, several potential team members wonder how participation will affect their performance appraisal, future assignments, and career opportunities given the organization's culture and previous lack of interest in teams.

John opens the launch meeting by thanking everyone for coming and reviewing the agenda for the two-hour session. He introduces Susan as the champion of the project. Susan gives a brief but upbeat presentation of how she came to the team idea and her vision for this particular team. John builds on Susan's remarks by outlining his expectations for the team and his role as sponsor in supporting that. He then turns the meeting over to Allison Smith-Thomas from corporate training. Because many people in the room do not know each other, Allison runs them through a fun, get-acquainted icebreaker. She concludes by emphasizing the importance of creating a relaxed, informal team climate. She also facilitates a concerns-and-questions exercise that allows everyone to have their issues addressed by Susan, John, and Judy. Most concerns center on how to deal with the demands of "serving two masters," as one person put it. Another common question is how team members' performance appraisals will be handled. Susan and John respond well to most of the concerns and questions, and John closes the meeting by asking the team to come up with goals, objectives, and an action plan that will translate the vision into reality.

TEAM DEVELOPMENT

Progressive organizations provide teams with training during the start-up phase. Hundreds of books and manuals and thousands of consultants are available to help design and deliver this training. Some subjects are basic, but the training curriculum will vary depending on the focus of the team, the expectations of management, and the budget. Usually it's best to use a short program to get the team up and running, and follow-up sessions designed to focus on specific skill gaps that emerge down the road. The initial training should focus on the following:

- Team members' styles and strengths
- Group dynamics
- Team norms
- Meeting management

- Goals and objectives
- Project plans
- Problem solving
- Decision making

For process improvement teams, start-up training may also cover tools such as flow charts, pareto charts, cause-and-effect diagrams, and other data collection and analysis aids. Other teams will need project management training to learn how to prepare project plans.

One week after the launch meeting, the team goes through start-up training. All team members, including the adjuncts, attend the two-day Basic Team Skills course. It was developed by an outside consultant for presentation by the corporate training staff. Allison Smith-Thomas is the principal trainer. During the program the team develops a set of operating guidelines or norms that cover such things as communicating during and outside of team meetings; decision making; making and keeping commitments; and sharing expertise, problems, and concerns. The team also learns how to write objectives and develop a plan and starts work on a project team document for the sponsor. A team-style survey helps members understand each other and their differences. John attends the first morning of training and participates in the styles survey, but then leaves to avoid unduly influencing or intimidating the others. One of the last exercises is to select a name for the team. The members choose CONPRO. On the surface it stands for "consumer process" but for them it means "contrarian professionals." The training is well received and the team leaves on a high, anxious to start working on the project.

Two weeks later the team completes the project plan; it is reviewed and approve by John with minor revisions. At a later team meeting, John reiterates his hands-off approach to the team, which is his way of saying that it has the power. Members are still somewhat skeptical, as the company has a traditional, top-down, controlling culture. For now, however, this is a nonissue: they have to get to work implementing their plan.

EARLY SUCCESS: PLUCKING THE LOW-HANGING FRUIT

Most teams hit the ground running. With the tools they gained in training and their natural esprit de corps, they move quickly to address the problem or opportunity that is their charter. They are energized by their power and freedom as well as the support of top management. As a result, they use their newfound energy and skills to score some early victories.

Indeed, teams and their sponsors should look for early successes that build team confidence and create momentum. Most team members have ideas they've been itching to implement but couldn't—sometimes simply because nobody ever asked their opinion. They often know about problems such as artificial barriers, stupid rules, or plain old "fat" in the system that can be trimmed or eliminated. For an example, see the following box:

CUTTING "CYA"

One of the authors' client companies created teams to reduce cycle time for certain products. In one case, a team set the goal of reducing the cycle from seventy-eight to twenty-nine days.

It was fairly certain it could reach the goal because, as one team member put it, the idea was to eliminate "all the 'cover your ass' time . . . [that was] built into the original process." Within two weeks of the team's existence it had a plan to knock twenty-five days off the cycle time. The team felt great and its management sponsor was thrilled.

During the start-up phase of a team, the leader necessarily plays a more prominent role than during its performance stage. Members of the team look to the leader for information, structure, and process. The leader often has information crucial to the team's success, such as what other teams are doing, input from the team's sponsor and other managers, changes in company direction, and input on how the team's activities are being viewed by others.

At the outset the team needs the leader's guidance in the form of suggestions ("Why don't we look into this area?"), targets ("Can we get this done by the next meeting?") or encouragement to use analytical tools introduced during training ("Let's spend the next meeting creating a process map."). Using a collaborative style, the leader should take responsibility for providing the team with frameworks for getting the work done. But the leader must make it clear that he or she is open to alternatives suggested by team members.

The *forming* stage is characterized by interpersonal tentativeness on the part of members as they try to decide what they are really being asked to do. Uncertainty is especially common in cross-functional teams where many members don't know each other. Early on, they tend to feel more comfortable with tasks than with each other. They would rather focus on their own work than on involving others. As a result, team process issues can get obscured or glossed over. It's important for the leader to be a process facilitator during the early history of the team. One quick and easy way to do this is to conduct a five-minute process check at the end of every meeting, where members assess the positive and negative aspects of the meeting. Sometimes this is called a "plus/delta" session.

The CONPRO team moved quickly in the first few weeks after its plan was approved. First, it created a real-time process map of the existing product development process. Team members were amazed at the number of steps and checkpoints, including many that seemed redundant or superfluous. Then they came up with five solid ideas for reducing the time without sacrificing quality checks. They uncovered other possible changes but decided to test the waters with a short list. John Chin met with the team to review the recommendations and develop a strategy for presenting them. He agrees to run them by Susan Vitale first, feeling confident she will be pleased. He recommends that team members discuss the five changes with their department managers to get their buy-in, and offers to help with managers likely to oppose the changes. Gary Gates asks that John attend when he meets with Ravi.

This cautious approach is effective. Everyone agrees that the five changes will improve the process and can be implemented immediately. Because the quarterly all-staff meeting is coming up next week, a presentation by Judy is added to the agenda. In the meantime, team members are encouraged to "talk it up" with their colleagues.

At a subsequent team meeting, the mood is upbeat as members do a quick review of their process to date. There are lots of high-fives around the room, as teammates feel very positive about their accomplishments. There is little interest in doing a serious debriefing of the process to date, including what might have been done differently. Allison Smith-Thomas attends this meeting and tries to warn them about the dangers of complacency.

It was nice while it lasted, but . . .

THE HONEYMOON IS OVER: WELCOME TO CYNICISM

It can be overt or subtle, but most teams—even well-intentioned, well-trained teams—experience a form of what professional baseball players call the "sophomore jinx": a period of early success that creates a sense of euphoria but leads to letdowns, performance plateaus, and negative reactions.

Tuckman (1965) called this stage "storming." As a result of it, he said, people assume that public conflict, loud disagreements, and angry words must characterize it. Such things can happen, but more often it surfaces as antigroup action and dysfunctional behavior. In corporate cultures where public disagreements are frowned upon, it's more likely to emerge as passive-aggressive behaviors such as showing up late to meetings, not completing assignments, and lack of participation in discussions. Other nonverbal messages in meetings include folded arms, smirks, rolled eyes, and bored expressions.

In such organizations, disagreements and concerns are usually expressed outside of meetings, most often in one-on-one conversations. Suddenly, members are frustrated with the failure of the team to move faster, a perceived lack of support from management, or the unrealistic views of their teammates. Things overlooked in the team's first stage or unexpressed because of the lack of interpersonal comfort now come out. In addition, because the first successes came easy—low-hanging fruit are the easiest to pluck—members are frustrated by the increased difficulty of solving the next set of problems.

In entrepreneurial cultures where the pressures are great and the inhibitions few, the conflict is more public. Team members openly disagree with the ideas and opinions of their teammates. If so, conflict management shifts to the team leader and ultimately to the sponsor, who must deal with the finger pointing, fault finding, and perhaps even name calling as members rush to occupy what they think is the high ground. They may accuse each other of a variety of high crimes, from lacking the correct vision to not working hard enough. Inevitably, much blame is placed on the team leader. It can get ugly.

Sometimes dissatisfaction is directed at a vague enemy: the "team thing" or "team process." The feeling is that the team approach is not so great after all. In some cultures it's more acceptable to attack a concept or a process than a person.

Dissatisfaction and cynicism in the early stages of team history must be addressed quickly and effectively. The situation will not correct itself; a young team has not had time to develop self-correcting norms. Members are not yet comfortable enough with each other or the team process to take on the tasks of assessing the problem and developing an improvement plan. An experienced leader can help, but usually the assistance of an expert team trainer, facilitator, or coach is needed. Also, renewed management support for the team is essential at this point. The sponsor, champion, and other key managers should express their continued belief in the project and renew their pledge of support.

Teams at this point need to take a hard look at their progress to date and examine the issues causing dissatisfaction. Sometimes an open discussion at a team meeting will work; in other situations individual interviews with team members or anonymous surveys are best for unearthing and solving problems. Any intervention must have focus on the future so that the team doesn't spend much time dwelling on past shortcomings. More attention must be paid to "How do we improve?" than to "Who do we blame?" The outcome should be a plan with a set of specific next steps that gets the team quickly moving forward. In addition, the plan should include "norms"—standards that encourage the open expression of concerns, a focus on issues rather than personalities, and an emphasis on problem solving rather than whining.

Several CONPRO team members run into each other at the company cafeteria and decide to have lunch together. At first they are uneasy because of unspoken feelings, but one person breaks the ice by talking about the team's lack of progress after its initial success. Pointed remarks are made about Judy's lack of assertiveness in pushing the team's agenda with management, the failure to deliver on action items by some team members, and pure and simple absenteeism by others.

The greatest criticism is reserved for two of the members' bosses who are making it difficult for them to complete both their team assignments and their regular department tasks. One member says she's working four more hours a week in order to get her team action items completed on time. They all reaffirm their commitment to the team's goal, but a few wonder out loud what's in it for them. Some believe that their work substantially benefits the company but those benefits are not shared with them. Others mention that although some nice words have been said about the work of the team there is little talk and no action toward rewarding people for working together to accomplish organizational objectives. One team member says his wife works at a company where cost savings generated by a project team are shared with team members and everyone in the plant receives an incentive payout if certain revenue and quality measures are achieved.

Others note that although the CONPRO core team members will get all the glory for this project, there should be some recognition for the "little people back at the ranch" who pick up the slack, cover for them, and do the grunt work that supports the team that keeps both the team members' departments of origin and the CONPRO team itself churning forward.

One team member agrees to talk with Allison about these issues. Allison has to restrain herself from saying, "I told you so." Instead she suggests an intervention that includes a discussion with Judy, which she thinks is essential, and interviews with all team members to identify some of the thorny issues facing them. Allison agrees to take the lead in talking with Judy.

At first, Judy is upset because she hears every concern as a criticism of her leadership style. But Allison explains that such reactions are common in new teams. To move forward, she explains, you have to identify and address the real issues as soon as possible. The good news is that these reactions have surfaced early on rather than later when they can easily derail a team.

Allison interviews each team member, summarizes the data, and presents the results at a team meeting. The team develops norms to address team behaviors, including attendance and completion of assignments. Judy agrees to talk with John and Susan about the cooperation of department heads. Allison says she will get HR and compensation involved in looking at team rewards and recognition and the performance management process. The team asks Allison to stay close over the next month or so to help ensure it stays on track with its established norms, to facilitate the meetings, and to keep an eye on other process issues. Judy asks Allison to provide her with some coaching and counseling during this time as well. See the following box for a quote about how really good coaches perform:

> *CHARACTERISTICS OF A GOOD COACH*
> Masterful coaches have a burning desire to help others learn, grow, and perform. They are highly perceptive in the gap between who people are today and their potential. They see leaders where others see followers. They see creative thinkers where others see those who can only follow the conventional wisdom. They see players who can win the big games . . . where others see only the drones. They see hidden strengths in meek people where others see only weakness and timidity (Hargrove, 1995, p.165).

YOU ARE ENTERING THE ZONE!

Athletes talk about "the zone" not as a place, but rather as a feeling that you can't miss and can do no wrong, an arena where everything—body, mind, and emotions—work in harmony. Every shot at the hoop is a slam dunk, every swing at the baseball is a home run, every tee shot is a hole-in-one, every toss of the football connects for a touchdown. Similarly, artists at times believe they have perfect perspective and jazz players think their improvisations are the ultimate.

Work teams may also enter a zone: everything crystallizes—goals are clear, the plan is feasible, members live the norms, management is supportive, obstacles are faced and overcome, meaningful work gets done, and, most important, progress toward the goal is clear. During this time, however, leadership should shift from the formal leader to those who are responsible for tasks and process requirements. Here leadership is seen more as a coordinator and facilitator function. As a result, everyone on the team feels responsible for its success and steps up to do what's necessary.

Champions, sponsors, and other members of management are thrilled by this. Team exploits are now regularly included in management presentations and there is growing acknowledgment—via e-mail messages, memos, written thank-yous, and other forms—of the team's exploits. The sponsor and leader take the team out to lunch and buy T-shirts for everyone. In the zone there is the quiet hum of progress, the sweet smell of success.

For team members, it feels great. But . . .

HITTING THE WALL

The zone eventually dissolves. The shots stop dropping, the hits stop coming, the passes miss their mark, and the golf ball slices. Reality sets in. You're a mere mortal. And for a team as well, the zone can carry it only so far. At some point, all the training, all the motivational speeches, all the informal recognition, all the good coaching and, all those good feelings of teamwork lose their impact.

One day the team may notice that management talks a good game but still practices command and control. Or that the corporate culture still values the lone ranger over the team player. Or that the top-rated performers are still the lone wolves who care little for sharing and caring. Or that the company's structure is still one with big functional silos with little cross-organization collaboration. And one day they look around and see a few haphazard, highly subjective forms of team recognition but no coordinated strategy that either rewards project teams or provides incentives for organizational unit accomplishments. They see nothing that encourages or celebrates collaborative behavior by rewarding the results of teamwork. Effective teamwork may still happen but it happens in spite of, and not because of, reward and recognition systems or management behaviors.

Over the next few months the CONPRO team makes great progress. The interventions by Allison, Judy's renewed confidence, Susan's presentation at a senior management retreat, and John's one-on-one sessions with department heads combine to put the team back on track. The team collects more data about the product development process, brings in key stakeholders to discuss what happens at their steps in the process, creates a more detailed process map, and does some out-of-the-box brainstorming about alternatives. It gets cooperation from people in various departments who provide information and ideas and readily give of their time. Everyone gets excited about the possibilities of dramatically improving the process. People suggest other areas that need to be changed. Judy provides monthly updates to John and Susan. Team members keep their bosses informed and often give reports at their department staff meetings. After the team meets a significant milestone in its plan, Judy has the whole team over to her house for a barbecue. John and Susan drop by. There are many good-natured toasts throughout the afternoon. Judy gives everyone a fun T-shirt with the team's name on it. The team is feeling good. Susan suggests to John that he nominate the team for a Chairman's Award.

Soon the team is ready to present its findings. It has devised a strategy to reduce the cycle time but retain important quality checks. The idea has been checked with the relevant stakeholders. The team conducts a dry run with John and he suggests a few subtle changes to make it acceptable to the scientific community. John talks with Susan and they agree that the team should present its report at a meeting of the Leadership Council, which is the top management team for the business unit.

The presentation to the Leadership Council goes well. With some changes, the council agrees to test the new process with one product. But first it demands a detailed implementation plan. Council members say nice things about the team. Susan, who's a member of the council, beams, and John is all smiles.

The team leaves the council meeting feeling upbeat and goes to the cafeteria for coffee. Allison joins them, there are more high-fives, and she suggests the team spend time at its next meeting doing a thorough review and debrief of the entire project, focusing on its teamwork component. This time, the team listens to Allison's advice.

At the next meeting Allison leads the team through a series of questions designed to bring out the positives and negatives of the project. The session goes quite smoothly. Sheets of flip-chart paper are taped up around the room. In general, members are positive about the work of the team, the training received, and the role of the sponsors. One question, however, has to do with management support and draws animated responses. Commented one person, "Well, Susan Vitale was fine although we didn't see much of her." Others agreed. Many people say good things about John Chin.

Finally, there is an avalanche of comments about the organization's overall support for a team approach: "I don't think management really cares about this whole team thing." "We're a democratic island in a sea of command and control waves." "We've all put in a lot of extra work but where's the payoff in our pocketbook?" "Nothing's really changed for me. My evaluation is still going to be based on my individual scientific work. This team experience was fun and I love you guys but it's still back to business as usual." "I don't need any more T-shirts." "I liked hearing the kudos from management but what about all the folks in the various departments that helped us out? Some people in my area put in many late nights for us—but what's in it for them? The organization reaps all the benefits from the improvements." "Some people in my area are wondering why they can't get on a team and get some of the glory. They're seeing us as some kind of elite who get lots of visibility with management." "Around here, the real heroes and heroines are still the star performers and they'll still be ones getting the bigger increases." "We come from different areas and we work well together but the walls between our departments are still high and thick." "We love you, Allison, but frankly, more team-building exercises are not going to change this system."

ENVIRONMENTAL OBSTACLES

Team building, coaching, facilitation, informal recognition, exhortation, and good intentions can only take you so far. At a certain point, teams come up against a variety of environmental obstacles. The key to moving forward is to ensure that all organizational systems are aligned in support of teams. (See the box on the next page for an explanation of how organizational units and teams differ.) Absence of even one part of the whole can bring the system crashing down. Four areas need to be addressed, and the following sections deal with them.

WHAT A TEAM IS AND IS NOT

Consider this statement: an organizational unit can act like a team, but a team is not necessarily an organizational unit, at least for describing reward plans.

An organizational unit is just that, a group of employees organized into an identifiable business unit that appears on the organizational chart. They may behave in a spirit of teamwork, but for the purposes of developing reward plans they are not a "team." The organizational unit may be a whole company, a strategic business unit, a division, a department, or a work group.

A "team" is a small group of people allied by a common project and sharing performance objectives. They generally have complementary skills or knowledge and an interdependence that requires that they work together to accomplish their project's objective. Team members hold themselves mutually accountable for their results. These teams are not found on an organization chart.

Corporate Strategy

Does the organization's strategy include the use of teams as a key success factor? Team-based organizations believe that judicious use of teams will help them achieve a competitive advantage in product quality, innovation, customer service, cost reduction, and other business-specific goals. Managers must believe, and act as if they believe, that teams are more than words in a vision statement and must be made accountable in their performance appraisals for doing so.

Some organizations are fond of saying, "We're all part of the team," but too often it is merely management-speak. This is especially common in conventional hierarchical organizations; they say the words but don't follow up with significant action. Their employees may read the articles and attend the conferences and come to believe that many companies have turned collaborative. Actually, though, few organizations today are genuinely team-based.

Others who want to quibble point to how they reward or recognize teams with splashy bonuses or profit-sharing plans. But these do not by themselves represent a commitment to teams; they're more like a gift from a rich uncle. If top management believes that only money and a few recognition programs ("team of the year" and that sort of thing) reinforces teamwork, they are wrong. These alone do not cause fundamental change in the way people and teams are managed.

But in a few organizations, teaming is a key component of the corporate strategy, involvement with teams is second nature, and collaboration happens without great thought or fanfare. There are natural work groups (teams of people who do the same or similar work in the same location), permanent cross-functional teams, ad hoc project teams, process improvement teams, and real management teams. Involvement just happens. You have a problem? You get a few people together and work it out. Managers believe and act as if teamwork really gives them a competitive advantage. Team players are valued. Managers are held accountable for support of teams. There are preannounced organizational unit incentives for hitting business goals, some project team rewards, and an abundance of recognition tools.

Structure

Structure refers to how work, people, and technology come together to implement corporate strategy. In a team-based organization, departments or functions are replaced by teams. Some structures make it easier for teams to succeed, others create barriers. Functional rigidity is often associated with managerial control, which strips teams of their power. Without significant empowerment, it is difficult for teams to make the best use of their resources. Teams must be accountable, but without control, without power, they are doomed to failure.

Proper structure comes from the top. The highest management team has to be a role model for everyone else. This is more than symbolism; senior managers must consistently demonstrate and explain to people how teamwork leads to business success. There can be no mixed messages or conflicting priorities from above.

Systems

All systems in an organization need to be aligned with the concept of teamwork. You cannot have a strategy that emphasizes teamwork and a structure that encourages collaboration that is not supported by the organization's relevant systems. Some such systems are the following:

- *Information:* Information that typically flows only up or down in an organization must be rerouted to teams at all levels. Teams cannot be accountable if they don't get accurate and timely information about their work. Also, they need current information that supports the team measurement system. And performance appraisals must hold people accountable for sharing, not hoarding, that information.

- *Performance management:* First, the evaluation system needs to include specific team behaviors valued by the organization. Second, performance on teams, especially cross-functional teams, needs to be considered in a person's evaluation. Third, as teams mature, some form of peer evaluation should be part of the overall performance management process.

- *Training:* Off-the-shelf training that focuses on individual knowledge and skills must be rejected in favor of that which emphasizes team-directed learning. Teams learn best when the members learn together and immediately apply their new knowledge to the team environment.

- *Rewards:* The rewards and recognition system must not focus on individuals (such as the employee of the month) but on teams, such that it fosters collaboration. Individuals should be acknowledged, but primarily for being strong team players. Teams should be recognized for accomplishments that support the overall organizational strategy. For a more detailed explanation of good team-based reward and recognition practices, see Chapter Six.

Culture

Culture is often a function of how long the organization has been in its core business. It is an expression of organizational values as they are translated into operational and behavioral norms. Culture shows in the organization's language, symbols, rituals, stories, myths, heroes, and heroines. It answers the following questions:

- What and who does the organization value?
- How do people behave?
- How do things get done?
- Who are the organization's stars?
- How is success defined?
- Who gets rewarded for what types of behavior or results?

Organizations that have long valued individual technical excellence, thinly veiled competition, solo action, and private deals need, instead, an emphasis on sharing information, working collaboratively, participative decision making, and team empowerment. A body of teamwork stories will then evolve and circulate that create heroes and heroines who helped the crowd stand out rather than stood out from the crowd.

There is a crucial link between culture and strategy. A team-based strategy is ineffective in an individually oriented, competitive culture. One way to foster culture change is to revise systems to support the new norms (for example, giving rewards that acknowledge collaboration rather than competition).

Allison presents John and Susan with a verbal summary of her feedback session with the CONPRO team. They are concerned but not surprised. Susan asks John for his recommendations based on the team experience to date.

Later, Susan once again gazes out her window. The CONPRO team experience has merely surfaced things she has known for some time. The culture, structure, systems, and management style of the organization are barriers to team-based operation. And they are interrelated. The culture is both a reflection of and a result of the structure. The systems reinforce the culture and create structural barriers. The management style is a manifestation of the culture as well as an influencer of the systems.

Susan is especially concerned about a few areas that have a direct impact on the success of BIZCOM and any future teams in the organization. First, the performance management system emphasizes individual accomplishments and encourages competition among people. The appraisal form still uses broad categories of traits rather than specific behaviors, does not include team-oriented accomplishments, and results in a ranking of people in each organization. Second, the reward and recognition program is limited, competitive, and focused on individual awards. Each manager has a discretionary budget that can be used for rewards, but collaborative efforts are rarely recognized. There is a series of annual awards that can be given to teams but instead usually goes to outstanding individual technical and scientific breakthroughs.

Susan sees several department heads walking across the campus to the cafeteria, and that alone tells her that management style and organizational culture must change if true teamwork is to become the norm. This is fundamental change, and it will take time, but it must be started. She thinks about getting some people in corporate organization development involved. Perhaps they can develop a culture survey to get a picture of where BIZCOM is right now. She also decides to coordinate the survey results with a management development process tied to behaviors of the desired culture. It's a tall order.

One thing is clear: she needs a plan that spells out where the organization is, where it wants to be, and how it will get there.

Sustaining high-performing teams requires an organizational environment and systems designed to support and champion teamwork. This book focuses on rewards, recognition, and incentives, but always in the context of an integrated, systemwide approach to change.

CHAPTER TWO

The Missing Link:
Meaningful Team Rewards

S usan Vitale is frustrated. She's pretty sure she hasn't paid enough attention *to her human capital—all BIZCOM employees. As vice president of operations, she manages people, labs, production, and money (through the budgeting and expenditures process). She's been adept at these, so operations is exceeding its budget expectations. Yet she knows something is amiss.*

Susan has left the management and leadership of more than a thousand people largely to Human Resources. But the CONPRO team's feeling that management could have played a more visible and hands-on role in championing and rewarding teamwork make her wonder about her management style.

Susan is scheduled to meet with General Manager Jerry Parker, a trusted peer. They have worked together and met at least weekly for a decade, and have a good relationship. They bounce ideas off each other and explore ways of meeting their respective business goals.

After ordering lunch in the executive dining room, Susan asks, "Do you remember CONPRO?" "Sure," Jerry responds. "I think it's one of our real success stories. Corporate thinks so, anyway. And I agree that it should be nominated for the Chairman's Award."

Susan pauses, then admits, "I thought CONPRO was pretty good, but it sure took a while to get there," she says. "We had a feedback session and I was surprised how negative some comments were about how the organization manages teams."

Jerry was surprised. "How can that be? Our employee opinion survey shows we're doing pretty good and people think this is a good environment to work in. We gave Rupert . . . uh, whatzisname? . . . the employee of the year award. Benefits are competitive and so is compensation. I talk about teamwork all the time."

"I know," says Susan, "but some of our best people tell us we talk teamwork but don't live it. If extra effort only means that they can work more for the same money, what does that say? We've got a problem. We talk a good game about the importance of people, but I'm starting to think we may be creating a pleasing work environment but not a place where performance is adequately recognized or rewarded. Especially team performance."

"If you think it's a problem, then it probably is," Jerry says. "What do we do?"

"That's another problem. I need a road map. Let's look at where we've been and where we are now. I went to a meeting last year and got some material on reward systems for work teams. I'll try to find it."

THE DISCOVERY PROCESS

Getting rank-and-file employees engaged in pursuit of organizational goals as individuals, as part of small work teams, or as broader organizational units, requires action and consistent follow-through by the management team. Unfortunately, management interventions that can spur such engagement—such as reward plans, communication devices, or training programs—are often created and implemented not as a coordinated system but independently. Even when part of a coordinated plan, they're often designed at cross-purposes. It's not at all unusual for companies to train people to work in high-performing teams but then publicly celebrate or reward only the work of outstanding individuals.

Reward and recognition systems, communication and performance feedback devices, and training tools must be aligned. This begins with vision and mission statements but becomes real through work systems, communications, management coaching, personal and professional development, performance measurement—and, of course, reward systems.

Improving where you're headed first requires understanding where you currently stand. Most organizations with more than a few hundred employees would be hard pressed to give good answers to most of the following questions:

Reward Systems

- Is there an inventory or audit of all reinforcement plans (social, celebrations, cash, noncash, and others) presently available at any level of the organization?

- What corporate objectives are supported by each reward or recognition plan, and how do managers know if they've been successful?

- Are the reward systems consistent with the organizational culture and management messages?

- How well do people understand how each plan works? For that matter, do they know that the plans exist?

- Who is eligible for each plan, and how many actually receive awards?

- How much is spent on each plan, and what is the average (or median if there is a wide range) award amount per person?

- What is the value contribution from the plans (performance improvement, reinforcing mission and vision statements, teamwork, customer success, maintaining or improving the organization's competitive position in the labor market, and the like)?

Communications and Performance Feedback

- How often are company or organizational unit measures and performance objectives communicated and explained to all employees?

- How often are employees told about the organization's successes, failures, and competition in the marketplace?

- How often are employees asked—and more important, listened to—about their ideas for improving company or business unit performance?

Training and Development

- How many personal or professional development programs are available? Are the programs aligned with corporate strategy and goals, including creation of a team-based culture? Or are most programs simply nice to have?

- What is the participation rate? Does scheduling make it easy for employees to attend needed training?

- Is training effectively integrated into the management coaching process for each employee, either through a performance management plan or a competency development program?

- Do reward plans reinforce training and development efforts?

As you move toward team-based culture, old strategies and practices must be maintained, redesigned, or thrown out. But conducting such a systems alignment audit is critical before installing a team-based reward or recognition system; doing the latter in isolation will greatly limit its impact. The objective is to create an integrated portfolio of practices that makes maximum use of human capital to improve business performance.

Susan's experience leveraging human capital has not been hugely successful. Management had sent out directives and established many measures of success (usually financial) since she'd been there. Management by Objectives (MBO) was the rage for awhile, and is now part of most managers' jobs, but Susan isn't convinced it makes a great deal of difference in people's or the organization's performance.

How can she create genuine accountability at the managerial and supervisory levels for supporting and rewarding teamwork? Performance management is a mixed bag. The organization now purports to focus on developing competencies and has encouraged managers to move people around in the organization, hoping that will increase their sense of satisfaction and develop more diverse skills in the workforce. The merit pay plan, however, means only a 3–5 percent raise to most employees each year, barely keeping pace with inflation. A few outstanding performers get 8–10 percent. Most employees believe they have a right to salary increases no matter what, and there are few if any incentive plans tied to organizational unit or project team performance. And there are even fewer recognition tools used to celebrate teamwork in the organization.

As the organization was preparing its application for the Malcolm Baldrige National Quality Award, continuous improvement project teams sprouted up everywhere. But most of what those teams suggested were simply integrated into departments' standard way of doing business, and team activity has dwindled away.

Employees of the month and the year are recognized, nominated by their immediate supervisors, and selected by a top management committee. But lately, Susan has had to beg to get nominations every month, and the quality of the nominations is dropping rapidly. Also, there is little peer-based recognition.

Any project team such as CONPRO is considered to be rewarded simply if it presents results to top management. The cookout was appreciated, but the T-shirts were misunderstood as representing the true value of their contributions. Probably a mistake to pass those out when she did.

A few years ago, Susan created a gainsharing plan for production. It was based on a complex formula measuring reduction of labor costs per unit of production against a standard. Engineering got tied up redefining standards and in the difficult practice of measuring performance against goals, and the plan simply lost momentum. Payouts shrunk and the plan was terminated not long after introduction.

But Susan figured it was time to take up the reward and recognition issue again. Well-designed team-based rewards have a unifying effect, offer an opportunity to create alignment and accountability, and spur performance improvement and collaborative behaviors. She knows rewards alone won't solve the problem, but they will get people's attention and give teams a sense that the fruits of their labor aren't going only into the organization's coffers.

Then she found the presentation from the Conference Board workshop. It described a reinforcement model for choosing and using various reward and recognition strategies.

THE ROADMAP: AN ORGANIZING MODEL FOR REWARDS

The reinforcement model is an easy way to look at your reward plan options. It begins with the organization's objectives and desired culture.

Business objectives tend to be straightforward. Profit, revenue growth, cycle time, EVA, financial return calculations, customer satisfaction, quality, new product development, and operating expense reduction are typical. Reward plans must be aligned with these objectives to ensure management support. Objectives that would be nice to accomplish are not as effective as ones that are key to success. Some objectives translate nicely into measures against which performance can be judged. Some require drilling down to find those activities, projects, and relevant contributory measures that, when addressed, will affect performance.

Susan ticked off the organization's primary business objectives:

- *Growth*
- *Cycle time*
- *Retaining the workforce*
- *Return on net assets*
- *Customer satisfaction, loyalty, and success*

The list could contain up to twenty objectives, all important at different levels of the organization, but she understood that people couldn't focus on more than three to five. If she had to put her people to work on just a few objectives, these would be the critical ones.

The best plans for losing weight or becoming physically fit aren't those that helped some mythical other person in a book you read, but are those tailored to *your* unique needs and lifestyle. The same is true with reward plans. The best are those that the organization will embrace as important to meet its needs and so will follow through on. That means all levels of management accepting the plans as business strategies to engage employees in meeting the objectives. And that is a matter of culture.

Organizational culture (and how to influence it) has been the subject of many books and much academic research. The organization's vision, mission, history, operating norms, strategy, environment, and structure form culture. For the purpose of discussing reward plans, culture can be described as how the organization utilizes its employees to get work done. It is more than work design. It is the way people are considered when there is a desire to improve performance.

One general description of the whole organization's culture is possible, although organizations are made up of a number of suborganizational units, each with a slightly different culture. Accounting has a different culture than marketing. Manufacturing has a different culture than customer service. Hopefully, they are aligned with the overreaching organizational culture, with the differences simply reflecting the nature of the work they do.

One of the keys to success in improving organizational performance is to ensure that reward plans reinforce the desired culture, or at least attempt to reduce the gap between the existing and desired culture.

Figure 2.1 is a way to describe organizational culture. It ranges from a focus on individual tasks and jobs to a collaborative and cross-functional team-based organization. How performance is improved is generally driven by the culture.

What part of the continuum should you target? Simply put, the desired culture should be the one that best suits the needs of your business. If your desired culture differs from the existing one, it's important to structure any new reward or recognition system to reinforce the ideal culture, the one you're moving toward. For example, if your most influential reward plan is to recognize and celebrate outstanding performers and you want a culture of collaborative teamwork, you've got a disconnect. An organizational unit incentive plan that rewards results through teamwork would be more appropriate, or could be added to existing plans. Reward systems need to be aligned with the desired culture.

Susan believes her present culture is hierarchical and somewhat paternalistic. The nice offices, day care center, employee gym, and excellent cafeteria are important for attracting and retaining employees, but they're strictly environmental benefits, almost table stakes for staying in the recruitment and retention game these days.

The prevailing management style of command and control stems from a time when cost control was paramount. But now revenue growth and rapid product innovation are the new totems. Management respects and values employees, but old traditions die hard, and the company still largely manages and views people— headcount—as a cost of doing business, not as a competitive advantage.

She believes moving to a team-based, collaborative culture would be the best fit for the organization's new strategic thrust. She needs employees to be focused on what's best for the business and, somehow, also make that the best for them. Equally important is engaging management in support of this new culture.

Figure 2.1. How Organization Culture Generally Drives Performance Improvement.

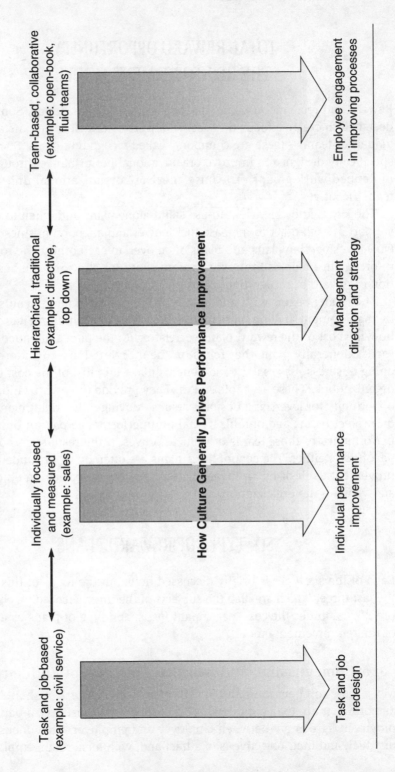

Organizational Culture: How Work Gets Done

Task and job-based (example: civil service)

Individually focused and measured (example: sales)

Hierarchical, traditional (example: directive, top down)

Team-based, collaborative (example: open-book, fluid teams)

How Culture Generally Drives Performance Improvement

Task and job redesign

Individual performance improvement

Management direction and strategy

Employee engagement in improving processes

TOTAL REWARD OPPORTUNITY: THE REINFORCEMENT MODEL

Reward and recognition plans run the gamut in organizations. Some plans are designed to create a focus on specific objectives or celebrate outstanding individuals or teams—these are commonly called recognition plans. Some plans are specifically designed to improve organizational performance through the work of defined work groups or teams—these are organizational unit and project team incentives.

The key is knowing when to use stand-alone plans and when to use them in support of each other to increase their power and affect on business objectives. Objectives overlap plans and plans often overlap each other. The role of the reinforcement model is to provide a framework for choosing the best combination of reward or recognition plans.

The model begins with a look at how the cost of plans (payouts) is viewed by management and the participant focus. The continuum in Figure 2.2 relates how the cost of the reward plans correlate with the plan's intended participant focus. Generally plans that focus on the individual are considered a cost of doing business. Base salary and benefits make up most of the cost of people in organizations. These are table stakes. They provide the organization with little opportunity for leveraging business results. Moving to the right, plans that focus on project teams and organizational unit performance pay off only when the performance of those teams or units improves. If the results are not there, the payoff isn't either. The cost of these plans are often offset or funded by the improvement itself or by an investment in meeting or exceeding objectives that add value to the organization.

SIX TYPES OF REWARD PLANS

Each of the six types is briefly discussed here, but the focus of this book is on the last three, which are also the subjects of the three succeeding chapters. Figure 2.2 combines the cost, participant focus, and type of plans as an overview of the reinforcement model.

Compensation and Benefits: The Land of Entitlement

Most basic compensation and benefit plans (see Figure 2.3) should be viewed as nothing more than entitlements—a cost of doing business, a part of the employment agreement between employee and employer. They focus on the individual, and their objective is to attract and, with luck, retain employees. They

Figure 2.2. The Reinforcement Model.

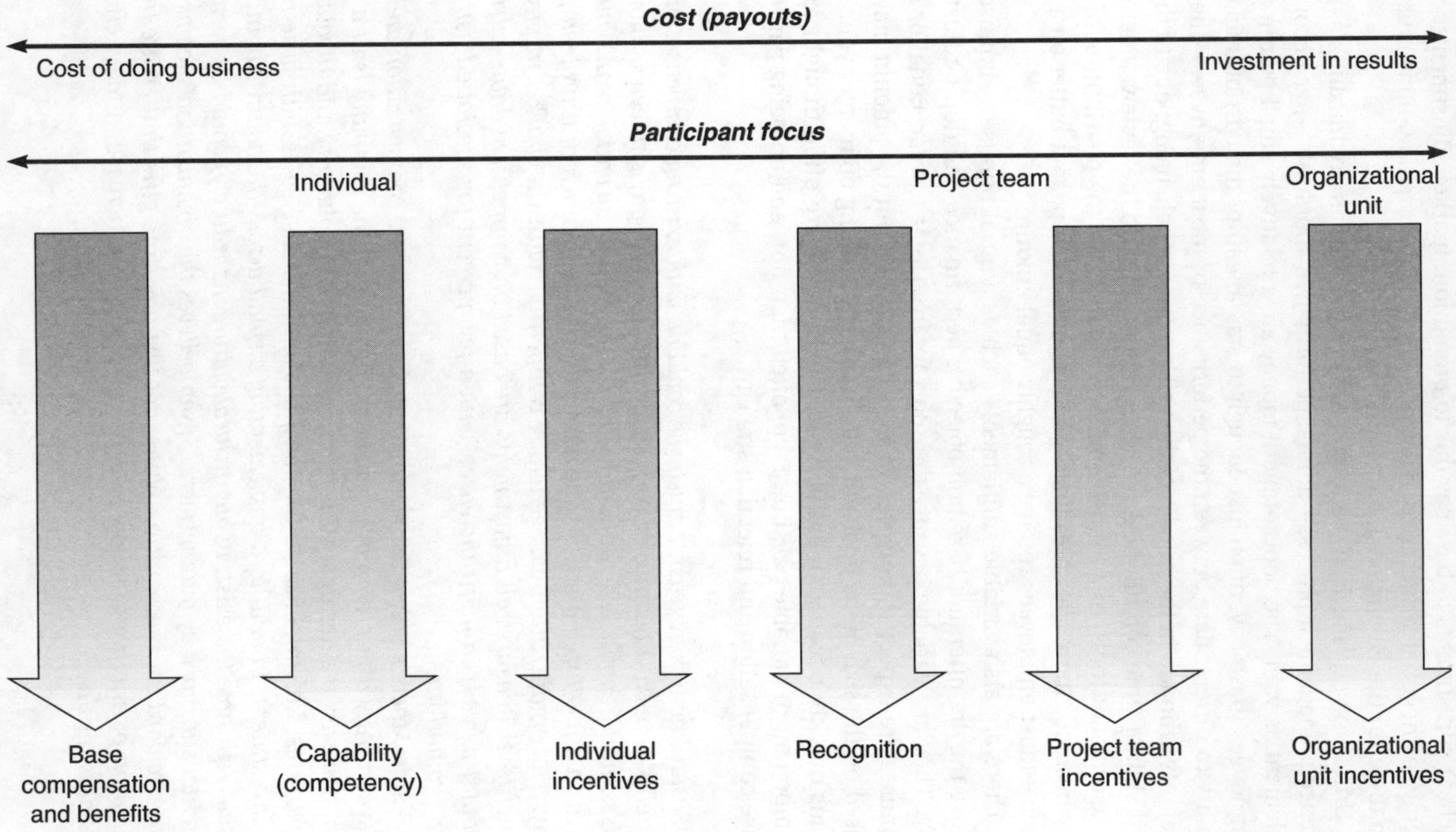

Cost (payouts)

Cost of doing business ←——————— Investment in results

Participant focus

Individual ——— Project team ——— Organizational unit

Base compensation and benefits

Capability (competency)

Individual incentives

Recognition

Project team incentives

Organizational unit incentives

include adjustments to base pay due to promotion, market adjustments, cost of living, or negotiated increases. They are simply what organizations must ante up to get in the employment game.

Unfortunately, much of the merit pay connected to an organization's performance management process—annual performance appraisals—has become entitlement as well. The pools of merit money are a relatively small percentage of employees' base pay, often just enough to stay ahead of the cost of living. The ability to differentiate between the performance of most employees—the great majority who fall in the middle of the bell curve—is challenging, due to the limited skill or time commitment of managers forced to do the reviews, ineffective measurement tools, or a limited employee pool. Thus, the distribution of merit pay becomes more like spreading smooth than chunky peanut butter on a sandwich—most employees receive a roughly equal amount.

There are also variable entitlements such as annual bonuses—bonuses because they're often not based on objective performance and don't adjust base pay. They are variable because they do vary from year to year. Equal or larger bonuses are expected, however, in succeeding years, but the amount may vary based on the size of the pool and your manager's shifting opinion of you. These plans quickly become an entitlement. The bonuses are often thought to be a component of variable pay, but, more often than not, end up being part of the base compensation and retention strategy.

Susan knew there wasn't much she could do with existing compensation and benefits to reward teamwork; corporate controlled base pay strategies, allowable raises, and benefits. The annual bonus (management incentive plan) only applied to a few top managers. She didn't think it was much of a problem, anyway. The organization was generally competitive with the market in pay and benefits. HR ensures all adjustments are based on competitive data—currently about 4 percent in merit increases. with a few percent for special adjustments and promotions.

Besides, there's only one measure that changes to core compensation and benefits can truly affect: employee retention. Turnover in the company isn't a problem, however; it's averaging 7 percent, including both voluntary and involuntary departures. Raising base pay or benefits would increase costs with little return on investment. In addition, implementing a small across-the-board pay increase would reinforce the existing hierarchical culture, as it likely would be seen as a paternalistic move by management. Susan believes the organization's teams need active reward and recognition plans, not just one-time gifts that create the expectation of another to follow with no corresponding increase in team effort or business results.

❖

Figure 2.3. Base Compensation and Benefits.

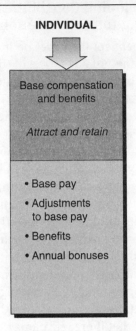

Figure 2.4. Capability.

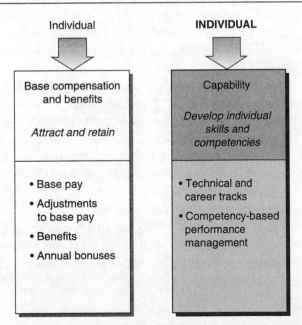

Developing Capabilities and
Engaging the Organizational Brain

Organizations are more dependent than ever on intellectual capital to compete in today's marketplace. Taking full advantage of that capital requires engaging not just the minds and capabilities of top product developers and computer programmers, but of the mail clerks, administrative assistants, and receptionists who have plenty of untapped, organization-specific knowledge to apply in pursuit of strategic goals. See Figure 2.4.

Special reward plans for technical and professional employees are increasingly being expanded to any job or role that falls under the heading of "independent contributor." These plans acknowledge that moving into management isn't the only way to improve your lot in an organization or achieve career desires. Many individual contributors don't have the desire—nor the complex management competencies—to lead, coach, or manage. It is not what they do best. Anyone who's worked for a manager ill-suited for the role understands how painful it can be for both parties. Technical and professional career tracks, and corresponding reward opportunities, increasingly allow for progression that doesn't include a stop in management.

It may go without saying that if organizations can do one thing to better develop appropriate competencies in the workforce it's to rethink the much-maligned performance management process. Performance management as practiced in most organizations is nothing more than a forced ranking system designed to generate a range of merit increases that falls within an organization's labor budget. In this use, critical skill development, goal setting, and coaching objectives of performance management take a back seat to the merit increase mechanism.

The role of traditional performance management is changing. As organizations continue to flatten out by stripping away middle management layers, there are fewer opportunities to move up in the traditional way. If organizations want to keep more of their valued employees, they need to find new ways for horizontal moves to keep them engaged, growing, and contributing. When such lateral relocation has the intent of broadening an employee's expertise, creating more big-picture thinkers, and creating a fresh enthusiasm for work, it can be a boon to both employee and organization.

Competencies are not traits or attitudes (loyalty, smartness, punctuality, and the like) but rather skills and behaviors that fall into three categories:

1. Job or role responsibilities
2. Facilitating competencies
3. Business and financial knowledge

The first indicates how well an employee fulfills his or her job description. What competencies are missing? What additional competencies need developing to take the employee to the next level?

The second, facilitating competencies, requires gauging how well employees work with peers and share their expertise so it can be useful to others. This is a critical competency for effective teamwork. Multisource feedback (often called 360-degree feedback) is a premier tool managers can use to find out just how well an employee functions as a team member.

Business and financial competency is how well employees understand finance and the profit-and-loss side of the business. Not surprisingly, the business and financial literacy level of nonmanagers usually ranks low. Developing more of those competencies at the front-line level can contribute to greater leveraging of human capital for the organization's—and the employee's—benefit.

Rarely, however, do companies directly reward the development of specific competencies within their workforces. Promotions, special assignments, or transfers into different roles to spur competency development do, of course, often lead to increases in base pay. The "add a competency, increase pay, or get a bonus" strategy—sometimes called skill-based pay—is very difficult to implement on a large scale in sizeable organizations, however. The sheer number of jobs, existing skill levels, skill development programs, certification, fairness, and other factors make the process so cumbersome it collapses under its own administrative weight. The real reward here is intrinsic. Employees feel they are learning, growing, taking on new challenges—and moving closer to their actualized selves.

Susan knows creating a formal, competency-based performance management plan out of what is now a haphazard development process is a crucial, but time-consuming, process. What she can do in the near term is to create more intensive training in team building, including more education around the team champion and team member roles. She can also insist that each employee's performance management review include a list of key teamwork competencies, and plan to develop any skills or behaviors deemed lacking.

Individual Incentives

An incentive is based on the certainty that if a specific, objectively measured objective is achieved there will be an award (see Figure 2.5). The required performance is specified in advance, as is the size of the award. The award can be cash, stock, time off, merchandise, travel, special assignments—anything of value to the recipient and consistent with the performance required. Quite often the size of the award increases as the performance increases, according to a pre-announced schedule. A sales commission plan is the most common of individual incentive plans.

Figure 2.5. Individual Incentives.

Individual	Individual	**INDIVIDUAL**
Base compensation and benefits *Attract and retain*	Capability *Develop individual skills and competencies*	Individual incentives *Improve individual performance*
• Base pay • Adjustments to base pay • Benefits • Annual bonuses	• Technical and career tracks • Competency-based performance management	• Sales incentives or commissions • Piece rate • MBO-based incentives

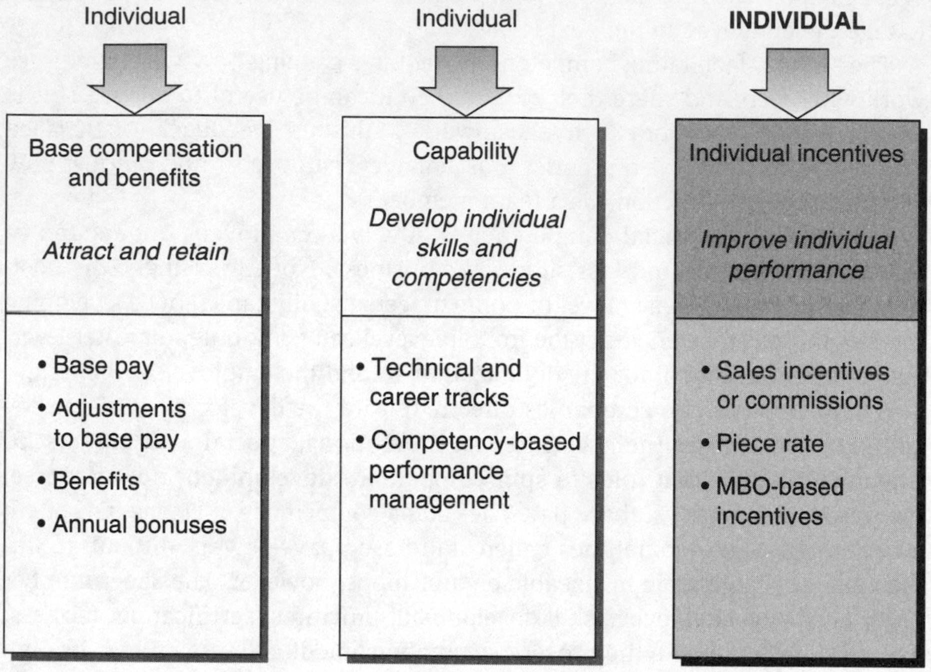

The effectiveness of the plan *as an incentive* is significantly reduced if management does not specify the linkage between performance and award. That's why use of an annual bonus that depends on management discretion—managers' largely subjective decision about how much of the bonus pool an individual will receive—is not an effective incentive to improve individual performance. It is the manager's subjectivity, not performance against published goals—objective data—that determines the reward. MBO-based plans attempt to create objectivity and are as successful as they are able to be truly objective.

Although still in use, time-honored individual incentives like piece-rate systems—where an employee earns more the more he produces—have grown rare in corporate America.

Susan quickly rejected individual incentives as a way to develop teamwork for all of BIZCOM. Almost by definition such incentives work against developing a culture of teamwork, and she doesn't believe they can help drive her primary business objectives. She decides to use them selectively for signing bonuses, but not to make it a general practice.

Recognition Plans

Recognition plans are investments in human capital and often reflect the culture of an organization (see Figure 2.6). These plans can apply to individuals, project teams, or permanent work groups (organizational units, by our definition). Recognition can take the form of a simple "thank you," a cash spot bonus, or a trip to Bali.

The critical distinction between recognition and incentive plans is certainty. Recognition is after-the-fact, awarded after behavior is exhibited or results accomplished; it is not "do this and get that" according to a preannounced schedule, but "we saw you do this—thanks." Recognition plans do not guarantee awards.

There are as many variations of recognition plans as there are creative minds. They are very powerful, and generally underutilized, tools for encouraging repeat positive performance and in building team morale. Getting the most out of a recognition plan requires ongoing attention and regular refreshing so that it stays meaningful to employees.

Most recognition plans fall into one of these categories:

- *Celebrating organizational objectives*—Picnics, pizza parties, special lunches, regular meetings to share accomplishments and challenges, and information-trading sessions are all examples of recognizing both the objectives of the organization and the importance of people in meeting those objectives. They are inexpensive, fun, significant, and make a positive cultural statement. They must be frequent, open, honest, and

Figure 2.6. Recognition Plans.

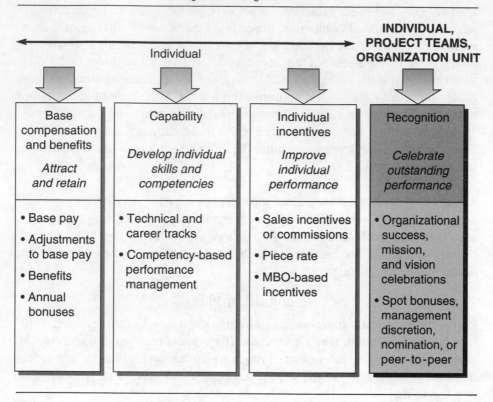

Individual			INDIVIDUAL, PROJECT TEAMS, ORGANIZATION UNIT
Base compensation and benefits *Attract and retain*	**Capability** *Develop individual skills and competencies*	**Individual incentives** *Improve individual performance*	**Recognition** *Celebrate outstanding performance*
• Base pay • Adjustments to base pay • Benefits • Annual bonuses	• Technical and career tracks • Competency-based performance management	• Sales incentives or commissions • Piece rate • MBO-based incentives	• Organizational success, mission, and vision celebrations • Spot bonuses, management discretion, nomination, or peer-to-peer

involving. They are about focus and celebration, rather than manipulation and hype.

- *Reinforcing outstanding performers as individuals, teams, or organizational units*—This is a formalized process of spot awards. They can be given at management's discretion, through a nomination process with a committee deciding who will be rewarded, or from fellow employees or customers. They single out contributors or teams of contributors to say "thanks" and "well done." They can be done in private (as opposed to secret) or in public. The awards can be cash, merchandise, special assignments, the opportunity to learn and develop, promotions, or a honest expression of "thank you." They can be time-based (monthly awards) or based on events (an accomplishment or contribution).

- *Reinforcing desired behaviors or activities*—These are generally social recognition of the completion of a training course, special project, or even changed behavior.

- *Service*—Recognizing years of service to an organization is the most common of plans, so common it is rarely mentioned when listing the active plans. It has become an entitlement, but does send the message that the organization knows you are staying with it and wants to celebrate the fact. The traditional pin or plaque is being replaced with a selection of items allowing the employee to choose something more meaningful and useful.

The number and visibility of recognition plans says a lot about an organization's culture. The more dynamic and meaningful the plans, the more appreciated the employees feel.

Susan decides to make a fundamental change in her two existing recognition plans, Employee of the Month and Chairman's Award. (Whether the chairman will agree is another issue.) She changes the EoM award to a spot bonus plan that allows any supervisor or manager to award individuals or teams up to $500 in cash or merchandise from a catalogue with no approval. For spot awards between $500 and $5,000, one-step-up management approval is required, and awards above $5,000 require the CEO's approval. These rewards can be given anytime, but only for work that contributes to a team's primary objectives or demonstrates desired team behaviors. But the awards aren't only at management discretion; nonmanagement employees can nominate peers or other teams for awards through their own managers.

She appoints a cross-functional, cross-level team of eight to promote and monitor the plan. At the end of each six-month period, two members rotate off and two other employees come on. When people rotate off, Susan recognizes them for their contributions with letters of thanks or other symbolic, noncash awards.

Project Team Incentives

Project teams are usually, but not always, formed by management to tackle specific projects or challenges with a defined time frame—reviewing processes for efficiency or cost-savings recommendations, launching a new software product, or implementing enterprise resource planning systems are just a few examples. In other cases teams self-form around specific issues, or as part of continuous improvement initiatives such as team-based suggestion systems. See Figure 2.7 on pages 40–41.

Project teams can have cross-functional membership or simply be a subset of an existing organizational unit. The person who sponsors the team—its "champion"—typically creates an incentive plan with specific objective measures and an award schedule tied to achieving those measures. To qualify as an incentive, the plan must included preannounced goals, with a do this, get that guarantee for teams. The incentive usually varies with the value added by the project.

Project team incentive plans usually have some combination of these basic measures:

- *Project milestones*—Hit a milestone, on budget and on time, and all team members earn a defined amount. Although sound in theory, there are inherent problems in tying financial incentives to hitting milestones. Milestones often change for good reason (technological advances, market shifts, other developments) and you don't want the team and management to get into a negotiation on slipping dates to trigger the incentive. Unless milestones are set in stone and reaching them is simply a function of the team doing its normal, everyday job, it's generally best to use recognition—after-the-fact celebration of reaching milestones—rather than tying financial incentives to it.

  Rewards need not always be time-based, such that when the team hits a milestone by a certain date it earns a reward. If, for example, a product development team debugs a new piece of software on time, that's not necessarily a reason to reward it. But if it discovers and solves an unsuspected problem or writes better code before a delivery date, rewards are due.

- *Project completion*—All team members earn a defined amount when they complete the project on budget and on time (or to the team champion's quality standards).

- *Value added*—This award is a function of the value added by a project, and depends largely on the ability of the organization to create and track objective measures. Examples include reduced turnaround time on customer requests, improved cycle times for product development, cost savings due to new process efficiencies, or incremental profit or market share created by the product or service developed or implemented by the project team.

One warning about project incentive plans: they can be very effective in helping teams stay focused, accomplish goals, and feel like they are rewarded for their hard work, but they tend to be exclusionary. Not everyone can be on a project team. Some employees (team members) will have an opportunity to earn an incentive that others (nonteam members) do not. There is a lack of internal equity. One way to address this is to reward core team members with incentives for reaching team goals, and recognizes peripheral players who supported the team, either by offering advice, resources, or a pair of hands, or by covering for project team members back at their regular job.

Some projects are of such strategic importance that you can live with these internal equity problems and nonteam members' grousing about exclusionary incentives. Bottom line, though, is this tool should be used cautiously.

One type of project incentive plan can help sidestep perceived equity problems, however: incentives for self-formed teams. Under this plan employees are encouraged to form their own teams—usually between five and eight people— to take on a specific objective and emerge with a way to make things better. Team-based suggestion systems are one manifestation of this plan, with cost reduction as a common target.

In well-designed plans, teams have the responsibility not only of coming up with an idea or solution, but of writing up a business and implementation plan, getting managers affected by the change to sign off, developing the cost justification (savings, or degree of performance improvement), submitting it to management for approval, and then taking an active role in idea implementation.

Again, a preannounced reward schedule—do this, get that, usually based on cost reduction—is used for all such incentive plans. Special consideration is given to projects for which cost reduction is not an appropriate goal.

Susan realized a good project team incentive would have made all the difference to the CONPRO team. It wouldn't have eliminated the usual difficulties most teams face in melding different styles and approaches to accomplish project goals, but it would have made team members feel more appreciated and forced Judy and other team members to agree on more quantifiable project outcomes as the basis of the financial incentive.

She decides to lay out guidelines for future project incentive plans. The guidelines include a payout range (20 percent of base pay maximum per team member for hitting preannounced goals, 5 percent minimum), time limit (no projects longer than twelve months), project goals (must focus on company business objectives), and participation (equal payout for all assigned core team members with the exception of the team leader, who earns one and a half times the

Figure 2.7. Project Team Incentives.

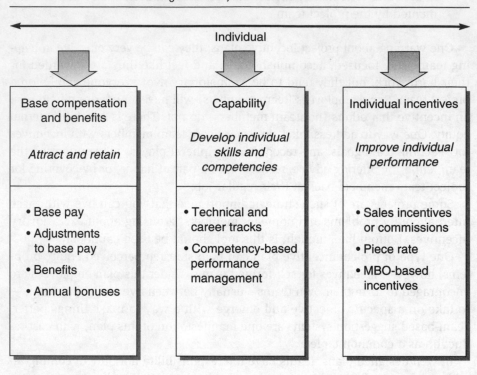

Individual

Base compensation and benefits	Capability	Individual incentives
Attract and retain	*Develop individual skills and competencies*	*Improve individual performance*
• Base pay • Adjustments to base pay • Benefits • Annual bonuses	• Technical and career tracks • Competency-based performance management	• Sales incentives or commissions • Piece rate • MBO-based incentives

Figure 2.7. Project Team Incentives (continued).

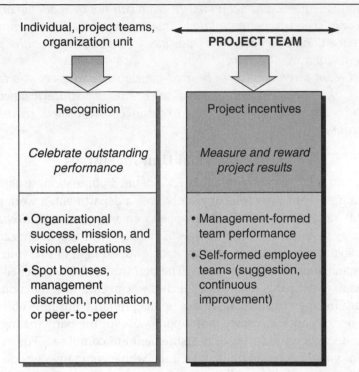

individual team member amount). The team can be composed of either full-time or part-time members, but not a mix. (A team can not be made up of three people who only spend 10 percent of their time on the team, and seven who spend 100 percent.) Champions are given guidelines for developing incentive plans, and Susan must approve any plan.

Project team incentives are to be used judiciously and every effort should be made to link the team's work to one of the company's strategic objectives. She also decides the plans will only apply to management-formed, cross-functional project teams.

Organizational Unit Incentives

Organizational unit incentive plans cover a defined population, usually an organizational unit—an entire company, a division, a department, a work group (see Figure 2.8 on pages 44–45). The unit appears on an organizational chart. Participation may be limited to certain levels of employees in that organizational unit (for example: everyone, all nonexempt people, all exempt, or everyone but those on the management incentive plan). The performance award schedule is pre-announced; participants know how much they can earn as a function of performance against the measures. It focuses on the primarily business objectives and can use performance measures most appropriate for the participating organizational unit. Sometimes levels of measurement are combined. For example, 25 percent of payout is based on how well the whole company does on return on assets, 25 percent on how well the division improves cycle time, and 50 percent split between two measures at the department level. All measures, however, should be aligned with the primary business objectives.

Organizational unit incentives can be the most powerful reward plan type to support a culture of teamwork. They can make a business strategy come alive. A good plan is a powerful way to leverage human capital to improve performance because of the following:

- It engages all or most of the employee base.
- It pays out only when the improvement occurs.
- It is based on results, not activities.
- It provides an opportunity to communicate, reinforce, educate, and engage employees for the accomplishment of specific and critical objectives.
- It can be measured for effectiveness.
- It is dynamic because it changes as business needs change.

Organizational unit incentive plans are usually announced for a year with the option to be revised, kept the same, or terminated, depending on the outcome of an effectiveness assessment.

One overlooked aspect of organizational unit incentive plans is the opportunity they provide to create accountability for all levels of management. Most managers are measured on their individual contributions rather than the accomplishment of their areas of responsibility and the performance of their people. The discipline of actually cutting a check based on performance against measurable objectives provides the opportunity *and discipline* to follow through, recalibrate, and actually find out what you got for your money (something lacking in MBO and traditional management measurement plans.)

Some organizational unit incentive plans are really awareness and communications plans in drag. It is rare that the plan designers realize they have designed a plan that is a methodology for the distribution of payouts based on a formula, rather than a plan that improves performance. These are long-line-of-sight plans. ("Line of sight" is the extent to which employees believe that they or their work group, department, or the like can actually contribute to affecting the measures.) Economic value added (EVA), earnings before taxes, return on capital assets, and customer satisfaction indexes are examples of measures often not understood by employees, making those measures have a long line of sight. Companywide measures, covering diverse divisions and departments and sometimes international operations, also contribute to a long line of sight. The existence of the plan has little affect on the performance because the measures are too remote to the average employee.

These long-line-of-sight organizational unit incentive plans can be effective if management understands what "effective" means. These plans are for communication of critical objectives, the opportunity to educate employees about the measures, and to reinforce the vision and mission. The question then becomes: Is the value of a plan worth the expense? Usually the answer is yes, particularly when the company has purposely decided to pay people slightly below the competitive labor market and make up the difference, and more, through the organizational unit incentive plan. The measures used in a plan for this strategy need to be calibrated to ensure a payout of at least enough to span the gap between the market and the organization's base pay, but it is the upside opportunity that makes it attractive to the employee. The fact that the payout is variable with overall performance protects the company from payout unless the performance is there.

Organizational unit incentive plans gives Susan the focus she is looking for. She makes a strong statement that this is a framework for action, with alignment to primary business objectives, to engage all employees in a common purpose: one that is good for the organization and good for them. She forms a cross-functional, multilevel design team that goes through a discovery process to ensure its members understand how the employees felt about the organization and what management would really support. They design the plan and present it to Susan after about four months, spending about a day every two weeks in

Figure 2.8. Organizational Unit Incentives.

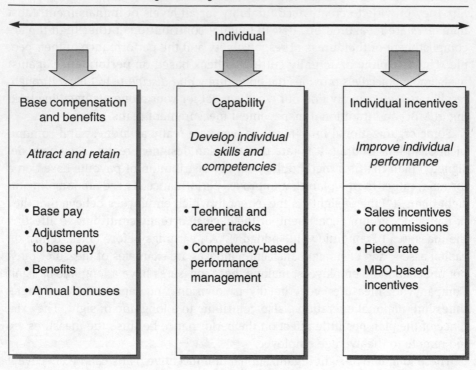

Figure 2.8. Organizational Unit Incentives (continued).

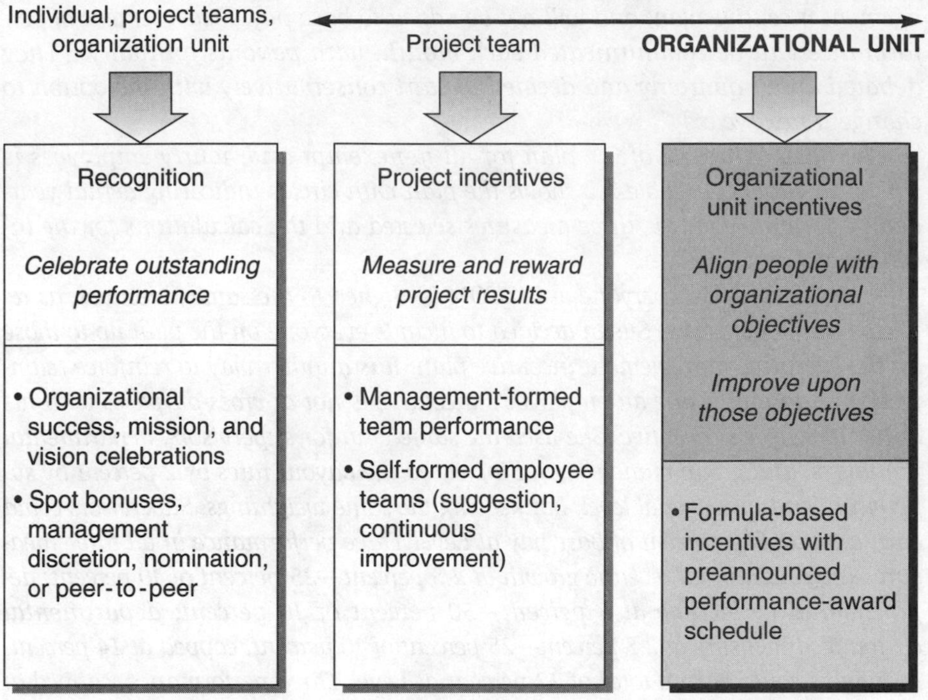

Individual, project teams, organization unit	Project team	**ORGANIZATIONAL UNIT**
Recognition	**Project incentives**	**Organizational unit incentives**
Celebrate outstanding performance	*Measure and reward project results*	*Align people with organizational objectives* *Improve upon those objectives*
• Organizational success, mission, and vision celebrations • Spot bonuses, management discretion, nomination, or peer-to-peer	• Management-formed team performance • Self-formed employee teams (suggestion, continuous improvement)	• Formula-based incentives with preannounced performance-award schedule

formal meetings. All payouts are in addition to their existing reward plans (base pay, adjustments to base pay, and benefits), do not apply to those on the management incentive plan, and will not be added to base pay. Measurement of performance will be communicated each month, with payouts annually. (They debated about quarterly and decided to start conservatively with the option to change it next year.)

The basic structure of the plan for all nonexempt and hourly employees is shown in Table 2.1. Table 2.2 shows the plan with circles indicating actual year-end performance for the three measures selected and the calculations for the incentive payout.

To make sure that everyone at BIZCOM is aligned to the same objectives, as reflected in the measures, Susan decided to include everyone on the plan up to those on the executive management incentive plan. It is another way to reinforce teamwork and to make sure an employee's incentive is not at cross-purposes with his or her manager's incentive. She used the same plan for supervisors, departmental managers, and group managers and increased the payout rates by 2 percent by supervisory and managerial level, but keeping the same weightings. Supervisors could earn a total of 10 percent of base pay at Level Three performance in all three measures (organizational revenue growth at 2.5 percent—25 percent of 10 percent; departmental cycle time at 5 percent—50 percent of 10 percent; departmental customized measure at 2.5 percent—25 percent of 10 percent, capped at 14 percent. Managers could earn a total of 12 percent at Level Three performance, capped at 16 percent, and departmental managers 14 percent and 18 percent, respectively.

The biggest surprise was how much difficulty the design team had getting agreement on the measures for each department. What were assumed to be tight measures (after all, they had been running the business with those measures for years) turned out to be not quite good enough when an incentive was tied to them. They began to call the process the "Drano effect." It forced people to confront the legitimacy of the measures and how they can be collected and fed back to the participants in a timely and creditable manner. Susan and the team agreed the process was worth it even if the "Drano effect" was the only outcome of the process.

She and the team presented the plan to the rest of top management after individual preparation by each decision maker. The presenter was a nonexempt production employee who served on the team. Her passion for the plan and insight about how the organization worked from the bottom up added a great deal of credibility to the process. The plan was approved if quarterly reviews are held for top management and a complete assessment begins two months before the end of the first year of operation.

THE MIX: LEVERAGING HUMAN CAPITAL

Susan understands that one size or type of reward plan does not fit all her business needs. She also understands the art of the possible. She cannot do everything

Table 2.1. BIZCOM's Organizational Unit Incentive Plan.

Measure	Weight	Match Previous Year's Performance	Percent of Base Pay by Performance Level for Nonexempt and Hourly Employees				
			Level One (90% probability of reaching)	Level Two (70% probability of reaching)	Level Three—Target (50% probability of reaching)	Level Four (30% probability of reaching)	Level Five (10% probability of reaching)
Organizational revenue growth	25%	0%	1% of base pay	1.5%	2%	2.5%	3%
Departmental cycle time	50%	0%	2%	3%	4%	5%	6%
Departmental measure, customized for unique needs	25%	0%	1%	1.5%	2%	2.5%	3%
Totals	100%	0%	4%	6%	8%	10%	12%

Table 2.2. Payout Example.

Measure	Weight	Match Previous Year's Performance	Level One (90% probability of reaching)	Level Two (70% probability of reaching)	Level Three—Target (50% probability of reaching)	Level Four (30% probability of reaching)	Level Five (10% probability of reaching)
					Percent of Base Pay by Performance Level		
Organizational revenue growth	25%	0	1	1.5	2	2.5	3
Departmental cycle time	50%	0	2	3	4	5	6
Departmental measure, customized for unique needs	25%	0	1	1.5	2	2.5	3

Payout Calculation:

Organizational revenue growth earns 2%

Departmental cycle time earns 6%

Departmental measure (customized) earns 1%

Total of 2 + 6 + 1 = 9% of base pay

at once. Her culture and management team need time to adapt to a more activist strategy in getting people aligned with the primary business objectives and improving upon them. In her case, base compensation and benefits are not the problem, nor are individual incentives. (Individual incentives can be a problem, as they are generally inconsistent with a culture of teamwork.) Performance management as a competency development process, as opposed to a merit increase tool, is a longer-term need.

Recognition (spot bonuses), guidelines for an expanded use of project team incentives, and an organizational unit incentive plan are quicker routes to performance improvement and her desired culture of teamwork. All have clear, but different, objectives and should be designed to complement each other. It is a mix of plans that can become the framework for action for the core employees and the management ranks. It is a carefully considered mix that reflects the degree to which the organization believes that people can make a difference.

Remember: an average plan, well implemented, will always do better than a brilliant plan, poorly implemented. Therefore, the key is to implement what you have designed, and that requires doing three things:

- *Gaining management ownership through supervisory levels.* Approval does not mean commitment. Management commitment is the critical distinction between plans that are effective and those that just limp along with support limited to lip service. It requires education on how the plans work and how they are tools to engage, educate, and motivate people to meet the organization's needs.

- *Rolling out the plan and operating it as a business strategy.* Effective plans constantly communicate performance to date, educate on the measures, and formally engage employees in contributing to success. It is also important to get feedback from the employees on a regular basis. You have time to fix something if you can find out what is not working earlier rather than later.

- *Assessment of effectiveness.* Management reviews of performance should be held quarterly. Two months before the end of an annual plan, a total review should be done, gathering information from employees and management obtaining performance data. Plans do not live forever. They require refurbishment regularly.

The rest of this book retells companies' experiences with recognition, project team incentives, and organizational unit incentives. The intent is not to suggest best practices (of which there are very few), but to show real experiences with reinforcement model plans for organizations wanting to move toward teamwork. All the companies had to customize the model to their own situation. All had their successes and learned some hard lessons. With luck, their experience will make yours more profitable.

CHAPTER THREE

Company Profiles: Recognition Plans

Recognition plans are investments in human capital—people—that often reflect the culture of an organization. They can apply to individuals, project teams, or permanent work groups (organizational units). Recognition can be a simple "thank you," a free trip overseas, or anything in between. This chapter examines five companies' team-based recognition plans that do not rely on a "do this, get that" formula. They do not, in other words, guarantee awards for anything other than exemplary performance.

CHASE MANHATTAN'S GLOBAL RECOGNITION EFFORT

An international bank based in New York with seventy thousand employees around the world, $20 billion in sales, offices in Europe, Asia, and Latin America, and a heritage that traces back two hundred years. Not a setting, perhaps, where you'd expect to see a thriving recognition culture that encourages employees to single out and applaud one another for daily acts of competence as well as near heroism. Nor, in this age of the ubiquitous ATM, banking by phone or computer, and the vanishing human touch, is it where you'd expect to see recognition plans built to celebrate top-notch service to the customer.

The senior management team at Chase Manhattan Corporation, however, seems to understand how the "soft drives the hard" in business, even in the consolidation- and technology-mad banking industry. Achieving the bank's goals is a function not only of a slimmed-down workforce with top-flight skills and knowledge—and the right tools and resources at its disposal—but of employees who feel valued and recognized for their hard work.

Why not create a formal mechanism that publicly champions acts—ordinary and extraordinary—that illustrate teams' or individuals' everyday commitment to excellence, refusal to lower standards, or willingness to take the extra step to help customers or coworkers? Such "soft" recognition tools, Chase knows, can build the kind of culture and support system that not only contributes to more satisfied employees and lower turnover, but that can distinguish a company from its competition. Chase's flourishing Service Star recognition program, for example, shines a light on positive employee actions large and small around the globe.

Chase Manhattan is the product of a 1996 merger between Chemical Bank and the old Chase, making the new corporation the second-largest bank in the United States after BankAmerica. Chemical itself had grown significantly with its purchase of Manufacturer's Hanover in 1991.

Because of that recent history of consolidation, the Service Star recognition program has a long lineage. Each of the three heritage companies had strong traditions of employee recognition. The key, says Don Barry, the corporate vice president in charge of incentives and recognition who oversees Service Star, was to take the best elements of each and coalesce them into one new, corporate-wide program that would create a universal "currency of recognition" across the global corporation.

THE SERVICE STAR PROGRAM

Service Star is built on peer-to-peer recognition. "It provides each Chase employee a voice to recognize the contributions of coworkers or teams for the things they do each day to support Chase goals or values," Barry says. Service Star has a strong team flavor, because teamwork is one of the corporation's six core values—the others being customer focus, initiative, respect for each other, quality, and professionalism.

The program recognizes employee acts at three escalating performance levels: Service Star, All-Star, and SuperStar.

Service Star

Any Chase employee can recognize another with a Service Star award. Employees are advised to look for colleagues or teammates who have provided outstanding cooperation, support, and commitment to achieving excellence. The award is a Silver Star pin with an accompanying plaque that displays multiple pins should employees receive them.

Colleagues fill out a short Service Star award form with information about the star performer being recognized and his or her nominated act, then forward it to the designated award program coordinator in each Chase business unit. There is no approval screening; the award form is forwarded to a fulfillment vendor, where it is scanned and stored for tracking purposes and for future consideration for higher levels of recognition. The fulfillment vendor generates a preaddressed thank-you card to the employee making the award and an award package with a certificate, a star pin, and a summary of why the award was made to the winner.

The coordinator forwards the award package to the recipient's manager, who informs the nominated employee of the recognition. To put a more public spin on the award, some business units hold weekly or monthly award presentations for all Service Star winners.

In 1998, nearly seventy thousand Service Stars were awarded to thirty-one thousand employees. Thirty-three thousand stars were awarded to recognize the achievements of individual employees and thirty-seven thousand to members of 4,600 teams. Across the corporation, thirty-eight thousand employees participated by either awarding a star, receiving a star, or both.

All-Star

The next level award, the All-Star, is given at the end of each quarter. Employees achieve this honor in one of two ways: either by accumulating three Silver Stars within twelve months (for Service Star–type actions) or by one extraordinary action. What defines extraordinary? According to Barry, it's "taking ordinary opportunities just that extra step that benefit a customer or a colleague."

Unlike the Service Star, this is a cash award: $750 (or the local currency equivalent), a Gold Star pin, and public recognition in their Chase business or region.

All-Star candidates' achievements are evaluated in an anonymous process, with winners selected by a blind peer review committee (nonmanagement) that has alternating membership. Blind means the committee doesn't know the nominated employees' names. Nominators are asked to include as much information as possible about the candidate's nominated act, including supporting documents such as complimentary customer letters (names on the letters are hidden from the review committee).

Plan administrators wanted to make the All-Star nominating process as easy as possible. If awarders identify Service Star winners that are exceptional, the awarder also has the option to mark an All-Star box on the Service Star form. That means that, in addition to receiving a Service Star award, the awarder requests the individual or team be included as a candidate in the All-Star selection process at the end of the quarter.

Chase had nearly a thousand All-Stars in 1998.

SuperStar

SuperStar is the program's highest-level award and is given at the end of the program year. To be eligible, employees must receive All-Star level recognition. The award process mirrors the All-Star selection process, with a blind ten- or fifteen-person peer review committee in each business unit evaluating applicants and selecting winners. Individual SuperStar winners receive $5,000 and a crystal trophy sculpture; team winners each receive the same $5,000. In addition, all Superstars and a guest attend the two-day Circle of Stars corporate recognition event in New York City with Chase's senior management team.

What is SuperStar-level performance? One Chase teller captured the SuperStar award for acting on her intuition to keep an elderly Chase customer from financial disaster due to fraud perpetrated by the customer's private nurse. Another employee took the initiative to overcome Mother Nature when a blizzard shut down her city so that no customers would be harmed. And there are other examples of employees who simply exceed everyone's expectations on a sustained basis. After two years, Chase has 226 inspirational stories like these.

Individual business or regions select such SuperStars. They attend the Circle of Stars recognition gala held in the spring of the following year. The two-day event mixes entertainment and business and is designed to celebrate achievements as well as take advantage of the wisdom of this extraordinary group of employees. The key event is the Leadership Forum, where Chases's chairman, president, and top managers work with the SuperStars in small groups to generate action items and ideas for increasing and cross-pollinating the kind of values-driven behavior this group displays. Senior managers uniformly comment about the powerful impact this group has on them each year. During the rest of the year the SuperStars are asked to share their experiences with colleagues through a variety of one-on-one sessions and presentations at large business meetings.

In 1998 there were 116 SuperStars, including the members of six teams.

Evaluating the Plan

As he looks back on the plan's first few years as a consolidated global program, Barry says Service Star has done much to support Chase's strategic goal of being "the employer and the investment of choice" in its markets.

"Most acts people are recognized for are the little things that make life easier and simpler for our customers and our colleagues, or for taking the extra step to help things go smoothly for a customer," Barry says.

There's no question that the plan received heavy use. There were forty thousand awards in 1997, seventy thousand in 1998, and twenty thousand in the first quarter of 1999 alone.

Although there have been a significant number of "above-and-beyond" or extraordinary acts nominated to date, Barry says what may be more important is the volume of awards given to people for simply maintaining a high level of performance each day. "No Herculean overnight drives or daring-do from these people," he says. "Rather, they were recognized for the consistent level of professionalism they bring to work each day, for small sacrifices they make to help teammates, or for their refusal to lower their standards in the face of daily pressures and stresses."

Another important by-product, he says, is that Service Star has helped bring to light for Chase's senior leaders the types of things employees in the trenches do each day to delight customers, reduce costs, or help boost Chase performance—small acts that can easily fly under radar.

"Senior managers might not hear about these kinds of acts until there is a program that unearths and celebrates them," Barry says. And that knowledge can ripple throughout the organization: "It increases awareness at the highest levels of Chase, and, with this spotlight on exemplary behavior, more employees want to get in on the act."

Lessons Learned

Wary of peer review committees? Don't be.

Concerned that peers might not hold their colleagues to the same exacting standards as management? That hasn't been the experience at Chase, Barry says. "The peer selection committees have proven much tougher judges than any management committee we used in the past for awarding winners in recognition programs in the heritage companies," he says. "For every seven hundred Service Stars, we see only nine or ten All Stars and one SuperStar. We also see the same diversity among recipients at the higher levels of recognition that we see at the service star level."

The peer review committees have cross-functional, rotating memberships that often include past All Stars and SuperStars. There's another benefit to using peer committees, of course: being judged by peers rather than management can help win skeptical employees over to the program.

Get your administrative ducks in a row.

The logistics of rolling out a global recognition program can be intimidating, particularly its tracking, reporting, and award fulfillment aspects. Because the disparate recognition programs that preceded Service Star had grown organically within various business units without much central coordination, "whatever tracking that was done wasn't being done in a universal methodology," Barry says. "Systems weren't compatible—people were doing tracking in Lotus Notes, Excel, or on yellow pads. We realized we were a bit out in front of our administrative headlights when we rolled this out."

But that quickly changed. Rather than add staff to handle the new administrative duties, Chase turned to new software and technologies, contracting with a consultant for database software and new processes that would centralize and streamline record keeping and award fulfillment.

"Every time someone gets recognized in Service Star, we need to record that information and hold a copy of it in some format, because when it comes time for our blind review committee to evaluate people's accomplishments, they need that information," Barry says. "We also need to get pins, plaques, notification and thank-you letters out in timely way to many people around the world."

The newly centralized process tracks all recognition activity around the globe, informs selection committees about who's eligible for All Star or SuperStar award categories, "and gives us reporting capabilities we never had before," Barry says. "We now know where nominations are coming from, where they're going, broken out by various categories and demographics. It makes it much easier to look across the company to see where the program is working and where it's not." The new system also eliminated the need for tens of thousands of paper files that were manually kept and the associated staff needed to maintain them. Finally, Chase is looking at a direct electronic award application process to eliminate all paper and the need to scan award forms.

Anticipate how the plan may play outside the United States.

If your plan will roll out globally or in select other countries outside the United States, remember that it may be viewed differently in other cultures. Chase, which operates the Service Star program in Asian, Latin American, and European units, ran into some unexpected resistance in the United Kingdom, for example.

"People aren't always accustomed to U.S.-style recognition there," Barry says. When Chase rolled out Service Star and attempted to hand out its Silver Star recognition pins to winners, many U.K. workers objected.

"It turns out that a fast food chain over there was doing a promotion at the same time that gave out small star pins to customers, and our U.K. people objected that Chase might do the same thing a fast-food company would," Barry says. Chase addressed the problem by issuing Service Star winners a recognition card in addition to the customary star pin. The personalized card thanks employees for their dedication to quality service and for demonstrating the Chase values.

Not everyone will climb on board (but you may be surprised).

In the program's initial stages, Service Star nominations came from areas that Chase management didn't anticipate would see much action. "I think it was a surprise to the investment banking division that they'd have any nominations, but they did," Barry says. "I think people across the company saw this as an easy way to say thanks to their teammates for making their life a little easier, thanks for serving that customer, or just thanks for doing your job well."

MARKEM'S REWARDS FOR TOP PROBLEM-SOLVING TEAMS

The success of Markem Corporation's recognition plan for problem-solving project teams is testimony to the power of continuous improvement and respect for a golden rule of reward design: that the best plans are works in progress, in need of continual care and feeding to adjust to shifting company objectives and any speed bumps along the way.

With headquarters in the small town of Keene, New Hampshire, Markem, a privately held company with sales of $250 million, makes high-tech, in-plant printing systems and supplies for those systems. If your product needs a label, date-stamp, or code, Markem Corp. has an answer for you.

Markem's award plan for the work of ad hoc problem-solving teams is the second generation of a plan originally designed for individual contributors at its main manufacturing plant in Keene. Markem has a strong global presence—60 percent of its sales are made outside the United States. With international revenues growing, Markem's CEO wanted rank-and-file employees tucked far away in southwestern New Hampshire to have a better understanding of the global nature of the business, and charged Barry Mallis, then Markem's corporate communications manager and now manager of training and development, with growing that consciousness. Mallis's answer was a program called Shop to Shop that awarded one front-line employee from each of Markem's three plant divisions with a week-long, all-expenses paid trip to Europe—accompanied by a management representative—to visit Markem customers in England, the Netherlands, and Germany. Fellow plant floor workers voted for the lucky traveler; managers—or anyone who'd previously traveled overseas—weren't eligible for the trip. The award criteria? Employees were asked to choose "someone who would best represent the division abroad in meetings with Markem employees and customers," Mallis says.

But this was no joy ride: the real purpose behind the plan was for the European travelers to return to the Markem home plant to spread the word about how the company's products were being used and received overseas, and any recurring problems cropping up. Each traveler made a formal presentation to their divisions upon return, highlighted by the customer feedback.

The plan worked well for a time, says Mallis. "Our employees could watch their printing systems and inks in use by customers halfway around the world who didn't speak a word of English, which to them was pretty amazing." Not to mention experiencing the thrill of traveling through Europe when many had never before been in a plane or traveled outside the country.

But problems soon emerged: voting became "something like a cookie bake-off," Mallis says, with workers making brownies and glad-handing in other ways to win votes in what had rapidly become a popularity contest; others considered the award criteria too open to interpretation. Perhaps most important, the award plan didn't support Markem's recent move to use of small, problem-solving work teams as part of a continuous improvement initiative. The goal of the ad hoc project teams, Mallis says, is to "address process-related problems people historically thought were too complex or unsolvable in the plant."

Any employees in the manufacturing plant can form such a team—usually of three to five people, no more than eight—to study chronic challenges in their work areas. To guard against teams forming for teams' sake, or without a mission-critical goal, prospective teams must fill out a standard form called the Team Charter that includes a mission statement (problems to be addressed), a description of problem-solving tools to be used, an estimated time frame for implementing solutions, and more.

Instead of abandoning the Shop-to-Shop concept, Mallis retooled it to encourage and celebrate the work of the ad hoc teams. The idea is for each team to target a small-but-impactful win that might be implemented after one to three months of problem study—to avoid the "solving-world-hunger" trap common to the embryonic stages of teamwork, Mallis says.

When project teams complete their work—completion defined as describing project processes and outcomes in a summary presentation to a team sponsor who is often but not always a member of management—they also can submit an award application to a five-person steering committee as part of the revised Shop to Shop program. Applicants must use measurable terms to describe and quantify business improvement or increased internal or external customer satisfaction from their projects (for example, reduced number or percentage of defects within a certain time; dollars saved or reduced paperwork; or improvements in customer feedback scores).

The award steering committee, using well-defined criteria as well as conducting face-to-face interviews with the team applicants, chooses five finalists for the award. But then—and this proved critical to the plan's success—voting for the winning project team is turned over to all plant employees. The winning team receives the same all-expenses-paid trip to Europe that individuals once got.

Here's how the voting works. The five award finalists are given fifteen working days to create two identical storyboard displays that highlight their projects—problems targeted, total quality tools used (fishbone or Pareto diagrams, plan-do-check-act, and the like), conclusions reached, solutions implemented, and reflections on the teamwork process. One set of the twin storyboards is displayed in a high-traffic spot outside the Markem employee cafeteria, and the other is placed on a cart that travels to all Markem departments for viewing for three days.

The idea is for all Markem employees—frontliners as well as managers—to view the displays and vote for a winner. All employees receive ballots with reward criteria, or what the finalists should be judged on, listed prominently on the back, and have five days to fill out and return them.

The winning team receives the week-long European trip, at an approximate cost to the company of $15,000 for the average five-member team, says Mallis. Although not all winners are enamored with overseas travel—one travel-phobic manufacturing worker needed a hard sell from his teammates to be convinced to step on a plane—most are thrilled with the opportunity, which often creates lasting memories. In between visits to customer sites, one winning team happened to visit Westminster Abbey in London when the famed Boy's Choir was rehearsing.

Recognition isn't just reserved for winners, however—all runner-up finalists are publicly recognized with bond certificates by top managers at an all-employee meeting, and every problem-solving team that completes its work (defined by making a formal presentation to a sponsor) receives a $50 gift certificate for each member to use at his or her choice of local restaurant, and a much-cherished pin representing the company's quality program. The work of all teams also is recognized in a bimonthly company newsletter.

The 1998 winner of the European trip, the self-named RATS or Remake Attack Team, was set to travel to Amsterdam. Even though Markem's business lagged a bit that year, and there was talk of sending the team to a more cost-effective locale like Canada, management stuck to its guns with the Amsterdam trip.

The RATS' team mission statement read like this: "To identify and implement effective corrective actions for three of the major occurrences of non-conformance due to operator error in fluid ink manufacturing." Target date for implementing solutions to the problems: three months. The four-person RATS team—a quality engineer (team leader), chemical stockroom employee, and two specialty ink mill operators—targeted a number of specific problems within that broad charter, says team leader Allen Blad.

Because most of the plant's workers had received three days of introductory training in the use of total quality tools like fishbone or Pareto diagrams, high-performance teamwork, and a seven-step problem-solving process, RATS had a strong foundation for attacking the problem—and refresher training was always available.

Meeting once a week for an hour on regular work time—then leaving with action items that often required working at home on personal computers—the team used flowcharts and fishbone and Pareto diagrams, then conducted an internal survey of the plant's mill operators to confirm its data. Finally, using a "Pokayoke" device—a Japanese tool to help "mistake proof" processes by eliminating chances of human error—the team eliminated some glitch-producing paperwork and solved a ink-lot tracking problem that was plaguing customers.

Results were immediate. In the nine months following this procedural innovation, corrective actions on lot numbers fell from twenty-two to only two.

Although the work was time-consuming and exacting, "once we began seeing results, it really motivated and excited us," says Blad. "And the prospect of winning the Shop-to-Shop award kept us going."

Evaluating Payback

Has this next generation of Shop-to-Shop, with its emphasis on team-based continuous improvement behaviors, corrected the popularity-contest problems inherent in the plan's first version? Although some level of politics is unavoidable in award voting, Mallis says there's strong evidence that employees now see the program rewarding merit rather than popularity, due in large part to clearer criteria and a voting process that samples all worker levels, not just management. As an example, he points to an ink operations team that won the Shop-to-Shop trip a few years ago—a largely unknown unit working in a remote facility. Hardly the big men on campus.

And what of Markem's payback from its significant annual investment in Shop-to-Shop travel and award program administration? Both hard and soft benefits abound, Mallis says, with the latter increasingly driving the former. Companies that consistently recognize and celebrate the work of their project teams reap enormous dividends, he believes. "The biggest ROI may be the perception among employees that management cares about them and their hard work on these teams," Mallis says. "Management is extremely visible throughout the process, from kick-off to assisting teams mid-process to reviewing presentations to handing out awards."

Adds Blad of the RATS project team: "Shop-to-Shop has triggered the spread of self-formed project teams in this organization. When winners come back from Europe and talk about their experiences, it makes other motivated workers want to find a real problem, form a team, and find solutions." Indeed, many a skeptical front-line worker has rethought his or her position on teaming. "We get crusty Yankee machinists who want no part of teamwork going in, but end up seeing the benefits," Mallis says.

The "hard" or financial and operational benefits of Shop to Shop are more obvious. Ideas implemented across the company by the best problem-solving teams, like RATS, show quantifiable, data-based results; time-eating or inefficient work processes have been streamlined, costly operator errors reduced, and customer satisfaction scores enhanced.

Despite the success, Mallis isn't done tinkering with the program. In the spirit of continuous improvement, he's looking for even more ways to recognize and promote use of ad hoc problem-solving teams within Markem. One way would be through use of a large magnetic whiteboard currently sitting in the company's maintenance shop. Mallis planned to permanently install the whiteboard out-side Markem's employee cafeteria—with "Continuous Improvement News" em-blazoned across the top—to continuously display stories of successful project teamwork in the plant, an idea gleaned from another company. (In 1999, the new board was prominently displayed with its first team "quality improvement story.")

The whiteboard supports Markem's corporate goal of "societal networking," giving greater visibility to continuous improvement initiatives that owe their success to use of grassroots, high-performance work teams.

MERCK: ALIGNING RECOGNITION AND INCENTIVES

Enlightened companies know it shouldn't take winning a big new account or a record-shattering profit level to find a reason to celebrate employee performance; they understand the power in recognizing the small daily acts of team play and sacrifice that ultimately lead to many of those "big bangs." Like Merck & Co., Inc., a worldwide pharmaceutical company, most of these companies also know how potent noncash team recognition tactics can be when used in tandem with financial incentives for project teams or organizational units.

The Wilson, North Carolina, pharmaceutical plant is part of giant Merck, charged with packaging many of its well-known prescription drugs along with manufacturing products such as cholesterol-lowering Zocor, the asthma drug Singulair, medications for AIDS patients, and others for those suffering from high blood pressure or ulcers. The Wilson plant is also the only nonunion man-ufacturing site in Merck domestically, and all 425 of its full-time employees are salaried.

Merck Pharmaceuticals boasts three reward plans with a strong team orientation:

- Reasons to Celebrate, a highly flexible, peer-nominated recognition plan
- Pay for Performance, a plantwide pay for performance plan tied to hit-ting annual goals in four of the plant's key operational areas
- A Team Stock Option reward plan for project and organizational unit teams that rewards extraordinary acts of teamwork, as well as team per-formance against predetermined goals, with Merck stock options

Reasons to Celebrate

This plan, says Vickie Cobb, the plant's employee development manager, is a way for "teammates to recognize teammates for extraordinary effort and ac-complishment, and to broadcast to the plant as a whole the achievements of those teammates." The plan emerged from the work of a cross-functional team of employees and managers charged with rethinking reward and recognition efforts at the Wilson plant. The goal was to find new ways to support and encourage Merck's burgeoning team-based culture. "Rather than having only top-down recognition, the team suggested to management a peer nomination process," Cobb says.

Any Merck team or employee can nominate any other Merck team or employee throughout the plant under Reasons to Celebrate. The recognition oversight committee created this list of actions that might warrant recognition, although nominators aren't limited to the list:

- Extra effort above and beyond ordinary and expected performance
- Improvements in the quality of teamwork
- Suggestions that result in product quality, worker safety, or process improvements
- Excellent customer service; cost or time savings; acquisition and use of new skills
- Perfect job attendance

Reasons to Celebrate is a noncash plan, following the thinking that cash awards provide a quick jolt of satisfaction but little feel-good staying power. Award recipients have little to remember their nominated actions by after the cash is spent. Instead, the menu of noncash reward items in Reasons to Celebrate offers a choice of gift certificates for one video rental a week for a year, courtesy time off, a new set of tires, membership fee at a health club, and more. The reward is accompanied by a letter of appreciation written by nominators and copied to two levels of a nominated employee's or team's managers or coaches, in addition to public bulletin board recognition.

Awards are limited to a $300 equivalent for individuals and $500 for teams. When a work team is given a Reasons award, it decides through vote which of the gifts it wants, or whether each team member wants an individual reward item.

What actions typically gets recognized? Cobb recently gave a Reasons award to a team of employees who volunteered to help her design and deliver a new training class to enhance plantwide knowledge of Merck's measurement of operational excellence. Six workers stepped forward, "finding time in very busy schedules to help deliver the course to everyone on the plant site," Cobb says. With the help of these part-time trainers—who delivered the content in time above-and-beyond normal work schedules—some 30 four-hour classes were delivered over a two-month span. Other project or organizational unit teams received Reasons nominations for quality or process improvement suggestions that helped Merck improve its bottom line.

Each business unit and support services group in the plant has a budget for the Reasons program. If there have been any rumblings about this highly successful program, they've come as a result of the sometimes uneven application of those budget dollars, Cobb says. "If we do get complaints, it's from those who feel their teams don't use their reward budgets as often as some other teams might," she says. "We encourage all teams to use their recognition budgets, but we made a conscious decision to leave award-giving decisions to the local team's discretion, to keep the process autonomous and decentralized."

Reasons to Celebrate saw one significant change in 1997. In the initial plan design, an independent, cross-functional advisory team was given power to approve or vote down all award nominations based on established criteria. But this oversight group often found itself coming back to the local team or individual making the nomination for more information. "We decided to return the decision back to the teams themselves," Cobb says. The advisory team had already been under pressure about why they were approving some nominations and not others, she says, "and we thought, who knows the details of a nominated act better than the team where the act originates? Who knows whether I'm exceeding job requirements better than my own team members?"

Plant work teams were similarly empowered to choose their own Reasons awards from the menu, rather than the prior process where the advisory team chose for them.

Pay for Performance Program

Merck Pharmaceuticals also has a plantwide Pay for Performance plan that rewards all eligible employees for hitting annual goals in four key performance areas: product quality, worker safety, customer satisfaction, and financial performance. The objective of this plan, Cobb says, is to "recognize the value of teamwork in helping accomplish plant goals, and to get everyone in the same boat pulling together toward those mutual goals. It's also another step toward developing a new team-based culture."

Each year plant management and department representatives gather to set new performance goals in the four categories, with each category weighted based on perceived importance:

- Product quality, viewed as the most important, 30 percent weighting
- Customer service, 25 percent
- Employee safety, 25 percent
- Financial performance, 20 percent.

If the plant's product quality goals are achieved, each eligible worker receives 30 percent of an $800 maximum possible payout, and so on down the line with hitting safety goals (25 percent of the $800), customer service (25 percent), and financial performance (20 percent). In 1996, "maxing out" on all four goals meant each employee would receive $600 (actual payouts were $525 per employee in 1996 and $575 in 1997). Maximum possible payout per employee increased to $800 in 1998.

Specific targets are set every year within each goal category. In 1998, Merck plant management identified two major targets in the product quality area: reducing product-related complaints and improving "straight-through" performance, or the cycle time from receiving incoming raw materials to manufacturing to getting product into customers' hands. Complaints are measured per pharmaceutical bottle manufactured or product lots received, and any market actions such as recalls are taken into account. In the worker safety category, two major goals in 1998 were to improve "lost time injury" and "recordable injury ratio," measures of the ratio of injuries sustained and worker time lost to total employee hours worked.

To improve employees' line of sight on how their individual actions affect safety goals—and because the two safety indexes can be challenging for employees to understand—a third measure was introduced in 1998: a "pyramid performance" tracking tool. Industry statistics show that for every lost-time worker injury, "there may be up to one hundred small injuries or events that add up to or result in that lost time," Cobb says. "It's like a pyramid, with lost time at the top, and the 'near-miss' or smaller injuries at the base. We believe if you can get workers to report and thus reduce the number of near misses that happen, you can reduce overall lost time significantly."

Every Merck work team now receives a pyramid tool to track its safety performance, and is awarded points for recording near-miss injuries, with points taken away for lost-time injuries. Each team or unit was asked to improve its 1998 point total by 5 percent over 1997. The upshot: employees are now more aware of how their small-unit safety performance contributes to or reduces plantwide payouts: hitting overall plant safety goals triggers 25 percent of that $800 individual reward.

Customer satisfaction goals include meeting promised delivery dates with the proper product quantity, and reducing the number of customer complaints tied to delivery or service-related problems. Merck takes pains to separate controllable from uncontrollable customer complaints, factoring only the former into the plant bonus formula. An uncontrollable complaint might result from a defective part arriving from a Merck vendor, holding up production and thus delivery performance; a controllable problem would be any required rework on a Merck line due to employee error that holds up production.

Finally, the financial performance incentive category measures whether each plant departmental area was "on plan," or met targeted revenue and profit budget for the year.

As with many companies using plantwide incentive programs, Merck made adjustments midstream to improve line-of-sight issues. One early change: communicating that the new incentive payouts weren't traditional year-end bonuses. "The year we rolled it out, we probably didn't do as good a job as we could have communicating that it wasn't a Christmas bonus," Cobb says.

Merck also rolled out a new training program called Operational Excellence, designed to improve rank-and-filers' understanding of how they can affect plantwide goals and thus their own incentive payouts. "We brought them all in, team by team, for four hours of education that illustrated with real-life, concrete examples how they can affect both their own team goals and the plant goals," Cobb says. "We also hold regular meetings to explain to employees what's making the numbers go up or down—like how the need for rework affects straight-through performance or customer satisfaction measures. Increasing communication to a monthly basis, and explaining in simple terms how measures are calculated, has helped line of sight tremendously."

Team Stock Options

Exemplary teamwork also is recognized through Merck's stock option reward plan. This award requires management rather than peer nomination and a series of sign-offs up through Merck's management ranks. Merck's area coaches (management level) can nominate work teams to receive stock options for performance that meet these five criteria:

1. Evidence of a total team effort
2. Performance with long-term significance, with impact ideally seen over five years
3. Teamwork with strategically significant objectives
4. A team that significantly exceeds performance in one or more of its objective categories
5. Ideas that are proven and implemented

A coaches' first-round nomination is sent on to a four-person awards committee (with members on two-year rotating assignments) that selects its winners and forwards those second-round nominations to another management selection team. That team sends its finalists—and suggestions for the number of stock options each should receive—on to a final step: approval and sign-off from executive management.

A 1998 winning team was honored with stock options for shortening everimportant cleanup and changeover time on a critical Merck production line, significantly boosting productivity.

The stringent multilevel review process has resulted in just one other team receiving stock options since the plan's inception, Cobb says—a reward rate that's triggered reevaluation of the plan by Merck's oversight committee.

OMI: LOW-COST, HIGH-IMPACT AWARDS

When your core business is the rather unglamourous but mission-critical work of wastewater and water management, creating a celebratory workplace environment—where even the smallest acts of team cooperation and sacrifice are publicly lauded—might not seem high on management's priority list. But Operations Management International (OMI), Inc., breaks the mold in many ways. OMI views its team-based recognition plans as crucial to creating the kind of fun, supportive culture that makes workers in the trenches look forward to arriving at work each day. All else being equal, these plans contribute mightily to employee retention, enhanced team productivity, and the company's employee-friendly reputation in a competitive industry.

Based in Denver, OMI manages over 130 water and wastewater and water facilities around the globe for clients in both government and private industry, including locations in South America, the Middle East, and Asia. The company's services range from facility startup and troubleshooting to complete public works and utility management.

OMI's multitiered recognition plan is designed to encourage and reward a variety of team as well as individual behaviors. "The core idea is to encourage anyone to recognize anyone else at any time—not just managers recognizing subordinates—for small as well as large acts that often go unrecognized," says Roger Quayle, OMI's vice president of quality. "We don't do employee-of-the-month here because we want situations where everyone can be winners. We want team members to recognize each other, their bosses, outside suppliers, and even customers."

In addition to cultivating a climate of mutual support, OMI's team-based recognition is designed to encourage behaviors tied to the company's total quality management philosophy and its home-grown Obsessed with Quality initiative, which stresses a single-minded devotion to customer service.

Tag You Win

The linchpin of team-based recognition is Tag You Win, an award given to OMI organizational units or project teams (as well as to individuals) for team performance consistent with OMI's mission statement. That, in essence, means "recognizing team members for the great things you see them do every day," says Quayle. In addition to natural work groups, two types of OMI improvement teams also are eligible for the Tag awards: focus teams and task teams. Focus teams are quasi-permanent, cross-functional teams with no established sunset; seven such teams work on ongoing continuous improvement initiatives linked to seven criteria of the Malcolm Baldrige National Quality Award. Task teams are formed at the companywide level to study specific issues—say, improving worker safety or community involvement—make recommendations, oversee implementation, then disband. Diversity is the hallmark of these teams, Quayle says: "Since we have facilities all around the world, we work to get geographic diversity, as well as diversity in management and hourly staff, on the task teams."

Tag You Win can be given by anyone to anyone; someone might give a Tag to an entire work team, or team members might give the award to each other for above-and-beyond time put in on a project. The award itself is a framed certificate presented at team or division-wide meetings. The certificate is accompanied by the award-giver's choice of "Quality Bucks," each worth a dollar toward purchase of OMI merchandise from the company store, a lunch or dinner celebration, movie tickets, a Wal-Mart gift certificate, and more. The idea is to tailor the reward item to the individual and the magnitude of the nominated action. Suggested spending guideline is $10 to $15 per person.

Quayle says Tag You Win is easily the most popular—and most effective—plan in OMI's recognition arsenal: "It provides the biggest bang for the buck, it's easy for people to use, and it's respected because it's a peer-to-peer award, not at management's discretion."

A large part of OMI's domestic business involves the privatization of wastewater water-treatment facilities historically run by city or county governments. In these situations OMI often inherits government employees with little experience being singled out for recognition. It's here where Tags have especially big pay-off. "We have people who've worked in plants for ten to twenty years and never been given a simple 'thank you' for work well done," says Quayle. "It's not unusual to have them tear up when being recognized. That's the biggest lesson from our experience: the impact you can have at the front lines with low-cost recognition."

Each organizational unit at OMI carries a recognition budget for Tag You Win, in addition to other rewards. If exceeded in a given year, "no one gets called on the carpet," Quayle says. "Budgeting for it drives it deeper in the culture."

When OMI assumes management of a new facility, it creates a cross-functional team—a mix of management and frontliners—to oversee reward and recognition activity there. Although employees are given corporately developed guidelines for "sample actions to be recognized" and "example vehicles for recognition" for Tag You Win as well as other reward plans, they're not limited to those ideas. OMI's bottom line: use the guidelines as idea starters, but have fun and fit the plan to your needs. Many employees heed the call; some OMI plants, for instance, allow employees who receive Quality Bucks to use them toward purchase of merchandise outside the OMI corporate store. Others devise new award categories altogether (for example, the Rock award, described in the following box).

THE GENESIS OF OMI'S ROCK AWARD

OMI employees are encouraged to let the creative juices flow in their award giving. A case in point is the organization's Rock Award, which grew out of an annual hike taken in the Appalachian Mountains by two managers in OMI's Atlanta office. Each year the managers competed to get the farthest the fastest. On one such hike, one of the managers decided to clandestinely place a good-size rock in the backpack of his competitor, who carried it for a full day before realizing his extra baggage. The result is the company's now-institutionalized Rock Award for "persevering at work under adverse circumstances."

In 1998, the Rock Award was given to OMI employee Max Edington at the spring regional meeting. Edington was selected for his sacrifices and hard work to develop a major base for operating services in Guam and for volunteering to serve as interim project manager for a very difficult new project start-up in Georgia.

The OMI facility in Fayetteville, Arkansas, puts its own twist on Tag You Win to encourage more recognition activity. Each time an employee gives a Tag to a peer, a single marble is placed inside a conelike piece of plant equipment called the "Cone of Recognition." When the cone fills up, the entire plant is treated to a celebratory pizza party. The cone filled at least three times in 1998, says Billy Ammons, the Fayetteville project manager.

A problem common to such recognition plans—growing stale after a few years of use—hasn't been the case in his plant, Ammons claims. In September 1998, two years into the plan, the plant had a record-setting 110 tags given by twenty-eight employees at an all-employee meeting, following an August where "there was a lot of overtime and team members pitching it to help others," Ammons says. He sees multiple payoffs from the Tag plan.

"People appreciate being recognized for the little things they do that typically go unnoticed, like staying late to help a team member finish a project, and it's improved camaraderie between departments," he says. "And since it's a peer-to-peer award, it makes it easier for those skeptical about management-driven reward plans to get involved."

Soaring Eagle

Another recognition is the Soaring Eagle award, reserved for team (or individual) performance beyond the ordinary, or that expands upon the normal team mission statement and exceeds expectations. This award is given to management-driven teams by regional business manager level or above. Team activities must be "measurably effective" to qualify. Team award recipients each receive a certificate bearing a bald eagle and the manager's choice of a Lightening Bolt check for up to $1,000 per team or gift certificates tailored to team members' particular interests, such as sports events or music concerts. Winning teams also receive big play in the company's newsletter, distributed monthly to 1,300 employees and clients.

One Soaring Eagle winner is a cross-functional task team that prepared OMI's application for the Malcolm Baldrige National Quality Award. When the application made it to Baldrige's second stage—consensus review—Bernie Miller, COO, gave the prestigious Eagle to the team. In addition to the certificate and accompanying award, the ten-person team was treated to a full-day guided pleasure hike in the desert outside of Scottsdale, Arizona, following a business meeting.

When the Fayetteville OMI plant earned a national award from the U.S. Environmental Protection Agency, a project team there received a Soaring Eagle during a plantwide meeting, along with a $300-per-team-member bonus.

The Golden Apple

The Golden Apple award embodies OMI management's strong belief in community involvement. Award recipients are typically volunteer project teams, with award options largely mirroring those for Soaring Eagle (company guidelines suggest spending $25 to $250 per team member for an award that accompanies a certificate). Again, actions must be fully documented and a regional business manager or above gives the award, usually at a ceremony that includes representatives from the local community. A cross-functional team formed by frontline workers in OMI's Denver office captured a Golden Apple for its plan to deliver food to needy people during the holidays. Working in conjunction with the Food Bank of the Rockies, volunteers purchased food in bulk from Sam's Club with contributed and solicited funds—including donations from OMI vendors—and filled up a huge conference room twice over with food donations.

Partners in Performance

This piece of OMI's reward schedule—not a recognition plan but an organizational unit incentive—has had mixed results, reports Quayle, with revisions under review at this writing. Partners in Performance is OMI's attempt to reward team members, as well as individuals, for helping to improve OMI product or service quality as well as productivity. Partners in Performance includes an individual cash and stock bonus plus a team cash bonus for each natural work group and program team. For the team cash bonus, each year representatives from all exempt and nonexempt employees working at specific OMI facilities come together to develop a strategic business plan that establishes business goals for the facility for the coming year. Goals are set in areas including worker safety, regulatory and contract compliance, customer satisfaction, budget effectiveness, and community involvement. If a given facility meets all of its goals—missing even one goal means no bonus—all workers receive a cash payout of up to $750, paid out approximately sixty days after the project anniversary date (the date when OMI assumed management of the facility). The delay allows enough time to measure how well the facility met its goals, say plan administrators.

The chief objective of Partners? "To help employees think and act more like owners of OMI, rather than just members of the payroll," Quayle says.

But because many OMI facilities have hit yearly goals with relative ease, the plan picked up a minor case of "entitlement-itis," Quayle says; many employees now expect the plan payout as a given. Although yearly goals originally were intended as stretch goals, that's not always been the case; setting performance targets that are ambitious yet achievable has been challenging. Quayle and other OMI top brass are now themselves part of a cross-functional team studying a new and improved version of the incentive plan. "We're looking to put more teeth into it," he says.

One change already has been made: as of 1999, the Partners in Performance cash bonuses are no longer prorated. Employees must be employed full-time at OMI for six months or more at their project's contract anniversary to be eligible for the team cash bonus.

Lessons Learned

Go beyond awards given at management discretion.

OMI knows awards given at management's discretion—such as employee of the month—create just one winner and many perceived losers. For that reason it built a collection of other team-based performance awards tied to strategic goals that can be given peer-to-peer, which carries greater credibility and sense of fairness with employees. This new system creates many winners, few losers.

Don't underestimate the power of low-cost team recognition.

In some plants that OMI had purchased and privatized, long-time frontline employees had rarely, if ever, received verbal or written thanks for doing high-quality work. Some of these employees were actually moved to tears when receiving one of OMI's Tag awards from a teammate for the first time.

Provide choice in recognition awards.

Particularly in decentralized organizations, it's important to let employees put their own twist on corporately developed award plans. Ask what they consider true rewards for meeting team or individual goals, not what management thinks might excite them. One team member might love company merchandise or tickets to a sporting event; another might prefer an open-ended gift certificate. Bottom line: provide employees with equally valued options tailored to their desires.

RALSTON PURINA PET PRODUCTS

It is a truism that nothing concentrates the mind of a salesperson like the prospect of a large cash bonus. But in the pet products division of St Louis–based Ralston Purina Company, another kind of currency increasingly holds sway: noncash awards and public recognition tied to both team and individual sales accomplishments.

When the customer development group (CDG) in the pet product group's western region—which sells the company's signature dry pet foods such as Purina Dog Chow, Cat Chow, and Meow Mix in addition to pet snacks and Tidy Cat cat-box filler—was reorganized in 1992, management asked an outside consulting firm to conduct a change assessment survey to see how people were dealing with the change. One portion of that associate feedback sent off alarms for management: sales associates felt the division was doing a less-than-stellar job of recognizing them for their accomplishments.

Enter the Western Region recognition committee, led by Janice L. (*note:* Ralston does not disclose the last names of employees), director of organizational performance. The committee came up with a scheme to implement a new recognition program, not only to boost morale and trumpet examples of top individual and team performance, but to "help improve communication within and between account teams," Janice says. "We identified that as a big problem—the lack of shared learning among sales teams. Our teams are geographically dispersed and isolated from each other, and it can be easy for them to get caught up in doing their own thing and meeting their own goals, and forget to get on the phone or log onto a web site to share their learning. But our teams won't continue to develop or reach their potential without that exchange of best practices."

One result of that lack of information sharing was teams reinventing the wheel—creating new processes when other, more efficient processes already existed on other teams. In other cases, members of the same team simply weren't keeping teammates apprised of practices on their own accounts.

"In some cases we had teams doing the same thing five or ten different ways. We needed to reduce those redundancies," Janice says. "Among other things, that variety made it difficult to document procedures for training purposes."

The sales account teams in CDG West each have five to ten members and sport a multifunctional structure. Each generally comprises a team leader (sales manager) and team members (account executives) and is supported by a customer supply chain manager and a business development specialist. Some teams call on only one account; others call on two or three.

The Recognition Plans

Using a cross-functional, cross-regional recognition task force representing every role in the organization—and after soliciting feedback from the region's salespeople—CDG West crafted a series of plans. The plans not only provide an impressive variety of recognition tools, they create the opportunity for more on-going, frequent recognition of team and individual accomplishments across all functions and roles. And the program goes beyond regional boundaries to include others—internal and external customers and suppliers outside the region—who deserve recognition for supporting or working for the teams. The region's managing directors and vice president purposefully stayed away from the design process, according to Mark B., team sponsor and vice president: "We didn't want to give people the impression we were directing or influencing design outcomes. We wanted to keep it strictly peer driven."

The program does not rely on big dollar awards, Janice stresses. In 1997, all regionwide recognition activities were administered with a budget of $5,000, which covered about fifty associates. As the region broadened its territory in the 1998–1999 fiscal year, that figure grew to $10,000 for 132 associates on the sales teams, which includes spending for cash as well as noncash awards.

Says Janice, "If you look at cost per person, we get a significant bang for the buck with our recognition program."

Most of the regional awards are presented at CDG West's annual awards dinner attended by the company's senior management (described in the following box). The national awards—for which Ralston account teams companywide are eligible—are also announced at this event.

NATIONAL RECOGNITION AWARDS

Ralston Purina's local reward and recognition programs supplement its national recognition program. In many ways, it is more meaningful for associates to receive a national award: the criteria for winning are more stringent and employees across the country are eligible, the awards are presented by the top executive team, and all winners are featured in a special publication received by all associates. The national recognition program comprises the following awards that were developed by a multifunctional national recognition task force:

The Business Excellence Award
This national award is given to all CDG sales teams that exceed their annual goals—called "high-performance targets"—in at least two of three categories: sales, share, and customer satisfaction index scores. The goals are created at the corporate level and cascade down to team and then individual goals.

Each member of the winning team receives a handsome trophy featuring a bronze dog and cat sitting atop a six-sided cube with Ralston's distinctive

(box continues)

checkerboard logo. The statuettes are presented by the vice president of CDG at the annual awards dinner. In addition, team members receive a year's supply of embossed business cards indicating their status. "This is a special award. I get associates calling me midyear to renew their business card order because they have used all their cards up," says Ken P., director of quality systems.

The Business Process Improvement Award
This recognizes the work of ad hoc continuous improvement teams. To qualify, the team must show "measurable, meaningful, documented, and sustained" improvement in the "efficiency, effectiveness, or adaptability" of a key business process. (Because these teams have only operated since the 1996–1997 fiscal year, 1998 was the first year they could qualify for the "sustained" part of those criteria.) These teams can be assigned by management or formed on the initiative of empowered associates. The award comes at the discretion of management sponsors, and winners receive their choice of classy desktop accessories— business card holders, pen stands, Post-it holders, or cherrywood coasters— each with engraved bronze insignia.

One project team captured the award in 1998 for improving a key financial process used by the sales teams. The ad hoc team created a new process with guidelines and procedures that greatly improves the odds that teams won't run into arrears on their checkbooks, and began training other sales teams on how to use the process in late 1998. The new measure of top performance for all teams: zero checkbook debt at the end of the year.

The Team Contributor Award
This award is given to team members who go above and beyond their normal role or assignment to provide outstanding service, assistance, and support to others. Recipients receive an engraved bronze checkerboard cube and a certificate of accomplishment. Awards can be presented as frequently as warranted based on value-added contribution and can be given by peers, managers, suppliers, or customers. Winners are written up in the annual national recognition newsletter.

"Associates give their peers in another department a cube for their help in solving a problem or improving a process," says Ken P. "It's especially meaningful when the cube is sent to the recipient's manager for presentation."

Best of Breed

Best of Breed is CDG West's centerpiece award, recognized throughout the region as the highest award a team or individual can receive. The award is given for "business excellence results that reflect consistent and sustainable improvement contributing to the overall success of CDG West and/or overall customer development group."

Any CDG West associate can nominate any sales team or individual for the award, and one final nominee from each geographic area of the newly expanded region (Western, Central, Southwest, and the multifunctional support group) is chosen.

All nominations are sent to reward and recognition committee liaisons. Each CDG West geographic area is assigned two or more such contacts to assist in program implementation, to field employee questions, and to handle award components. The R&R committee reviews all region finalists and selects one Best of Breed winner and runners-up. The winner receives $500 (recently increased from $250) along with a commemorative item. Runners-up receive a smaller cash award along with a commemorative item. The R&R committee believed increasing the top award from $250 to $500 was just enough to pique associates' interest. "This is the award most cherished by our people," says committee member Donna A. "It's like receiving an Oscar to them. It's a very secretive process, too—winners aren't revealed until the night of the awards dinner."

All Best of Breed nominations are reviewed against two formal criteria: First, "efforts must reflect measurable results in support of one of the following: Business process improvement measures of efficiency, effectiveness, and/or adaptability; improvements in financial contribution, sales volume, share, or customer satisfaction scores." And second, "significant innovation, creativity, or application of new learning must be evident in approach or solution and yield positive results in areas such as, but not limited to, the following: strategic planning, promotion planning, category management, retail solutions, business development, supply chain, and/or customer relationships."

Team member Keith R. was awarded the region's first Best of Breed in 1997 for, quoting the region newsletter, "contributing significant improvements to the category management, forecasting and budget processes that resulted in increased team and individual efficiency and effectiveness, throughout the region and the total U.S. Keith is continually looking for ways to improve our business process and build more integrated customer relationships."

Another team member, Bill S., won Best of Breed in 1998 for his innovative work to improve the supply chain with his team's main customer. This customer had formed an internal task force to examine processes in its distribution system. Bill was instrumental in helping the customer create a new, more efficient methodology to supply its retail outlets. His recommendations significantly reduced supply chain costs for Purina, as well as for the account. Bill also received the Outstanding Logistics Support Award in the fall of 1997 from the account.

The Top Dog Award

This team-based peer award, uniquely designed to increase intra-team recognition, provides a way for account teams to recognize teammates for "outstanding accomplishments that assist in meeting the team's goals." Within CDG West, each team leader picks one team member as Top Dog for the first quarter. That award winner then works with the team leader to pick the second quarter Top Dog, and so it goes through the third and fourth quarters. Although four different team members can share the award over a year, there's no requirement to name a winner in any given quarter.

Top Dog winners are given a $50 cash award against their team's recognition budget to spend on virtually whatever they choose. Ralston feels that leaving the choice to the winners, rather than providing an approved menu of awards to pick from, is critical. "We debated it for awhile," says committee member Steve B., "and wondered about allowing someone to buy, say, sports gear with the $50 if they so desired. In the end we thought it much more important not to put restrictions on what winners could buy, and it's worked out well. Most associates take their spouses out to dinner or buy company gear."

The recognition committee did think it crucial to include a commemorative award item along with the cash—cash disappears, but the item reminds associates over and over that they were recognized for their work. In 1998, an engraved glass paperweight was given along with the cash; in 1997 it was an inscribed glass mug. "Finding different award items each year is important," says Steve, "to keep the recognition from growing stale to multiple winners of the award. Giving the same item repeatedly can be the death of a recognition program. That's one reason we asked associates to help design the program. We wanted those designing the program to be the ones most likely receiving the awards."

Because employees are usually curious to see what others have done to receive Top Dog—and because the committee wants to provide winners another splash of public recognition—winners' accomplishments are detailed in the region's quarterly newsletter. Although the Top Dog nomination process might be the most subjective of all of CDG's recognition awards, "I have yet to hear much carping, or have anyone call me complaining that someone got an award that didn't deserve it," Janice says. "And I encourage people to be brutally honest when I'm out working with them. They're not shy about letting me know if they feel there's something wrong with our recognition programs."

The Bulldog Award

This team-based award is given twice a year to individuals on teams who "through perseverance and tenacity" overcome a major obstacle in completing a key project, closing an outstanding sale, or implementing a critical program. Nominations can be submitted by any team member for anyone via e-mail to the appropriate team leader and assigned recognition liaison.

In 1998, ten people in the region received the award, a denim shirt featuring a Bulldog's face surrounded by the words "For Tenacity and Perseverance." Shirts are custom-ordered to fit individual winner's sizes, says committee member Jennifer M. "We don't just order large or extra-large sizes. Speaking for all the smaller people, too many of us have those oversize shirts piled up in dressers or hanging in closets that we never use because they're too big. We just hate to get rid of them because they represent our Purina pride."

Thanks Notes

CDG West also encourages team members to recognize each other, team leaders, suppliers, and even customers in more spontaneous ways by distributing Thanks notepads. The idea is for associates to jot a note of appreciation on the pads—which say "Thanks" in bold letters along the top, followed by ". . . for going the extra mile" along the bottom—to recognize peers' good efforts or above-and-beyond work. No specific ground rules are given for use, although, committee member Donna A. says, "they're not to replace verbal feedback or recognition. They're more of a supplement to provide recognition anyplace, for anyone, at any time."

The R&R committee encourages sales team leaders to "role model" use of the notes every week. "We suggest that leaders spend thirty minutes at the end of each week thinking and reflecting on actions of their team members that might warrant a Thank You note, then start writing," says Donna. "Once the team leader role-models use of the notes, others on the team are likely to start using them too."

The pads have been such a hit that the region exhausted inventory each of the past two years; internal surveys also confirm that the Thanks notes are well received. "People report that they're hanging onto their thank-you notes, putting them in rainy-day files for times they might need a little boost or simply want to reflect on past accomplishments," says Donna.

Evaluating the Regional Recognition Plans

Although Janice L. has done no formal return-on-investment (ROI) tracking of the regional recognition program, she says there's ample evidence of "heartfelt" ROI throughout the region. "Our associate satisfaction surveys confirm we're doing a much better job of recognizing good performance than in the past, and our management takes the leap of faith that it has contributed directly to improved regional performance," she says. "The surveys also tell us the program has enhanced quality of worklife and is influencing associate satisfaction."

Recent responses to one question on those surveys—which average an impressive 80 percent response rate—is particularly telling. The question reads: "I receive meaningful recognition for a job well done." The average score across CDG West increased from 3.4 to 4.4 (on a five-point scale) a year following roll-out of the recognition program.

Successes and Lessons Learned

Playing Johnny Appleseed: Spread best practices.

It's critical in team-based recognition programs, Janice L. says, to get the word out about why winners won, not only to counter any perception of playing favorites but also to get more mileage from the process by disseminating "best practices" of your award-winning teams.

In addition to publishing an annual booklet that details accomplishments of all recognized teams in each award category—handed out to all at the region's yearly awards dinner—the regional recognition committee publishes a quarterly newsletter called Recognition NewsNotes. The newsletter features associates who have received team, individual, or regional recognition, with a description of their nominated acts.

"Besides giving people public recognition, the newsletter shares learning across team and regional boundaries, critical because our teams are spread out across the western U.S.," says Sandy V., a committee member. The newsletter also lists phone contacts for winners so others can readily follow up for more information or idea swapping.

Coordinate regional and national award programs.

Consistency in program design may be a hobgoblin for some, but a corporate human resources group usually favors a uniform application of reward and recognition programs across an organization. It's important to be sensitive to that, says Janice L., whose CDG West group built its local recognition program on its own initiative and prior to the rollout of the national program. Having a go-getter in one region receive $500 for hitting a goal while his counterpart in another region receives little or nothing can create friction.

"Even though we have permission to do our own thing here, we have to be careful not to discount the national program," Janice says. "We supplement the national program with our regional program and emphasize the importance and meaningfulness of the national effort."

CHAPTER FOUR

Company Profiles: Project Team Incentives

As you may recall from Chapter Two, project teams are usually, but not always, formed by management to tackle specific projects or challenges within a defined time. In other cases teams self-form around specific issues, or as part of continuous improvement initiatives such as team-based suggestion systems. This chapter examines project team incentive plans in several companies and reviews their experiences.

GREAT PLAINS SOFTWARE

In the new high-tech world, it takes more than high pay or annual bonuses to keep top team members productive, motivated—and off the competition's payroll. Challenging projects, team camaraderie, and recognition for achievement are more important than ever.

Cutting-edge technology, reliable quality, and system compatibility are little more than table stakes in the software business; they get you in the game, but do little to guarantee enduring success. All else being equal, Great Plains Software, Inc., has long believed its distinctive customer service and technical support keep it ahead of the crowd.

Great Plains achieved its award-winning level of customer care by transforming what once was purely a functional organization into one featuring smaller line-of-business work groups and teams designed to serve distinct customer segments. More important, its management came to understand that competing on service requires an exceedingly well-trained and highly committed workforce, one not possible with a turnstile mentality to employee retention. Great Plains' most recent annual turnover rate averaged 3.5 percent in an industry that often averages 20 percent. One reason for the low turnover is a culture that regularly celebrates and publicly acknowledges the hard work of its many project teams, its permanent work groups, and the organization as a whole with a plethora of noncash recognition and cash incentives that travel far beyond paychecks as rewards for a job well done.

Founded in 1981, Fargo, North Dakota–based Great Plains is a leading provider of enterprisewide business management software, serving some forty-five thousand clients in over 125 countries on six continents. Its leading products, such as Dynamics and Dynamics C/S +, are designed to meet a broad spectrum of business application software needs of midsized businesses. Available in eight languages, the Dynamics product family is designed for businesses standardizing on Microsoft Windows' NT technologies and seeking accounting, human resources, or fully integrated enterprisewide solutions. The thousand–employee company also is well known for its cornerstone product line, Great Plains Accounting, a feature-rich accounting solution for small to medium-sized companies.

Behind Great Plains' sales and earnings success is its unique culture and operating strategy. In both 1998 and 1999 *Fortune* magazine named the company to its list of "100 Best Companies to Work for in America." The fun, familial atmosphere, emphasis on meaningful recognition for project and organizational unit teams, and employee-friendly policies are designed to do more than create a pleasing work environment: they drive the company's impressive sales growth. Sales were $85.7 million for fiscal year 1998, up 50 percent from the previous year. For the nine months ending February 28, 1999, operating income was $11.9 million, a 60 percent increase over the comparable nine-month period in fiscal 1997. *Business Week* named Great Plains one of its "100 Hot Growth Companies" in 1998 for its three-year run of sales and earnings growth.

Great Plains added more honors in 1998: two of Arthur Andersen's prestigious "Global Best Practices" awards in the categories of Exceeding Customer Expectations and Motivating and Retaining Employees. In the latter category, judges specifically cited Great Plains' use of companywide and team-based recognition, along with stock ownership opportunities for all employees working twenty or more hours per week. "In knowledge-based businesses like ours, retaining and motivating team members is essential to the organization's success," says Doug Burgum, chairman and CEO of Great Plains.

Burgum and other top managers believe that even in today's high-tech world, customers place a premium on caring and efficient postsale support from carbon-based life forms. Great Plains retains 80 percent to 90 percent of its clients from year to year by making customer service its top priority; service, support, and maintenance also account for some 40 percent of company revenue. That customer support was recognized with the distinguished STAR award from the Software Support Professionals Association in 1998; Great Plains' CustomerSource Web site, providing around the clock on-line technical support to customers, was named Best Overall Support Site in 1998 by the Association of Support Professionals.

To encourage exemplary and everyday acts of good team play and customer service, Great Plains uses a variety of financial incentives and recognition tools for project teams and permanent work groups.

Project Team Incentives

Great Plains makes heavy use of project teams in its 250-employee global product development group, which works on new software releases or upgrades of existing products. Management is fervent in its belief that these teams should be specially recognized and given incentives for their contributions to the company's success.

Recognition usually comes in a mix of modest cash incentives for hitting product deadline and quality goals, and noncash recognition for accomplishing milestones during a project's life. All of Great Plains' unit managers or team leaders carry a budget for such discretionary recognition spending to use as they see fit in some combination of preannounced cash bonuses and spot recognition.

According to Jeff Young, vice president of global product development, project teams can have as many as a hundred members, but most usually contain about fifteen. The average project span is six to nine months. In Young's group, as throughout the rest of the company, cash bonuses for team members are usually tied to hitting two goals: product release deadlines and quality standards.

On a typical software project, team members share equally in a two-part preannounced bonus: half of the bonus is delivered upon hitting the targeted release date of the product, the other half for accomplishing product quality or functionality goals. The latter incentive is linked to market performance of the product ninety days following release; that payout usually requires a near-zero level of detectable bugs as determined by a combination of three measurement tools:

1. Customer satisfaction survey scores
2. Experiences of specific "referenceable" customers identified in advance
3. Calls to customer support lines reporting problems with the released product

Says Young: "This part of the incentive has made project teams acutely aware of what happens after the product leaves the building."

Cash bonuses usually aren't large—often only a few hundred for each team member. But coupled with spot recognition of the teams during and after the project, most team members accept it as a sincere thanks from management for the extra hours and hard work put in to get quality product out the door, often on brutally tight deadlines.

Why use cash incentives for project work that some might interpret as part of everyday work duties? Explains Young: "We don't look at a paycheck as recognition for a job well done. These special incentives allow us to place a big asterisk next to those things we think are critical to business success, and allow teams to participate in the organization's success."

Young also believes this spirit of recognition contributes to low turnover in his group. "Right now the average turnover in a technology development group around the country is about 18 or 20 percent, and we've been running about three and one-half percent the last two years," he says. "We know our culture and how hard we work to genuinely appreciate people is part of that. People in these jobs can always find a headhunter who'll offer them a little more money, or another company offering a chance to work with whiz-bang technology. But if you consistently let people know in meaningful ways the company wouldn't be as successful without their hard work and smarts, all else being equal they'll be more apt to stay."

Project team leaders also are encouraged to celebrate milestones throughout the course of projects to keep morale high and momentum strong. A nine-month project might have four or five significant milestones, and the typical project team in Young's group celebrates hitting them with team dinners at local restaurants, team bowling events, picnic lunches, or other off-site celebrations, all of which come out of the leader's discretionary recognition budget. Each significant project also closes with a formal celebration, often held away from the office. "If we achieve additional functionality or higher quality levels earlier than expected in a development cycle, team leaders will usually celebrate that, too, with informal awards or celebrations," Young says.

Often those celebrations are small, impromptu affairs. One project leader promised his team, which had fallen behind a milestone target by a few days, that he would personally serve each team member a large hot fudge sundae if they cranked it up a notch over the next couple days and made the deadline. They did, and he served.

Great Plains used this combination of cash incentives and noncash recognition recently for the team that worked on its "Royal Troon" project to deliver support for the new Euro currency across the company's entire software line. The new product gives European businesses three implementation options for transitioning their Great Plains' business management software to the Euro.

The team's cash bonus was tied to creating such support by January 1, 1999, when the Euro was released in eleven European countries; hitting that date meant having product ready to be shipped by December 15, 1998.

A series of recognition events celebrated big milestones along the way, and the project's end was capped with a Vegas-style celebration, where a vice president of international sales and marketing spoke to the team about the impact the Euro product already was having on the market. The team spent the remainder of the day playing Vegas-style games using "Great Plains dollars," and could use accumulated dollars at afternoon's end to bid on different prizes, from DVD players to golf balls.

"I've been here ten years, and some of the biggest reaction I've seen hasn't come from the cash bonuses, but from teams recognizing a sincere thank you from the organization when they see it, in whatever form," says Young. "A gift certificate to a nice restaurant or for a weekend getaway is a way for the company to say 'we understand you missed a few dinners or weekends with your family during the course of this project, and here's a small way to make up for it.'"

The Friends' List

Those not on a core project team but who nonetheless play some role in the team's success also are recognized through use of a Friends' List. At the end of each project the core team creates a list of those both inside and outside the organization who somehow helped the project along. That list can include those who participated in software beta testing, those in the product support group who aided in product testing, coworkers who covered for core team members while they spent time on a special project, or sales and marketing employees who helped develop postrelease reference sites. People on the Friends' List receive their choice of gift certificate and a formal thank you letter signed by the entire core team.

Project team leaders also are encouraged to recognize outstanding individual performance on teams; specifically, to set aside part of the overall team bonus to recognize what they consider the top 10 percent of individual performers. Behavior such as going above and beyond to get a project back on track, overcoming unforeseen obstacles, or helping out teammates in a pinch is recognized with small cash bonuses or gifts personalized to a team member's interests.

Young himself awarded a team member who'd put in many extra hours working on an acquisition project with a personally engraved shotgun. "From a dollars perspective, it probably wasn't much in relation to the amount of work he put in," Young says. "But from a trophy value perspective, it was pretty big to him. Every time he hunts, he sees the engraving on the gun and remembers the success of the project, and how Great Plains acknowledged him for his work."

THE "I" IN "TEAM" AT GREAT PLAINS

In addition to publicly calling out acts of exemplary teamwork, Great Plains believes it important to recognize individual excellence as well. The company's Pioneer Awards, presented with pomp and circumstance in an annual ceremony, do just that. The individual awards all tie back in some way to the company's heritage on North Dakota's Great Plains, and celebrate the corporate mission and values in action. Here's a sampling:

The Heritage Award (Excellence in Customer Service)
"Heritage reveals who you are and what you're about. As human beings, we need to identify with more than a paycheck or product—we need a context of values and ideals that give meaning to what we do every day. That's heritage, and from the beginning Great Plains' heritage has been customer service. This award honors an individual who has shown resourcefulness, determination and personal integrity in overcoming obstacles to do what's right by the customer."

The Pathfinder Award (Excellence in Team Supervision)
"In the age of pioneers, every expedition relied on a pathfinder. A great pathfinder not only guided the expedition, but kept everyone else close to the meaning of their journey, pointing ahead to the shared dream they were pursuing until the destination came into view. This award is given to the modern-day pathfinder, a supervisor who's guided and inspired his or her team through another challenging year. In demonstrating resourcefulness, determination, and compassion, they've earned the day-to-day respect of each individual on their team, and contributed to reaching departmental and company goals."

The Jesse James Award (Excellence in Innovation)
"For more than a hundred years, Wild West outlaws captured our imagination with their daring. Today, we can't afford to forget that Great Plains began as a start-up. We rode into an industry run by the East and West coasts, and became a contender right here on the prairie. This award honors an individual who's reminded us of our outlaw heritage: taking chances, acting with daring, and breaking old rules to introduce new opportunities."

The Harvest Award (Excellence in Quality)
"Harvest time is the true test of quality. That's when everything is above ground, out in the open, the results of months of planning and work are there for everyone to see. The consistent, day-in day-out effort which seems to go unnoticed for so long is justified by the rich harvest. This award is given to a person who has made an exceptional commitment to quality, which they've demonstrated in their everyday work, month after month."

The ZeZula Award ("One Who Helps")
"In the 1870s, the great-grandfather of Great Plains' current CEO, Doug Burgum, was an army surgeon at Fort Rice, an isolated post in a territory that would

eventually become Bismarck, North Dakota. When the doctor visited Dakota Indian reservations to look after the sick, his wife would accompany him. In honor of her spirit of friendly helpfulness, they gave her the name ZeZula, which in the Dakota language means 'one who helps.' This award honors an individual who has used his or her skills and knowledge to help others in the Great Plains community. They have not let job descriptions or personal differences stand in their way, but have taken action where necessary and lent support where needed."

The Sodbuster Award (Perseverance in the Face of Obstacle)
"Some of the earliest pioneers in our area were called sodbusters because they broke fertile ground and, when necessary, fought Nature herself to create a rich, sustainable livelihood. They persevered against considerable odds, doing what was necessary day after day. They challenged themselves and those around them to keep the faith with dreams held in common, no matter the hardships endured. This award is given to an individual who's done the work of a true sodbuster— someone with the pragmatic stubbornness necessary to punch through barriers, and the intelligent flexibility to roll with the inevitable punches."

Other Recognition

Special recognition isn't just the province of project teams at Great Plains. Permanent work groups and the organization as a whole also are recognized through a series of formal quarterly and yearly awards, and plenty of business units have their own, more informal team-based recognition. Although the latter awards usually are customized to suit particular work environments, all publicly celebrate evidence of Great Plains' values and vision in action.

Most of these awards are peer-nominated. "We feel no one knows good performance as well as the people who work next to you," says Mike Slette, Great Plains' vice president of human resources. "These recognition plans are as effective as anything we do at keeping the organization's mission and shared values at the top of employees' minds in day-to-day work."

In 1996 Great Plains reorganized from a purely functional organization to one featuring a mix of functional and line-of-business work groups. By creating smaller work groups or teams focused on smaller customer segments, management felt customers would benefit from greater expertise and more nimble, efficient product support.

"We realized our success depended on the success of all these little teams added together, and it made sense to create company-wide reward and recognition plans specifically for team performance, without losing sight of individual accomplishments," says Slette.

Here's a look at some of the other ways Great Plains recognizes and rewards teamwork across the organization:

Companywide President's Awards

The President's Awards recognize the work of teams and individuals on a quarterly basis. Both permanent work units and teams—those that show up on the organizational chart—and project teams are eligible for nomination.

The top award for teamwork is called, appropriately enough for Great Plains' location on the vast prairie, the Roaming Buffalo. Bestowed annually or quarterly—the latter only if nominations are received—the Roaming Buffalo is given to the work team that "exemplifies excellence in teamwork, team spirit, and the ability to work together to produce high-quality results."

Any Great Plains employee or team can nominate a team for the award; nominations are submitted to a management review committee via corporate intranet. True to company form, every nomination is reviewed by CEO Burgum. "We get hundreds of nominations at the corporate level, but he reviews each one," Slette says.

The Roaming Buffalo winner receives temporary possession of a trophy featuring a large Buffalo statue, and the team's name is engraved on the traveling prize. Runners-up receive honorable mention team certificates; both winner and finalists are recognized at an annual all-employee meeting.

A product development team won the Roaming Buffalo in December 1998 for meeting a strict deadline and quality standards for release of Great Plains' new Dynamics 5.0 product. The twenty- to fifty-person rotating team—with titles like software engineer, product planner, software supervisor, product planning supervisor, and quality assurance—worked for six months on the release, and was cited specifically by the nominator and review committee for staying on track despite unplanned additions to the project. The nominator had this comment: "The team is tireless in its work. What I admired most was its dedication and ability to continually absorb delays, work odd hours and test the product regardless of the chaos that came its way."

Another team captured the Buffalo for creating a more efficient testing method to measure how Great Plains' software products print on a variety of printers on the market. The old testing process required printing between one hundred and two hundred reports—on each supported printer with each supported driver on each supporting operating system. Combinations requiring testing were huge; 450 hours were spent on printer testing for Great Plains Dynamics 5.0 alone.

The team devised a new paperless testing process that greatly reduces the time required, essentially turning testing into an automated overnight process, with no loss of accuracy; the new process can determine if a report is printed one pixel differently than before.

Such a solution might seem like a bit of a yawner, but it was received with great fanfare at Great Plains. "Some might think it a bit strange to be in an all-company meeting and have this roaring standing ovation for a team that's figured out how to more efficiently test software on printers, but that's our culture," Slette says.

Many of the companywide team awards are presented during Great Plains' annual Pioneer Days, a week-long event held each June. Almost every employee attends the event at Fargo headquarters. As part of the week, a special Info Day is held, a kind of internal trade show designed to expose disparate work teams to each other's work and mission, to help them better understand how all pieces fit into the whole and the value of cross-functional work. For a half day at the Fargo Convention Center, the work teams man individual booths, much like at a typical trade show, to discuss their team goals, objectives, and recent projects with coworkers; in 1998, fifty such booths operated. Throughout the day employees roam the booths to learn about their peers' work, and individual departments and work teams sponsor contests and activities with special prizes and giveaways, including round-trip airplane tickets.

"We'd grown rapidly, and found teams could get so caught up in their own areas that certain silos were starting to form in the organization," says Slette. "It was becoming easier to lose touch with what was happening around the rest of the company. Info Day is one way of breaking down the walls."

Business Unit Awards

Great Plains also encourages business units to create their own informal award plans to spotlight good teamwork. Many of these awards are modeled on the companywide President's Awards, with a local touch.

The Heritage Customers Group, which manages Great Plains' oldest product line—Great Plains Accounting—does as good a job as any unit in using local awards. The unit gives a semiannual Outstanding Teamwork Award to the permanent group or temporary project team that's accomplished goals over the past six months instrumental to the success of the entire unit; peers nominate and then vote on the winning team, which receives a small trophy. The Heritage Group also gives a Teamwork Champion award to the individual or team outside of its unit that has demonstrated extraordinary teamwork in assisting Heritage.

The group also bestows a litany of semiannual noncash awards for individual excellence, including awards for internal and external customer service ("going the extra mile to assist others within the department, or in assisting external customers"), innovation ("for stepping out of the box to solve a problem in a new way, or saving time/money by implementing a solution that didn't exist six months ago"), and a milestone award given to the team member who's taken on some new challenge—either voluntarily or assigned—and as a result grown professionally or personally in the previous six months (see the box on page 82).

Kindness Cards

It's difficult even for the smallest acts of good team play to slip underneath radar at Great Plains. Employees regularly reward each other for daily acts of kindness or competence through use of Kindness Cards that the company prints up and distributes to business units. The cards make giving compliments an easy and institutionalized process; some carry the slogan "You Put the Great in Great Plains" across the top, with space for a personal message below, and others say "Gotcha" for a job well done.

Slette says the cards are a valued keepsake around the organization. He was on the receiving end himself when he helped a coworker jump start a stalled car during a bitterly cold stretch of winter a few years ago. "I still have the card," he says. "When you get them, you tend to keep them."

COMMUNITY HEALTH CARE

If you think team-oriented suggestion systems are more hassle than they're worth, Community Health Care, Inc., has a few surprises for you.

It's difficult to argue with the implicit logic of team-based suggestion systems. For nonmanagement employees who at times can feel powerless, participation on idea-generation teams creates a way for voices and ideas to be heard, offering financial rewards along the way. For the organization, it's a way to gather and apply cost-saving or revenue-building ideas that might otherwise go unharvested, and teach employees about the power of project teamwork along the way.

Yet pitfalls abound. For one, team-based suggestion systems often demand a good deal of employee time above and beyond normal workloads. Other problems such as long turnaround times on idea review, poor or absent explanation for why some ideas are approved and others aren't, limited internal support for teams, lack of detailed plans for moving ideas from approval to implementation, and too-small rewards for accepted ideas can easily derail such plans.

Suggestion plans can also be a hard sell on the heels of other organizational change, particularly in the wake of workforce restructuring or downsizing. Employees have long memories and are naturally skeptical of new "win-win" programs handed down from management.

Neither challenge kept Community Health Care (CHC), of Wausau, Wisconsin, from success with its team-based suggestion plans, however. CHC is a nonprofit integrated health system providing a full range of health care services in northern and central Wisconsin. The 2,300-employee system encompasses a regional network of physicians, hospitals, home health care providers, some twenty outpatient clinics, and a medical equipment company.

Before implementing the project team suggestion system, CHC management had strongly considered a new gainsharing program, a version of an organizational unit incentive. But gainsharing was ultimately nixed, says Steve Solomon, CHC's vice president of human development, because of potential fallout from the organization's recent restructuring. "We looked at gainsharing primarily from the aspect of helping to educate our employees about business operations, and how that new literacy might impact organizational success," Solomon says. "But we felt no matter what we'd do to communicate that emphasis, due to our recent history gainsharing might be perceived narrowly by many only as an attempt by the company to improve its financial situation."

So a team-based suggestion system—strictly voluntary for employees— seemed a more viable and less risky way to meet CHC's corporate goals of enhanced business literacy for employees, increased cross-functional teamwork, and a resulting boost to the bottom line.

How the Plan Works

Employees from any part of CHC's network can participate in the suggestion program, with one stipulation: they must be part of a team. Employees are encouraged to form their own five-to-seven member project teams—the more cross-functional participation, the better—to research ideas in two areas: cost savings and revenue enhancement (employees can only serve on one team at a time.) CHC management at the director level and above is not eligible to participate on the idea teams, but physicians are.

To be eligible for the program, a team must create at least $1,000 in first-year estimated net savings or revenue, and accomplish one or more of the following objectives:

- Save supplies or materials while maintaining or improving product or service quality
- Reduce or avoid unnecessary costs
- Reduce the frequency of equipment and facility repairs
- Improve or streamline procedures
- Improve methods of handling materials
- Reduce, simplify, or eliminate paperwork
- Reduce the cost of contracted services
- Avoid duplication of effort

In other cases, it's more difficult to assign a quantifiable dollar value to suggestions—process efficiency and customer satisfaction ideas are two examples. In those cases, ideas are evaluated using a separate point-scoring matrix; teams research and document their ideas and complete a scoring grid. If the idea is approved, the team receives award points based on a score calculated by an evaluation committee.

In the program's initial run in 1998, each team was given a twelve-week window to submit ideas. Management believed the condensed time frame would create energy around the new program and result in a flurry of idea creation. It wasn't disappointed. Evaluation committees approved some $400,000 in cost savings or revenue generating ideas from eighty-three self-formed teams. Although some were "big-bang" ideas, many came in the $2,000 to $5,000 range. "You get a lot of smaller dollar-impact ideas in programs like this," says Solomon, "but they add up quickly, and are usually easier to implement than bigger ideas."

Each project team chooses a leader, who receives a full day of formal training in how to complete idea submittal forms, properly calculate savings from suggestions, write implementation plans, manage team dynamics, and more. "We want well-thought-out, well-documented ideas," Solomon says. "We also want to ensure teams are on the same page, and that they calculate things like depreciation, reimbursement, or revenue in the same way using the same process. Training helps with that."

When teams finish developing an idea, it's written up on an official form and reviewed by a designated team sponsor for thoroughness, accuracy, and eligibility. The sponsor sends it on to one of eight evaluation committees for review, each a three-member group of managers with a specific area of expertise—for example, a nursing evaluation committee or a purchasing and materials evaluation committee. Ideas are funneled to the appropriate committee based on content, and as part of idea review a committee identifies the CHC manager most likely to oversee implementation should the idea be approved. The implementation manager and a designated implementation team put approved ideas into practice.

Because long turnaround time on idea review is a problem that sometimes plagues and often cripples suggestion systems, CHC built an incentive to encourage its evaluation committees to make timely decisions. If a committee takes some action on an idea within two weeks—be it approval, veto, or sending the idea back to a team for more information—the committee can earn up to 500 award points (each equivalent to one dollar) to be split equally among its members. Evaluation committees also can earn points for the percentage of ideas they approve that also are successfully implemented.

Database software warehouses every idea generated in the CHC system—who created it, what evaluation committee reviewed it, how long the committees had it, and, if an idea has been approved, what its implementation deadline is. One human resources employee manages the database on a full-time, project basis.

If an idea isn't approved, evaluation committees must give teams a detailed, written explanation; a half-day of training teaches committee members how to deliver the bad news in a constructive and educational way. Solomon says these explanations prove invaluable in helping employees better understand CHC's business, and to craft ideas with greater chance of acceptance in the future.

What's in It for Team Members?

Rather than cash awards for approved ideas, suggestion team members receive points to apply toward reward merchandise of their choice. The points—each equal to one dollar—are deposited electronically to an "Exclusively Yours" American Express awards card each team member receives, a concept created by St. Louis–based Maritz Corp., the consultant CHC used in plan design. Essentially a debit card, Exclusively Yours can be used by team members to purchase merchandise from an extensive awards catalog, or from a select number of area retailers such as Macy's and Eddie Bauer, where it functions as a credit card. In cases where team members can't purchase products on site—at a distant Spiegel's store, for example—they can use the card to order by catalog. In addition, most major airlines, hotel, and rental car companies also accept the awards card.

IDEA REJECTED? TAKE IT TO THE APPEALS BOARD

When an idea evaluation committee rejects a CHC team's idea, and the team disagrees strongly with the decision, the team isn't forced to live with that decision—it can take its grievance to an appeals board within CHC.

A team leader, with the agreement of the team's sponsor, can request reconsideration of a nonapproved idea within thirty days of the original final decision date.

An idea may go through the appeals process only once, and all decisions by the appeals board are final.

TWO TEAMS, ONE IDEA?

What if two teams submit the same idea? It happens—suggestion teams within the same company or division can end up working on cost-saving or revenue-building ideas that are essentially the same.

Which team, then, should get the credit and accompanying awards? CHC set up the following guidelines to deal with the possibility.

During the initial forty-eight hours of its twelve-week suggestion program, CHC equitably divided award points among teams for duplicate ideas that are submitted and approved in that period.

Following those first two days, the first qualified idea received and documented by a team sponsor (to be passed onto evaluation committees for review) is considered first for award points.

On occasion duplicate ideas expand or build upon the value or application of a previously submitted idea. In these situations, teams are rewarded for the difference between the initially approved idea value and the expanded value of the duplicate idea.

The two teams that create ideas with the largest dollar impact in a defined period receive a four-day, all-expenses-paid trip to San Francisco accompanied by their significant others. For every $300,000 that CHC exceeds its overall goal of $2 million in impact from the program, another top-producing team is sent on the San Francisco trip.

CHC management applied trophy-value thinking in opting for debit cards over cash awards. "If you give a team member $50 or $100 cash, they may end up using it on a perishable like groceries, which means they'll have nothing to reflect back on to remind them of their award," says Solomon. "But if they buy a TV set, clothing, or company merchandise with the card points, each time they use it or see it they'll be reminded of what they did to earn the award."

Points are awarded to team members based on the dollar impact of their suggestions. An idea that leads to cost savings of $50,000 would reward each team member with 880 points, for example, a $25,000 idea 440 points, and a $3,000 idea 80 points. Points are deposited directly to the team member's card.

Half of the points are awarded on idea approval, the other half upon successful implementation. "It's a problem common to many such suggestion systems—ideas get approved but many are never implemented," Solomon says. "It becomes like having 'funny money.' Teams identify thousands or millions in potential savings, but without the right mechanisms and follow through in place, much of it doesn't come to fruition."

In addition to points earned for the idea, each team member receives twenty-five bonus award points for submitting the team's first qualified idea; another twenty-five is awarded to each member if the team has two or more members from another CHC unit when that first idea is submitted. The latter incentive helps spur more cross-functional involvement on teams.

Creating accountability for implementing ideas—and not letting the hard work employees put into developing top ideas go to waste—is a theme driving the program. Before any evaluation committee can formally approve an idea, those most likely to oversee the idea's implementation must be brought into the process. This person—or people—must sign a document that explains the idea and creates a timetable for implementation; that deadline is then entered into a corporate database for monitoring.

For their critical role, these "idea implementers" also are recognized with awards. Implementation managers and their teams can earn up to a third of what a project team earns for creating an idea.

Creating a Support System for Teams

CHC understands that, in many cases, suggestion teams are only as effective as their internal support systems. Each team is assigned a sponsor—a manager who acts as advisor and mentor throughout the idea creation process—with each sponsor overseeing four to five teams. Sponsors review teams' ideas for thoroughness and accuracy before they're passed on to evaluation committees. Because of the importance and time demands of the role, sponsors also are eligible for awards—like idea implementers, each sponsor earns a third of what teams receive for approved and implemented ideas.

CHC also designates resource people throughout the organization to assist suggestion teams. When teams need additional data or information to develop ideas, they're encouraged to turn first to these resource people, subject matter experts who volunteer their time and are given formal training for the role. One thrust of that training is to function more like librarians than judge or jury. "It's easy for resource personnel to be judgmental, because teams often come to them with ideas the resource person may have already tried without success, or has certain opinions about," Solomon says. "But we teach them it's not their job to evaluate whether something is a good or bad idea. Their job is simply to give teams the information they're looking for."

Like the rest of the team support system, resource personnel also are given incentives for their time and effort: each receives a flat 400 "points" for their work.

The Year One Report Card

CHC management sought $2 million in impact from the program—a combination of cost savings and additional revenue—in its first fiscal year. That target was based on a projection that, given CHC's structure and employee population, 50 percent of employees would form teams and each generate five to ten ideas with X dollar impact. Based on the Maritz data, 30 percent of all generated ideas could be expected to be approved and implemented.

The actuality: approximately $400,000 in cost savings and additional revenue was approved in the suggestion program's first twelve weeks; as of this writing, some $200,000 of that total had been successfully implemented. Solomon claims there is "another $7 million worth" of team ideas in various stages of review and analysis. "If you assume up to 30 percent of those ideas will be approved and implemented, we should hit our goal of $2 million in year one," he says.

If CHC does achieve the $2 million, Solomon expects approximately $1 million to fall to the bottom line after expenses including award payouts to employees, plan administration costs, consultant fees, team travel, and more.

In the plan's initial twelve-week run, eighty-three teams formed across the 2,300-employee organization to research and submit ideas. That was fewer teams than anticipated, but those that did form were more active and generated higher-quality ideas than CHC management expected, Solomon says. "About 80 percent of our teams were active, meaning they submitted ideas on a regular basis," he says. "The average team submitted five to seven ideas."

Lessons Learned

Play up the plan's "teaching moments."

Although realized cost savings or added revenues are the program's most obvious payoffs, Solomon says team suggestion systems are also a potent way to teach the troops business literacy and big-picture thinking. The requirement that evaluation committees provide a detailed, written explanation to teams when ideas are turned down—and are trained to do so in a way that educates, doesn't patronize or scold—"is as important to the success of the program as the actual rewards given to team members," Solomon says. "Employees will sometimes submit ideas that say, in essence, you guys—management—are crazy for doing X when you could be doing Y. But the written explanations provide the all-important 'why' behind why something is or isn't done in our environment, why management might do one thing over another. And that 'why' is critically important to laying a foundation for educating employees about our business operations."

It's not atypical in a health care setting, for example, for some employees to submit ideas for new medical procedures that they believe can generate significant new revenues for the organization. But often those employees fail to factor in mitigating issues such as reimbursement scenarios. "A new procedure may generate new revenue, but if it's primarily for a Medicare population, for example, CHC may actually realize only 50 percent of those revenues," Solomon says. "We assume our employees know that, but that's not always the case. That's what we consider a teaching moment."

Likewise, employees often assume their organizations can save money by purchasing from supplier X instead of supplier Y. That might be true— pencils as a single item might be cheaper elsewhere—but it becomes a teachable moment when the employee discovers the company has a volume purchasing contract with supplier Y that saves it over $500,000 annually.

Use process awards to recognize the plan's peripheral players.

To develop strong ideas, suggestion teams need to draw upon a network of resources in the organization—team sponsors or advisors, subject matter experts who function as librarians of a sort, and idea evaluation committees. Don't just reward suggestion teams for their work. If you want a well-oiled and productive suggestion system, make sure you recognize or award those peripheral players as well.

Consider awards that pay half on idea approval, half on implementation.

To create more accountability on teams and others in the organization to see approved ideas through to implementation, CHC pays teams half of their award upon idea approval, half on evidence of successful implementation.

Be up front about the time investment.

At CHC, employees are granted one hour of paid time per week—upon approval of their supervisors—to work on the suggestion program. But researching and developing good ideas usually takes more time than that. Some areas of CHC, such as nursing, found their normal workloads were far too high in year one to warrant participating in the program. "We make sure people understand that up front—that to do this right will take up a chunk of their personal time," Solomon says.

Yet CHC also stresses the extracurricular work can have a generous payoff for employees as well. At a Houston-area health care organization Solomon once worked for that ran a suggestion program similar to CHC's, one of the top idea teams, made up primarily of operating room employees, spent a number of "nights, lunch hours, and some weekends" working on an improvement idea, he says. "Not only did the idea win the San Francisco trip for the team, each team member earned in excess of $10,000 for their work."

BAYER CORPORATION

Team-based achievement awards spread the recognition wealth and create ambassadors for continuous improvement where they're needed most—on the front lines.

It's all too common for workers on special-mission project teams, asked to work the extra hours necessary for the project's success—hours that often result in significant cost savings or process improvements for the organization—to receive nothing more than a slap on the back or quick thanks from management for work well done.

Token recognition might suit some workers, but the fallout from appreciation so out of proportion to effort is employees reluctance to again make similar sacrifices—and missed opportunities to create hundreds or even thousands of ambassadors for the continuous process improvement in your company.

Bayer Corporation wanted to do things differently. The company's recognition program leaders envisioned a noncash program that not only would recognize examples of exemplary project teamwork in ways recipients might remember the rest of their lives, but would work to avoid the winners-and-losers syndrome by spreading the recognition wealth far and wide.

Plan architects also wanted a program that would encourage teams to carry the continuous improvement flag throughout the organization, spreading lessons learned and lighting fires across all eleven divisions of Bayer's diverse empire.

Thus was born the President's Achievement Awards for project and organizational unit teams. Bayer, a research-driven organization based in Pittsburgh, has more than fifty plants across the nation that manufacture not only its trademark aspirin but products including Alka Seltzer, Flintstones vitamins, spandex, the flavoring for Tuna Helper, foam used in in-line rollerblades, organic pigments, fibers, plastics, rubber, and medical diagnostic equipment. Bayer employs more than twenty-three thousand people and had 1998 sales of $8.1 billion.

Aleta Richards, manager of continuous improvement who oversees Bayer's corporate recognition efforts, spells out the organization's philosophy on recognizing team and individual accomplishment, exemplified through the President's Achievement Awards (PAA): "It's important to us to amply reward outstanding team-based contributions, and the PAA does that in a large way," she says. "The teams' experiences with the PAA often motivate others to tackle continuous improvement projects—participants often become ambassadors for the awards back in their divisions, encouraging others to get involved. That kind of role modeling through recognition is a powerful process."

How the President's Achievement Awards Work

Any Bayer team working on a continuous improvement project—be it an ad hoc project team that won't show up on an organizational chart, or an intact, organizational unit team—can apply for the annual President's Achievement Awards. According to the self-nomination criteria, teams applying must have "successfully completed continuous improvement activities—the review of the current status of a process, method or operation, and the resulting improvement or innovation as a result of team work, problem-solving and ingenuity." (See the box on the facing page for more on the award criteria.)

Although involvement on continuous improvement projects (CIPs) is mandatory in some Bayer divisions, many other project teams are pulled together on workers' initiative. One such team formed in Bayer's agricultural division when workers there decided a vendor wasn't distributing the division's products as efficiently or as swiftly as possible. As a result of its work, the ad hoc team—comprising more than twenty frontline representatives from warehousing, credit, product management, customer service, and other areas—contracted with a more progressive vendor to create a direct distribution process through Bayer that delivers products to customers' doors faster and more cost-effectively. The team went on to be recognized in the PAA process.

All PAA nominees fill out an award application form that describes the purpose and scope of their continuous improvement project, boundaries and barriers in decision making, supporting documentation, resources, methodologies, tools and budgets used in the process, completion dates, and measures of team success. All team members sign the form, and it's sent on to a Bayer recognition selection committee in the team's division—the first tier of the PAA's multilevel screening process. Most teams that complete the form and include the required supporting documentation—indicating they've successfully executed

---

CRITERIA FOR THE PRESIDENT'S ACHIEVEMENT AWARDS

Selection of finalists for Bayer Corporation's annual President's Achievement Awards is based on measurable performance criteria divided into two categories. Category A rates work teams on "continuous improvement" behaviors, and how the team "functioned as a team unit." Specific points are given for initiative and ingenuity (five points), continuous improvement process skills (five points), and teamwork and cooperation (five points).

Category B assesses "measurable" results from the teams' projects, with points awarded for linking team results to corporate objectives (five points), financial and nonfinancial effects of the project (five points), and team efficiency (five points).

In a criteria handbook given to all potential award applicants, examples are provided and questions posed for all award categories to help applicants understand what performance achievement looks like in concrete terms. Take the "initiative and ingenuity" category, for example. How might that look in practice, out on the plant floor? In describing the criteria, the handbook states "there are processes your team uses that may not actually need 'fixing,' but that present an opportunity for improvement. Did your team identify and pursue such problems, demonstrating an entrepreneurial attitude? What were the consequences of inaction? Who assumed risk?"

One Bayer work team demonstrated its initiative by "proposing and accepting new inventory responsibility, in spite of a 40 percent manpower reduction."

Under the award's "teamwork and cooperation" criteria, applicants are asked to answer these questions, among others: Were team resources assigned and used effectively? Did your team focus on improvement rather than on fixing blame? Did your team leverage the diverse opinions and thoughts of its members? Was the team open to ideas from employees outside the team? Were authority and decision making delegated to the appropriate level?

---

a continuous improvement project—are recognized with Bayer's minimum-level Quality Excellence Award (QEA). Other divisions require teams to achieve a minimum score on the PAA criteria to qualify for the QEA.

Even if these teams progress no further in the awards process, Bayer wants to ensure they're adequately recognized for effort expended and contributions made. In 1998, 201 teams were recognized at the QEA level, usually with celebratory lunches or dinners held in their respective divisions. The names and accomplishments of QEA winners also are published in division newsletters.

From these QEA teams, divisionwide operating or selection committees—a mix of management and the rank and file—identify five teams to represent each division in the companywide PAA selection process. With eleven divisions, that means fifty-five teams move ahead in the process. From these contenders, a PAA selection committee, with one representative from each division or service group, selects ten finalists based on written applications and personal interviews with the teams.

What makes the process unique is that the ultimate winner—the Bayer team that receives the coveted President's Awards Cup—is chosen not by yet another selection committee, but by a vote of the other nine award finalists. The peer vote represents a significant change from the original voting process (see Rethink the "Olympic Model" in the lessons learned section that follows). Each finalist team receives a booklet detailing the work and accomplishments of all ten finalist projects, examines that work, and then ranks the other finalists 1 through 9 (teams can't vote for themselves.) Once an intimidating twenty pages or more, these team project summaries are now limited to six pages. When all ten finalists arrive in Pittsburgh for an awards reception and ceremony, each team leader turns in the rankings by sealed envelope to a PAA oversight committee. The winning team receives the traveling President's Cup to great fanfare during a reception attended by Bayer's president and division heads.

The 1998 Cup winner was an eleven-person project team in Branchburg, New Jersey. The team tackled a problem with a Bayer film product that caused the chemical properties of the film to change, making it unusable to customers. The team created an innovative method to stabilize the chemical properties, resulting in a U.S. patent and six team members being cited as inventors. The fix helped the product generate record sales in 1997 and the first half of 1998.

True to Bayer's philosophy, the nine Cup runners-up also get a big dose of recognition: along with the winning team, they're wined and dined over three weekdays at Pittsburgh headquarters that include sightseeing events, receptions, and other activities that celebrate their accomplishments. Each team member also receives a PAA Finalist trophy and a team photo with Bayer's president; a larger team photo is put on display back at the team's worksite. (Award administrators were considering a change in late 1999 that would allow all finalists, not just the Cup winner, to host the President's Cup at their location for a time to diminish the feeling of losing at the finalist level.)

Julie Spaid worked on a project team at Bayer's Middletown, Virginia, site that was a PAA finalist in 1997. An associate human resources representative, Spaid served as a process facilitator on an eight-person cross-functional team with members from manufacturing and maintenance that tackled a problem with a critical piece of equipment at the facility. The Hematology Business Unit had created a new product that required a unique vial, and the project team sought a better way to fill, cap, and label the vials without purchasing expensive new equipment.

Using continuous improvement tools and training—and Spaid's help facilitating the problem-solving process—the team solved the vexing problem by designing and creating a new machine from obsolete equipment, helping it meet its quality, safety, and throughput goals and resulting in its nomination for the PAA from Bayer's diagnostic division. The team went on to become one of the ten finalists. There was disappointment, but little ill will, about not capturing the top prize. "The voting process was thorough and fair—the criteria were quite clear, and each finalist team really had to do its homework on the others," Spaid says. "And I think all the teams appreciated being judged by a jury of their peers."

The finalist recognition, and attending the lavish three-day celebration at company headquarters with some of Bayer's top brass, created a lasting impression on the team, Spaid says. Bayer sent a luxury bus down to Virginia to pick up the team—each member was allowed to bring a spouse or guest—and transport it to Pittsburgh for the awards celebration, which was purposely held over workdays rather than a weekend. "From the moment we arrived we were treated like royalty," Spaid says. "It was a big deal for our little site in Middletown to be recognized in that fashion." Each evening when team members returned to their hotel rooms they found a fresh gift from the company on their bed; all finalists also were given ample free time to explore Pittsburgh or attend structured events.

Participating in the PAA benefited the team in other ways as well, Spaid believes: "Implementing the CIP process helped our group stop pointing fingers, and start focusing on fixing problems, not so much on who caused them. Ever since, our team's been spreading the word about the power of the problem-solving process, and about participating in the President's Achievement Awards."

Of the thirty PAA award finalists from 1996 to 1998, twenty-two were organizational unit teams and eight were cross-functional project teams. And fulfilling management's intentions, the award process helped light a fire under work teams to pursue more continuous improvement activities. "After the annual awards ceremony, the planning committee now gets calls from managers all around the world asking about criteria for the coming year's award," Aleta Richards says.

Evaluating Plan Payoffs

What is the organization's return from implementing the PAA concept? What is the payback from the employee time spent preparing and judging nominations, and from dollars spent on the lavish award ceremony?

Richards says this one's a no-brainer: "Every year we tally up the cost savings or productivity improvements realized from the work of the hundreds of PAA teams around the organization, and they greatly outweigh whatever we spend over the year on reward and recognition. As long as that continues to be the case, the PAA will go on."

The Cash Complement

A second, pilot incentive plan provides a cash complement to the noncash PAA rewards. Called Productivity Plus (PP), the plan, managed by Bayer's corporate HR group, is a "do this, get that" incentive designed to boost Bayer's performance in three areas using improved teamwork: worker safety, and financial and operational results.

"The idea behind Productivity Plus is if your team can identify some improvements in areas like cost reduction or safety, then make that improvement, it will receive a financial reward," Richards says. "If you save X amount for the company, your team is entitled to X amount of that savings."

This self-funding structure means teams create PP plans with the hope their performance and productivity improvements will fund their own financial rewards. As teams show actual dollar savings and bottom-line gains, they're entitled to a reward that's part of that savings—if other financial triggers also are met. No bottom-line gains, no team bonuses.

Richards believes the plan has potential to form an effective one-two punch with the President's Achievement Awards: "To meet some of the Productivity Plus goals, teams will naturally need to use the kind of continuous improvement tools championed in the PAA award process. We're working now to make a stronger link between the two plans."

Successes and Lessons Learned

Video summaries explain why winners won and spread best practices.

Until 1996, summaries of teams' work and achievements in the PAA were often as long as twenty pages—an intimidating prospect both for those who had to write them and for the judges. To help get the word out in more digestible form and cross-pollinate lessons learned from each team's experience, video summaries were introduced.

The Corporate Quality Department now creates a three- to four-minute video highlighting goals, process improvement work, and accomplishments of each team; a Pittsburgh-area vendor interviews the teams and produces the videos. The videos are made available companywide for viewing, which has helped quell some of the typical debate about why certain teams won and others didn't.

"Most people viewing the videos can clearly see why team X might have been named a finalist or a winner," Richards says. The videos also prove an easy-to-use internal benchmarking tool; by watching the videos, those in Bayer's consumer medicines division might be able to pick up useful ideas from the industrial chemicals group, for instance. If a manager or work team wants more information on a particular team's work than the short video can supply, they can access a database on Bayer's intranet. "If I see a video on a team that's done a substantial job with waste reduction, I can hop on my computer, access the intranet, and pull up much more detailed information on what that team has done to help my own situation," Richards says.

Rethink the "Olympics model."

In the PAA's original version, Bayer used an Olympic-like awards format, with only the top three team finalists—from hundreds of applicants—recognized with gold, silver, and bronze awards based on selection committee review. But like the Olympics, gold medal winners tended to draw too much attention, whereas silver and bronze winners, not to mention other finalists—despite impressive performances—were largely overlooked. The recognition committee installed a new system in 1995 that takes the choice of the President's Cup winner out of the hands of a management-driven selection committee and places it with peers. Ten finalist teams now vote for an ultimate Cup winner among their ranks, and all ten, not just the top three, are recognized in grand fashion. "Our internal surveys show finalists welcome the change, in large part because it's now a peer voting process," Richards says.

Recognition plans are like software: most need periodic upgrades.

The corporate committee overseeing Bayer's recognition activities constantly looks for ways to improve the PAA awards process—particularly ways that tie award criteria more closely to shifting corporate objectives. Aleta Richards recently led a team from Bayer's corporate quality council in reexamining PAA criteria, using this question as a guide: "If we could imagine the ideal President's Cup winner, what criteria should that team have to meet to be so honored?" The visioning led, for starters, to a change in the "ingenuity and initiative" portion of the award criteria, an area that had been covered only tangentially under existing categories but was never singled out for separate emphasis. The committee voted to give it more weight.

The committee also added new criteria under the PAA's "teamwork/cooperation" category that measures whether teams are recognizing and supporting their outside resources. "It's nice to be recognized for your own team accomplishments, but are you recognizing the people that helped you get there—your managers, mentors, or sponsors?" Richards asks. This desire to continue the cycle of recognition is formally addressed via a question in the PAA criteria handbook: "Did you recognize and thank the individuals outside your team that contributed to your team's success?"

Bayer also has begun examining results of nominees' continuous improvement efforts through a different lens. "In the past a team might show results that saved its division thousands of dollars, but we didn't look as closely at costs or inputs involved in creating that savings," Richards says. "In other words, did the team spend $100,000 to save $100,000? What was the true bottom-line impact of the team's work? We're also looking more closely at how team members have to stretch outside their usual capabilities to achieve goals."

In addition, the planning committee is attempting to revamp future PAA ceremonies. The group hopes to change the focus of the ceremony from its Pittsburgh base and spread the significant team results throughout the country. The PAA finalist selection process will remain the same, but the committee plans to broadcast the ceremony, via satellite, to each finalist location. This multisite celebration should allow more employees to participate in the recognition activities.

LOTUS DEVELOPMENT COMPANY

At Lotus Development Corporation, cash bonuses and quality of team life were strategies for rewarding project teams for success. Stand out as an individual? You get rewarded, too.

For one team at Lotus, a high-stakes challenge came along that not only would test the limits of teamwork, but might make or break careers. The mission: reengineer the process by which software pioneer Lotus and its parent company, IBM, fulfill worldwide orders for both companies' desktop software products, and install new SAP enterprise resource planning (ERP) systems as part of a consolidation of operations in 140 countries into just five Lotus administrative centers running from a single computer system.

The end game: increase customer satisfaction and operating efficiencies by making all IBM and Lotus desktop software available for the first time through a single contract, and improve the company's ability to react more swiftly to market changes and new marketing initiatives by creating a single, worldwide software fulfillment system. And oh yeah—make it all happen in eighteen months, even though the project team members were working elbow-to-elbow and ego-to-ego for the first time.

The preeminent challenge, says Larry Raymond, a director of reengineering who led the project team, not only was to convince team members that meeting the project's deadlines was vitally important to the fortunes of Lotus and IBM, but to keep highly marketable team members from jumping ship during the lengthy reengineering and SAP configuration work. Even those having only a few months' experience with SAP implementation were hot commodities, receiving calls or offers almost daily from headhunters. For other technical experts or business analysts named to the team, the promise of lucrative, independent consulting beckoned.

So how to keep team members both content and on deadline? For Raymond and other Lotus leaders, part of the answer was to tie weighty cash bonuses to meeting project milestones—sums that not only would reward efficient teamwork, but would be large enough to address "opportunity cost" distractions, compensating for additional monies that might be gained through leaving the project midstream for a new job and a base-pay hike that, in some cases, Lotus might not be willing to match.

Most know Lotus (based in Cambridge, Massachusetts) as maker of the Lotus 1–2–3 spreadsheet and the omnipresent Lotus Notes software, which allows users to communicate and collaborate across corporate networks of disparate computers. The company, acquired by IBM for $3.5 billion in 1995, also has long been known for its employee recognition practices, family-friendly work schedules, and company-run day care.

The reengineering and accompanying implementation of SAP systems was designed to change the way orders for Lotus products such as Notes, cc: Mail, and Domino Servers as well as IBM desktop software such as DB2 and Via Voice, were fulfilled to customers in the 140 countries IBM serves. Lotus wanted to consolidate the order fulfillment process in a few central locations run by one computer system, creating new efficiencies.

The project team featured twenty-three "conscripts," as Raymond calls them, employees volunteered to the project by their managers for particular areas of expertise. This cross-departmental team—all assigned to the project full-time—included mostly supervisors or staff workers from finance and accounting, order management, contract management, and materials management; a reengineering specialist and SAP project development leader joined team leader Raymond on the management team. (Including outside consultants, more than forty people worked on project development at any given time.) That represented just the core project team, however. When all was said and done, more than a thousand employees had a hand in the project.

"The core team of twenty-three couldn't handle project deployment as well as development, so we created small, supporting teams in Lotus locations around the world to prepare administrative centers in their locations to receive the new SAP systems," Raymond says.

To prepare the core team to collaborate at the highest levels, all of its members went through high-performance team training designed to develop a common vision, learn to negotiate differences, and understand when to stand their ground as individuals. To the latter end, Raymond employed an educational video based on the 1986 Challenger space shuttle disaster. "The video discusses at what point team members should dig in their heels on issues they truly believe in, and in what situations compromise is a better solution," he says

Tying Bonuses to Project Deadlines

As mentioned, the completion of the project and installation of the SAP systems coincided with the launch of a new, unified contract between IBM and Lotus; the companies' products had been sold separately under independent contracts since IBM's acquisition of Lotus in 1995.

That confluence of change raised the stakes for the project. "We were reengineering and installing a new global system at the same time we were moving our customers to a new consolidated contract," says Raymond, "so meeting project deadlines was absolutely critical."

Team leaders believed cash bonuses would help focus attention on those deadlines. "Information Services (IS) projects have a reputation of being late, so we had to get the team over any willingness to accept that as an inevitability," Raymond says. "We knew we'd hit the dates based only on the strength of the weakest link on the project team."

The bonuses were designed to reward "bookend" performance on the project. The first bonus was tied to hitting an April 27, 1998, deadline for launch of the new customer contract, which required having the new SAP system up and running for all North and South American country locations. Both events, of course, also depended on successful and timely completion of the stage-setting reengineering effort.

Team leaders decided to vest this front-end bonus; team members would be eligible for the monies upon making the April 27 deadline, but the bonus wouldn't pay out until July 1. "We did it to make sure people didn't see April 27 as an end point," says Raymond. "There's a lot of emotional release upon hitting a major milestone, but we needed to keep pushing ahead. In hindsight we were glad we vested."

The April milestone was met, and all core team members received a bonus Raymond describes only as being "in the thousands" of dollars.

A second bonus—half the amount of the front-end payout, which was considered a more critical deadline—was pegged to hitting a November 1, 1998, deadline for full, worldwide deployment of the new SAP system. That meant, Raymond says, "ending up with just one functioning system sitting in one computer center running order management for all global locations."

Unlike the front-end bonus, this one was not vested. "We were concerned that vesting the back-end payment would make it look too far off, and not serve to keep people committed through the life of the project," Raymond says. This deadline also was met, and immediate payouts were made.

The project had critical midterm milestones as well. Two included SAP deployment in all European countries by the end of August and all Asian countries (except Japan) by the end of September. Team leaders decided not to tie cash bonuses to hitting these dates.

Rewarding Support Teams in the Field

Although the core project team captured most of the attention, Lotus also made sure to recognize the work of the small supporting teams that enabled system implementation in the field.

Each Lotus region held a celebratory party for the teams at a local restaurant, and teams received cash bonuses of $200 to $1,000 per member, the amount depending on how a regional steering committee viewed the team's contribution to project implementation. Those criteria included "contribution to the local installation, primarily the effort to install and support early days of the start-up," Raymond says.

For its success, the core project team was honored by the company with its 1998 "Make Something Happen by Working Together" award, given since 1991 by Lotus for examples of exemplary teamwork. To capture the inscribed Steuben glass bowl, Lotus teams or work groups must, according to award criteria, accomplish the following:

- Make a significant contribution to executing Lotus business strategy
- Demonstrate Lotus operating principles in teamwork efforts
- Show a commitment to achieving "best customer satisfaction" internally, externally, or both
- Effectively work across organizational or geographical boundaries to collaborate or influence others

The award reflects Lotus's active recognition culture; many of its divisions regularly use awards to celebrate team and individual performance. The Lotus information services group, for example, gives a biannual team excellence award for cross-functional project teamwork—the award being a team plaque and $100 American Express gift certificates for all team members—and also gives an Excellence in Customer Satisfaction award for outstanding customer service provided by teams.

Rewarding Individual Performance on Teams

Project team leaders believed it imperative to reward individual performance on the core project team as well. In preproject contracts that all team members signed, discretionary cash bonuses were dangled—above and beyond the team bonus—for evidence of certain well-defined behaviors.

Bonuses were awarded at three performance levels, at the discretion of Raymond and the system development manager. "We were clear up front that this would be our judgment call," Raymond says. The top bonus—again in the thousands of dollars—was reserved for the project supernovas, or what Raymond calls the team's "indispensable spark plugs." These employees contributed to the project at a level above and beyond team norms, with a pattern of assumed responsibilities, accountabilities, and leadership, often picking up the slack for others and keeping the team churning forward toward goals (see box on the next page for specific criteria used to determine extraordinary individual contribution to teams). Only three team members were given this top-level individual bonus.

OUTSTANDING INDIVIDUAL PERFORMANCE ON A TEAM

Leaders of the project team that reengineered a Lotus/IBM order fulfillment process and implemented a new worldwide SAP system felt it crucial to reward not only strong team performance but also exemplary individual performance.

But how could they grant such discretionary cash bonuses in a way that proved fair and equitable?

Team leaders decided extraordinary individual performance had to meet specific criteria, described in contracts each team member was asked to sign. Says Larry Raymond, project team sponsor: "This statement is as close as we could get to being precise about the kind of behaviors we were looking for."

These are the criteria as laid out in contract language:

"Extraordinary individual contribution means qualitative and quantitative work beyond the team norm that has a material impact on the avoidance or solution of obstacles and critical issues. It may be manifested as: leadership, whether delegated or informally assumed; extensive personal effort to prevent or resolve a crisis; or sustained fault-free work beyond the team norm that brings a high level of 'stability of operation' to a portion of the system. The judgment of the project team manager and project team sponsor regarding extraordinary contribution to the team's achievement shall be binding."

The next bonus level—about half the dollar value of the top award—was reserved for those who, although perhaps not showing the same level of leadership or overall responsibility for team progress, "threw themselves into the system deployment, often making important personal sacrifices in terms of being away from homes and families for weeks at a time, or working over weekends," Raymond says. "This bonus level was for sheer effort and volume of work, accompanied by a high level of quality." Five team members were given this bonus.

The third or bottom bonus level—half the dollar value of the midlevel bonus— was for those "who'd done a high standard of work, but not necessarily above and beyond, or who hadn't made the personal sacrifices others may have," Raymond says. Ten team members captured this bonus.

Only five of the twenty-three core team members received no individual cash bonus.

Raymond admits giving these discretionary bonuses was a delicate issue, but team leadership thought it important to acknowledge exemplary solo effort. "Our HR department was very careful about it, and I was required to provide a detailed, written explanation of why the people who got the bonuses qualified for them," he says.

Raymond wrote this, for example, as part of his justification of a top-level individual bonus given to one team member: "Charley [fictional name] assumed leadership of the configuration integration whenever the system development manager was not available, and took responsibility for many areas that would have fallen between the cracks. He was consistently going beyond the call of duty."

Retaining Top Employees in a Seller's Market

The team and individual cash bonuses, although not guaranteed, did play a substantial role in retaining some of Lotus's more valued employees during the project, Raymond believes. The job market was such that once a team member had a few months of SAP experience, it was likely he or she could command a base salary 50 percent higher than what Lotus might be willing to pay. A business analyst paid $60,000, for instance, might be offered another job during the project paying $90,000.

Rather than face the costly prospect of multiple base pay increases, Lotus used other tactics to help keep top employees on board. The one-time cash bonuses, for instance, "kept people thinking their compensation was at least in line with the market during the project," Raymond says. A team member who received both the team bonus for hitting project deadlines and the top-level individual bonus could have earned up to an additional 30 percent of salary over the eighteen-month period.

In addition, to help retain employees who'd acquired an extraordinary level of skill in areas deemed critical to company success, Lotus created a special quarterly skills payment, which didn't require altering standard salary bands. The payments will continue, Raymond says, "until in our estimation we have a broad enough base of those particular skills that we no longer have to use special compensation tactics to retain them."

Lotus, of course, also wanted to increase the odds team members would stay with the company far beyond the special project's end. And team leaders understood that had as much to do with creating challenging jobs and assignments, opportunities for influence, and a feeling of belonging as it did with putting extra dollars in pockets. "Beyond money, what keeps people from looking for greener pastures is the feeling that they're part of something bigger than themselves, that they're recognized and appreciated for their work, that they value relationships with coworkers, and that they can have a real impact on the company," Raymond says.

To that end, team leaders held a number of celebratory events throughout the project to help build team camaraderie and cohesion and to offer a chance to blow off steam during a stressful process. Included were team dinner cruises in the Boston Harbor, clam bakes, pizza parties, and outings to comedy clubs and bowling alleys. Indeed, two of the ground rules in the team's charter were to have fun and to treat each other with civility even under tense times or dead-line pressure.

The collection of reward and retention tactics appears to have paid off. Only one core team member left Lotus during the project, Raymond says, that for a higher-paying consulting job. Another was transferred internally from the project after completing her principal project work; she received the stage-one team cash bonus, but not the stage two. Three other team members left Lotus for other opportunities following the project's end.

"Money is only a dissatisfier, not a motivator," says Raymond, referring to Herzberg's classic "hygiene factor" theory. "We didn't believe the cash bonus would be the only way the team motivated itself to meet deadline dates. We knew true performance would be ground out day by day, and that team spirit and loyalty to teammates and team goals would be the things that truly mattered and made a difference. These are things that couldn't be written into any contract."

UTILICORP UNITED

UtiliCorp United, Inc., understands that its senior managers don't have a monopoly on good business ideas. Overlook the brainpower available closer to the front lines, the company knows, and you're missing a chance to unearth numerous ideas for doing the organization's business better, faster, and often cheaper.

Where one frontline brain might do wonders if turned loose to ponder new cost-cutting, process efficiency, or revenue-building ideas, UtiliCorp figured five could quintuple the creative power. So in 1995 the company launched a project team suggestion system that continues to enhance its bottom-line performance.

UtiliCorp, based in Kansas City, Missouri, is an international electric and gas company with more than 4.5 million customers across the United States, Canada, the United Kingdom, New Zealand, and Australia.

UtiliCorp's current team suggestion system builds on the success of an earlier idea program. That program, dubbed Think Big, was designed with a short life span to draw employee attention and create maximum impact. Over a three-month period, Think Big asked employees to form suggestion teams of up to five members—on their own, not by management decree—to research and develop ideas that might in some way reduce UtiliCorp's costs or increase revenues.

Why a suggestion system built around cross-functional teams and not individual contributors? "We felt teams not only would improve the quality of ideas, they would foster team building across functions and more awareness of how employees fit in as part of UtiliCorp's whole," says Dave Sisel, senior manager for financial support. "We encouraged teams to pull together as many different kinds of expertise and viewpoints as they could."

Think Big was heavily promoted across the organization with a video featuring the CEO's endorsement of the program, wall posters, articles in the company newsletter, and kick-off meetings held at UtiliCorp sites around the country.

One unique aspect of the plan: use of noncash awards rather than cash for approved ideas. "UtiliBucks" are deposited into team member accounts for use toward a catalogue of functional, as well as deluxe, merchandise awards (one UtiliBuck equals one dollar). The objective of this type of award is to extend the memory of the recognized act or idea; employees remember how they earned the video camera a lot longer than what they did with the same number of cash dollars, Sisel notes. For approved cost savings or net revenue ideas with an impact of between $500 and $1,000 over twelve months, for example, each team member earned fifteen UtiliBucks; for ideas with a bigger impact—between $5,001 and $10,000—each member received 150 UtiliBucks. The cost of the awards was "grossed up"—W-2 statements reflected award value, including taxes—and UtiliCorp paid the taxes, increasing the perceived value of the awards.

The promotional blitz worked: 85 percent of UtiliCorp's then four thousand employees joined some type of suggestion team during Think Big, which translated into 650 teams that generated about 1,600 cost-savings or revenue-building ideas in the three-month span.

Interest ran high in part because Think Big had high incentives, says Sisel. Teams that had ideas approved for $1 million or more in cost savings or additional revenue, for instance, received the equivalent of up to $20,000 after tax—per team member. Sisel says several ideas paid out at that award level.

Ideas ran the gamut from the innovative to the commonsensical "how-come-no-one's-done-this-before?" variety. To qualify for submission in Think Big, ideas required a minimum projected impact of $500.

One team suggested a new way to refinance debt UtiliCorp had incurred as part of a foreign acquisition. Total savings? Approximately $4 million in taxes. Another team came up with ways to use sources other than coal to fuel Utili-Corp's boilers at lower cost.

When the dust settled, some $16 million in ideas had been approved on the heels of the three-month program, Sisel claims, with $15 million implemented as of this writing. About 87 percent of that $16 million, or $13.9 million, represents cost savings, and the remaining $2.1 million additional revenues. What did team members reap for their hard work and creative thinking? $2.97 million in Think Big awards.

Over three years, the net bottom-line contribution from the program—with all related expenses deducted—was $22.6 million. (That figure exceeds $16 million because of the compounding effect of idea impact over three years.)

Tweaking Plan Design

Although Think Big exceeded management's expectations, the plan's condensed time frame and frenetic nature created administrative headaches and strain in some quarters of the company. Project teams put in plenty of time above and beyond normal work hours to research and develop ideas, and the one hundred evaluation committees charged with giving thumbs up or down on ideas often found themselves swamped. "It took the committees several months beyond the program's end just to clear ideas out of the pipeline," Sisel says.

As management debriefed on Think Big, it decided a slower tempo was needed: a suggestion system that retained the best qualities of project teamwork but was more of a long burn than one-time splash. "We didn't want the new program to take over people's lives to the extent Think Big did," says Sisel. Management also wanted suggestion teams to be more accountable for helping to implement their ideas.

The revised program, named Suggest One, is a less structured initiative with no defined time frame that builds on Think Big; teams now submit ideas more as an extension of their day-to-day business than as part of a one-time program.

The slower pace hasn't stemmed the tide of quality ideas, however. The first idea implemented under Suggest One came from Minnesota employee Randy Carlson, who invented a way to help customers more efficiently and safely locate underground gas lines in their yards before starting a digging or excavation project. The tool helps locate plastic natural gas lines that don't have what's known as a tracing wire, a mechanism often buried with the gas piping so UtiliCorp's metal detector–like locators can identify where the pipe lies. The new tool also allows UtiliCorp technicians to feed a tracing wire into the pipe but keep the gas from leaking out.

Carlson's invention is roughly the size of a roll of quarters and costs around $70; in past years, an $8,000 machine was used for this duty. Price isn't the main advantage of the innovation, however: safety is. It's more accurate than guesswork or pricey electronic equipment. It's faster, too.

For their ingenuity and hard work, Carlson and six members of his implementation team each had $600 in UtiliBucks deposited in their merchandise accounts—possibly more later if the idea exceeds its anticipated $87,000 value.

In another case, a Suggest One team in Nebraska spent months trying to convince the Nebraska Department of Revenue that a new UtiliCorp customer service center qualified the company for a $600,000 tax break. State tax officials finally agreed, and the team's idea was finalized not long after. "It was an excellent idea that required lots of research, and it required plenty of perseverance getting to the right people inside and outside the company," says Don Nordell of UtiliCorp Energy Delivery, an idea advocate for the proposal.

Lessons Learned from Act I and Act II

Teams now receive UtiliBuck awards based on an idea's implementation, not just its approval. A team that generates an idea with projected twelve-month revenue impact between $5,001 to $10,000, for instance, would have 25 UtiliBucks deposited in the idea originators' accounts upon idea approval and 90 more in the implementation team members' accounts upon idea installation; if the idea's impact fell between $100,000 and $150,000, team members would receive 25 UtiliBucks at approval and 800 at implementation.

"This is one of our biggest lessons learned," says Sisel. "It moves us away from the 'here's my idea—now someone else go implement it' syndrome." Teams now can receive award payouts at three points in the program: at concept origination and approval to proceed, idea implementation, and under a one-year equity gain scenario. A team's idea is considered implemented for purposes of payout once that implementation has begun; in most cases that means whenever changes are in place and beginning to show results. In other cases, implementation is official when action has been taken "that would require a specific act of management to stop or change the course of implementation events," says Sisel.

Another key change with Suggest One: teams or individual employees have a chance to reevaluate the impact of their ideas at the idea's annual anniversary date and be rewarded an "equity bonus" if their idea yields additional savings or revenue over and above the amount approved at implementation. "The objective is to keep teams involved to ensure payoffs from their ideas are maximized," Sisel says.

Suggest One also replaces predecessor Think Big's three-person idea evaluation committees with "idea advocates," mid- to low-level managers assigned not only to evaluate the worthiness of a team's ideas but to advise it on idea development. UtiliCorp made the change to speed the idea review process and provide a new consulting resource for teams. "Many evaluation committees under Think Big had difficulty finding time when all three members could meet," Sisel says.

The new structure creates a dual role for idea evaluators, freeing them to provide more one-on-one coaching for teams than was possible using multiple-member committees. Each advocate receives formal training in coaching and facilitation skills, team building, how to set milestones and objectives, use of quality tools such as flow diagrams and pareto charts, and more. It's all designed to help advocates provide teams with the resources and advice to develop winning ideas.

Any ideas with projected impact of $100,000 or more still must pass through a second screening process, a review by an evaluation committee made up of senior managers.

Think Big only accepted ideas with a clear or immediate financial benefit, but Suggest One opens the door to ideas that target operational improvement—including suggestions to improve process efficiency or customer service. Although usually more difficult to assign a dollar value to, these types of improvements have no less tangible—and often more long-term—payback to the organization. Awards are proportionally smaller for these types of suggestions, however.

The overall award schedule also was altered to match Suggest One's new structure. The maximum payout for approved ideas, for instance, fell from $20,000 per team member (in UtiliBucks equivalent) for ideas with $1 million or above impact in Think Big to $2,500 for ideas valued at $500,000 or above under Suggest One, Sisel says. At the lower end, awards for ideas with a net impact from $10,001 to $20,000, for example, fell from 300 UtiliBucks per team member to 200, with 175 of the latter coming upon idea implementation. Management felt higher payouts were well suited to the shorter Think Big program, but lower payouts more appropriate for a program that has no limit to the number of ideas teams can submit. "Over time, employees have an opportunity to earn even more for their contributions," Sisel says.

Under the Think Big program, employees who formed a team were essentially stuck with it; if they wanted a new team to work on a new idea, they couldn't create it. Under Suggest One, teams now can reconstitute from idea to idea, and individuals also can submit ideas, although teamwork is still strongly encouraged.

Ideas can only be created for use outside the originating team's own department. If the suggestion team has strong cross-functional membership, its idea should apply to the area with the smallest amount of team representation. The stipulation is designed to avoid rewarding teams for work that might be considered part of their normal job duties. "People here are expected to continuously look for ways to improve things in their own work areas," Sisel says.

Is it realistic to assume workers without expertise in other parts of an organization can generate ideas to improve processes or outcomes in that area? It is at UtiliCorp, especially with five heads at work instead of just one. The idea to use alternative fuel sources to lower costs, for instance, came from an environmental engineer who was familiar with fuel technologies but who had never worked in a UtiliCorp power plant.

Because Suggest One doesn't have the defined time frame or special project emphasis of Think Big, Sisel and others have to work a bit harder to keep the suggestion system upmost in the mind of busy employees. "When things appear to settle down, we create new promotions and a new energy to jump start it," he says.

CHAPTER FIVE

Company Profiles: Organizational Unit ("Group") Incentives

The growing use of incentive plans for organizational units is part of management's response to a vexing challenge: how to continually build shareholder value while acting on increasing evidence that an organization's people are its only truly sustainable competitive advantage.

Properly designed and implemented, organizational unit incentives acknowledge the increasing importance of engaging all parts of the organizational brain—not just in management ranks—in helping a company thrive in ever-competitive global markets. The incentive's key weapon: tying employees' focus and energy more tightly to the organization's strategic business goals.

In their best use, these incentive plans (often called by such names as group, gain-sharing, or goal-sharing plans) give a broad employee population a new voice and a stake in company success, asking as much of their minds as of their hands. These plans use the power of teamwork to rally work groups, divisions, departments, plants, and entire companies around a common cause—the win-win proposition that when a work team, department, or company accomplishes its key measures of success, the employees will share in the financial gains.

The best of these plans can be characterized as "employee engagement with rewards." The engagement (employees taking action to improve unit performance) is supported through business literacy, communications, and awareness of business objectives. The plans' most obvious and immediate payback is improved performance and more cash or other awards in the hands of workers. But the gift that keeps giving is a workforce more aligned with divisional and corporate goals, more educated about the specific decisions and actions that contribute to profit or loss, and with luck, more committed to an organization's ongoing success.

Organizational unit incentive plans also create new accountabilities. The structure gives management the discipline to set specific unit-based goals and encourage employees to work as a team to accomplish them. You might argue that this should be part of a manager's normal charge, but engaging employees often gets a low priority. The plans also make employees equally accountable to each other, and to management, to meet incentive plan targets.

Of course, expecting such incentive plans to translate precisely from design on paper to implementation in the field is inviting failure. Speed bumps are many on the road to instituting a plan that does the following:

- Seems fair and motivating to both management and employees
- Uses metrics that make employees stretch but not so far that they lose motivation
- Produces results that management feels more than justify the time and effort spent on the plan

ROCKWELL AUTOMATION

Employee engagement: to some it's the secret weapon in an arsenal of once-potent competitive tools increasingly dulled by unforgiving markets or encroaching global competitors. Those competitors might easily match your state-of-the-art technology, your pay or benefits package, even your product line. But can they match how engaged your workforce is—from the front lines up—in finding ways to wring out waste and inefficiencies while ratcheting up productivity and profits? Can they match the ownership mind-set you've created in the trenches, where frontline employees tailor daily decisions and actions to how they'll affect the organization's quarterly or annual objectives?

Creating such engagement is part of the strategic drumbeat at Milwaukee-based Rockwell Automation, the largest arm of Rockwell International Corporation, the former defense industry giant and current electronics automation powerhouse. With $4.5 billion in annual sales, Rockwell Automation produces more than 500,000 products in eighty countries with brand names that set the standard for industrial automation solutions. The brands include Allen-Bradley, Reliance Electric, Dodge, and Rockwell Software, under which programmable controllers, industrial motors, human-machine interface devices, sensors, software, and more are manufactured around the world.

One way Rockwell Automation works to increase employee engagement is through a group incentive plan designed for the business unit or site level. Called the Critical Success Measures Incentive Plan, or CSMIP, the plan serves three key purposes, says vice president for human resources Mary Jane Hall:

- To link and reward employee and business performance at the business unit level to improve local results

- To better educate Rockwell's employees throughout the organization about their unit or site's key business measures ("critical success factors"), and how those factors link to overall company success

- To increase employee engagement and interest in meeting business goals and reward them outside the normal merit levels when they attain or exceed those goals

CSMIP also is an outgrowth of Rockwell Automation's annual "Best Place to Work" employee satisfaction survey. A pattern of responses identified "a better connection between performance and rewards" as a key employee desire.

The Birth of CSMIP

The challenge to develop a meaningful organizational unit incentive plan for employees located at sites throughout the United States, often in significantly different lines of business, is a daunting one. Two or three broad measures for the ten thousand potential participants would have been too remote to be meaningful; employees would have great difficulty seeing how their individual actions could influence the measures. On the other hand, driving the performance measures down to each Rockwell Automation work group would have created more than a thousand separate plans, not practical to administer.

What Rockwell needed was one overarching incentive plan that would meet key business objectives, reinforce performance goals that employees could accept as meaningful and controllable, and create a greater sense of ownership and engagement in each of the diverse unit management teams.

Rockwell Automation formed a steering committee with representatives from the major stakeholders in the organization, including finance and human resources to craft such a plan. Debates were healthy and frank. The outcome was a design framework with a few guidelines, such as payout targets, maximum payouts, and the use of a modifier that would reflect Rockwell Automation's overall annual performance. The framework was then given to nine champion committees. Training taught managers how to adapt the framework to suborganizational units with meaningful measures and performance levels. Working with line management, the champion committees created a localized plan structure that addressed the objectives of CSMIP.

Rockwell Automation defines a business unit as a "significant product grouping with independent profit and loss accountability." One example is its Motion and Information Group; other business units are further segmented into specific geographic sites, such as the company's Twinsburg, Ohio, site. Some of the incentive plans covered Rockwell Automation business units with only a few hundred employees; some were larger units. In the plan's inaugural year of 1997–1998, 128 CSMIP incentive plans operated throughout Rockwell Automation.

How CSMIP Works

The CSMIP framework concept is detailed but relatively simple: by improving local performance at the business unit or site level and overall performance at the Rockwell Automation level, employees can receive an award or bonus based on a percentage of their annual pay. Rockwell Automation performance as a whole enters the incentive pay equation through a modification of the payout based on operating return on sales, or OROS. A unit or a site's performance on its four chosen critical success measures, as well as Rockwell's overall OROS performance, are then used to calculate employees' annual CSMIP payouts.

Consider, for example, the hypothetical XYZ business unit within Rockwell Automation. As a first step in the plan, XYZ—and all participating Rockwell Automation business units—selects four critical success areas to measure for the year. The CSMIP steering committee of senior leaders signs off on all units' goals, applying two dominant screening conditions: all measures must have a significant effect on business success and have a short line of sight so employees can directly impact the measures. XYZ unit, then, selects these four measures in its fiscal year:

- Profit before taxes (as a percentage of forecast plan)
- Sales growth
- On-time product shipments using the original promised date
- Scrap reduction

For each of the four measures, three incremental performance levels or targets are set. Level one constitutes a "meaningful improvement" the unit expects to achieve in the measure over the course of the fiscal year; level two is a "substantial improvement," or the midpoint between level one and level three performance; and level three is "exceptional improvement," designed as a stretch target. Table 5.1 shows the four measures of performance at each of the three levels.

In terms of probability of achievement, Bob Bilsborough, the plan administrator, estimates that achieving level one performance has a 70 percent probability for any given unit, achieving level two about 50 percent probability, and level three a 30 percent probability.

Table 5.1. Example of a CSMIP Performance-Reward Schedule.

| | Performance | | |
Performance Measure	Level One	Level Two	Level Three
Profit before taxes (as percent of plan)	100 percent of plan	103 percent of plan	106 percent of plan
Earns (as percent of pay)	*0.5 percent*	*1 percent*	*1.5 percent*
Sales growth	10 percent	13 percent	16 percent
Earns (as percent of pay)	*0.5 percent*	*1 percent*	*1.5 percent*
On-time shipments (as percent of promised dates made)	90 percent	92 percent	94 percent
Earns (as percent of pay)	*0.5 percent*	*1 percent*	*1.5 percent*
Scrap reduction (as percent of raw material scrapped)	15 percent	13 percent	11 percent
Earns (as percent of pay)	*0.5 percent*	*1 percent*	*1.5 percent*

The maximum employee payout for local performance is 4 percent of pay. As Table 5.1 indicates, the total potential payout for hitting level three performance in all four measures reads as 6 percent. But that's set higher simply to reinforce greater performance on each measure. If the business unit hits level three performance on all four of its key measures, the payout would be capped at 4 percent of annual pay.

Here's where Rockwell Automation's operating return on sales (OROS), a gauge of the company's overall performance, comes into play. When business units or sites operate more effectively, as is amply explained to all employees, Rockwell Automation as a whole should be more profitable—there's a direct link between business unit performance and overall divisional performance. To integrate the company's overall performance, CSMIP plans include the OROS variable. OROS is defined as operating earnings divided by sales. Essentially, OROS captures, as a percentage, how much Rockwell Automation earned for every dollar in sales. A 12 percent OROS, for example, means that Rockwell is earning twelve cents for every dollar in sales.

The OROS performance modifies the earnings by applying a multiplier according to the schedule in Table 5.2. Integrating that OROS figure, the CSMIP payout for each eligible Rockwell Automation employee is a straightforward calculation.

Table 5.2. Use of Organizational Performance Modifier.

	OROS			
	<9 percent	9–10.9 percent	11–12.9 percent	≥13 percent
Modifier	0.5	1.0	1.5	1.75

Assume XYZ unit performs at the levels highlighted in Table 5.3 for the year and OROS is at 12 percent (shown in Table 5.4). Local earned payout would then be: $1 + 1.5 + 0.5 + 1 = 4$ percent.

Table 5.3. Performance Example in CSMIP.

Performance Measure	Performance		
	Level One	Level Two	Level Three
Profit before taxes (as percent of plan)	100 percent of plan	103 percent of plan	106 percent of plan
Earns (as percent of pay)	0.5 percent	1 percent	1.5 percent
Sales growth	10 percent	13 percent	16 percent
Earns (as percent of pay)	0.5 percent	1 percent	1.5 percent
On-time shipments (as percent of promised dates made)	90 percent	92 percent	94 percent
Earns (as percent of pay)	0.5 percent	1 percent	1.5 percent
Scrap reduction	15 percent	13 percent	11 percent
Earns (as percent of pay)	0.5 percent	1 percent	1.5 percent

Table 5.4. Modifier Performance Example in CSMIP.

	OROS			
	<9 percent	9–10.9 percent	11–12.9 percent	≥13 percent
Modifier	0.5	1.0	1.5	1.75

Factoring in the OROS modifier, the total annual payout for XYZ employees is: 4 percent local × 1.5 OROS = 6 percent of pay. For a Rockwell Automation employee earning $30,000 per year, that's an award check of $1,800.

The Report Card: First-Year Results

Of the 128 CSMIP plans running in Rockwell Automation's United States and Canadian operations in fiscal year 1997–1998, 108 paid out by hitting one or more of their four performance targets. In other words, only twenty plans provided no payout to participants.

The average employee payout was 3 percent of annual pay, with a range of 1 percent to the 7 percent allowable maximum. Bilsborough says this "modest" first-year performance is partly a result of "the year not going quite according to plan [financial forecasts]. But in a relatively tough market for us, we only had twenty plans that didn't pay out, which we consider very good."

Rockwell Automation management believes payout levels are but one yardstick to measure the plan's first-year success, however. Other gains can be traced, at least in part, to introduction of CSMIP. Some areas of the company improved inventory management dramatically, for example, and others saw improvement in cash flow, product quality, and on-time delivery performance.

"Inventory management and reduction is a key thrust for us, and many of the CSMIP plans around the company had inventory measures in them," Bilsborough says. "We got plenty of attention, effort, and focus around achievement of that goal. Surveys show employees really thought they could impact inventory levels—there was strong line of sight."

But how much of a given Rockwell Automation unit's improvement on operational or financial targets can be attributed directly to the incentive plan? Bilsborough posed the question on a postmortem survey sent to managers in units where the 128 CSMIP plans operated.

When asked, "What percentage of the gain in your chosen measures would you attribute directly to the plan?" the average response was 15 percent, he says.

On that same survey managers also cited these as the biggest payoffs from using CSMIP in the first year:

- Improved understanding among front liners and first-line managers about their unit's—and the company's—annual business objectives. "We consider that among our biggest successes," Bilsborough says.

- The incentive plans were "somewhat effective" in fostering improved teamwork and in making the pay-for-performance linkage tighter.

- Greater interest and engagement among employees in their unit's business objectives.

- Ample evidence of positive employee relations and a boost to morale.

As the profile was written, Bilsborough was adding quantitative data to this largely qualitative ROI research by "valuing out" financial gains from the first year of CSMIP. He'll take the cumulative financial gains possible to isolate from the plans, subtract the plan payouts, and then divide by the payouts for that valuation figure.

Successes and Lessons Learned

**The more engaged first-line managers are,
the more successful the plan is.**

It's little surprise that the most successful CSMIP plans at Rockwell Automation—measured not only by payout levels but by improvements in manager-to-employee communication, employees educated about how they can affect unit goals, and units' operational or financial performance—showed a greater degree of first-line manager involvement and ownership.

"Groups that had more frequent, open, and detailed communication from management to staff concerning progress against plan goals—where employees were given a chance to have their say—tended to have the highest employee and management satisfaction with the plan," Bilsborough says.

Rockwell Automation found that employees tend to move through three stages during a CSMIP plan: *awareness* (I am aware of the plan and know generally how it works), *understanding* (I understand how payouts are calculated and what I can do to affect my unit's business measures), and *full engagement* (I fully understand how the plan works, and I know which groups outside of my immediate work team I can engage to help improve unit or groupwide performance and affect systemic change).

"Those management teams that worked hard to facilitate a rapid move through awareness to understanding, and sometimes on to engagement, tended to have better-performing plans in year one," says Bilsborough.

To nudge first-line managers to communicate more frequently with their employees about the plan, Rockwell Automation created a number of devices. Each unit using CSMIP receives a large poster frame in which to publicly post its four measures of monthly performance. The frames are hung in a prominent place so workers can easily check them for progress against goals like accounts receivable days, on-time performance, and the like, and read management's kudos or urgings if progress has been derailed. Many managers hold monthly or quarterly meetings with employees around the poster frames to keep attention focused on the plan.

In the plan's second year, each manager will receive a scripted guide that will make it easier to have more regular, fifteen- to twenty-minute conversations with employees about the incentive plan. "The focus will be on what the organizational unit can do to impact plan goals, and who else a team or unit might work with outside its own area to help get those results," Bilsborough says. "Our main focus going forward is education—educating employees about how they can impact measures, and that there will be rewards for them as well as the organization if they do."

Many Rockwell Automation business units used temporary project teams (called WIN teams) in support of CSMIP goals. "CSMIP links with our continuous improvement philosophy," Bilsborough says, "and some of our organizations use WIN teams very effectively in pursuit of CSMIP goals." Relying heavily on WIN teams, for example, a Rockwell plant in Greenville, South Carolina, improved accuracy of its packaging and shipping by 70 percent over a year, a Control and Information group decreased its excess inventory balance by 77 percent, and a Standard Drives group reduced its annual warranty costs by 40 percent.

Once payout levels from the plan's first year became known in December, discussion about CSMIP ratcheted up significantly around the company. Sensitive issues, such as why one unit got bigger payouts than another, surfaced. "Here's where you really have to communicate the intent of your incentive plan," Bilsborough says. "People need to really know how the plan works, and what went into one unit receiving a larger payout than another. It drives acceptance of the plan—and accountability for results."

Make sure performance measures don't cloud line of sight.

Bilsborough acknowledges that despite an initial goal to use only short line-of-sight measures in plans, a few Rockwell Automation units or sites had year-one measures that extended too far beyond the horizon.

"Worldwide profit before taxes, worldwide inventory days, worldwide gross margins—employees may not have felt a whole lot of ability to impact those measures," he says. "Our goal in coming years will be to create subsets of those measures for CSMIP, or smaller pieces that drive the longer line-of-sight measures, so employees feel they have more local control."

Already the plan is being tweaked to drill deeper down into business units or sites, creating incentive plans for smaller work teams or functions within the unit to avoid measures that might encompass the work of ten thousand employees.

Management also is considering a change to the minimum performance threshold that triggers plan payouts. In year one, "the annual operating plan was the annual operating plan was the annual operating plan," says Bilsborough, meaning all units had to achieve the annual operating plan for level one performance on their particular measures to trigger any payouts.

That threshold was set figuring Rockwell Automation would continue its aggressive growth from previous years. But 1998—year one of the plan—proved more difficult than anticipated.

"Since our primary goal is improved performance, we may set the new level one trigger differently, to exceed prior-year performance, but to be somewhat below our coming year plan," Bilsborough says. "Not across the board—only in areas where we may have very aggressive budget plans." In other words, payouts in 1999 for hitting select performance measures were to be linked to improving on 1998 performance, but they wouldn't necessarily have to meet aggressive 1999 forecasts.

Rockwell Automation learned another important lesson about setting goals during this virgin voyage: beware of linked measurements. Some units chose a package of sales growth, margin, and profit before tax (PBT) as their CSMIP measures, for instance, increasing the odds employees might not receive any payout at all.

"If you miss your sales growth target, you may also miss your margin and PBT, depending on your mix and other factors," Bilsborough says. "In the future we'll strive for a better balance between operational and financial measures, and work to help local units avoid some of those financial linkages."

MID-STATES TECHNICAL STAFFING SERVICES

In this company's unconventional self-funding plan, team members aren't forced to wait for yearly or even quarterly incentive payouts. If the company hit its short-term profit goals, they pocket bonus checks immediately.

Most organizational unit incentives are designed within the safe guardrails of tradition. Consciously or not, designers follow a timeworn path—they create plans tied to the traditional financial reporting periods of the calendar. Most of these plans pay out monthly, quarterly, or annually simply because that's when accountants make financial data available. That schedule is logical, convenient—and the way it's always been done.

But Steve Wilson didn't want to be bound by that tradition. Wilson, founder of Mid-States Technical Staffing Services, Inc., a temporary help agency, wanted a group incentive for his organization that wasn't handcuffed to time-honored reporting periods. If Mid-States' financial information was available on a more frequent basis—weekly or even daily—he reasoned, why should he be bound by the monthly-quarterly-yearly payout schedule everyone else uses? Why not pay a bonus immediately to employees whenever they reach a given performance milestone, and not make them wait until the end of a quarter or a year rolled around?

Wilson believed such a plan would not only create a more visible link between pay and performance but also aid a company like Mid-States whose income has a strong seasonal ebb and flow.

Bingo! Wilson's innovative Bucket Bonus plan was born.

Wilson founded Mid-States in 1986 to provide client companies with temporary technical employees, and later opened a division offering contract engineering services. The company grew quickly, doubling in size the first few years.

The growth eventually earned Mid-States a place on *Inc.* magazine's list of the 500 fastest-growing small companies in America.

In 1997, Mid-States was purchased by temporary staffing leader Modis Professional Services of Jacksonville, Florida, and now operates under the name ENTEGEE, continuing to supply companies with temporary technical and engineering staffing.

Prior to introducing the Bucket Bonus plan, Wilson had launched a number of traditional group incentive plans at Mid-States with little success. As a labor-intensive service business, Mid-States did not have consistent month-to-month, or even quarter-to-quarter, profitability. Earnings were a year-long roller-coaster. Much of Mid-States' new hiring, for instance, was done in the first quarter of the year, so most of the company's profit margin in the first few months went to state and federal unemployment taxes, social security tax, Medicare, and other expenses related to hiring new employees. Profitability would typically improve in April and May, fall with the holidays and vacations during the summer, pick up substantially through most of autumn, then drop dramatically from late November through the end of the year.

Wilson needed to find an incentive plan to accommodate that seasonality. Though employees' performance was consistently strong, traditional bonuses paid out for monthly or quarterly profitability were erratic. For a while, Wilson tried periodic discretionary bonus payments, then went to a single, year-end bonus. But none of the plans created a consistent link between performance and pay. One of Mid-States' managers at the time, Dave McCracken, says the annual bonus produced a "Santa Claus" effect. Like children on their best behavior before Christmas, employees busted their humps for six to eight weeks before the end of the year in hopes of maximizing their bonus. As soon as the bonus was paid they reverted to normal—good, but not exceptional—performance.

How the Bucket Bonus Plan Works

Wilson knew he needed a new approach. Inspired by discussions with a fellow participant at a CEO leadership forum, he came up with the Bucket Bonus plan.

Here's an overview of how the plan works (for more detailed information, see the box on the next page).

At the start of the year, Mid-States' management decided how much profit it needed to fill up a symbolic bucket. If the yearly profit target was $450,000, each of six buckets might total $75,000. Later, as the company grew, the bucket size would be bigger. To make the plan possible, Mid-States had to keep track each week of its year-to-date pretax profit.

Whenever the company filled the "bucket" with $75,000 pretax profit—regardless of the calendar date and whether it was the middle of a month or a quarter—the fifty or so employees at Mid-States eligible for the plan were paid a bonus, or a percentage of the bucket sum. In other words, they weren't forced to wait for

STEVE WILSON'S DESIGN AND IMPLEMENTATION GUIDELINES

If you want a simple and effective incentive plan for a small or midsize organization, and you don't want intricate details in your bonus design, you can adapt Mid-States' Bucket Bonus template to your work environment, says plan founder Steve Wilson. As you gain experience, you can review and adjust the plan to your unique circumstances. Wilson outlines the plan as follows:

- *Identify two critical numbers.* In this incentive plan, your first critical number is annual profit. The second critical number will determine whether the bonus payouts are doubled. Mid-States' second number was sales growth, but it can be anything you choose: percentage of revenue from new products, quality ratings—whatever reflects your company's strategic objectives.

- *Set the bucket size.* Determine the dollar amount of pretax profit you want for the year. Multiply that amount by 1.35. Divide by 6 (buckets). You can adjust the bucket size up or down somewhat to a round number, if you like.

- *Determine the bonus pool.* If you like, you can borrow Mid-States' formula: 5 percent of the first yearly "bucket" paid out as bonus to employees, on up to 20 percent of the sixth bucket, with the amount doubled if you hit your target for the second critical performance goal chosen.

- *Determine the distribution formula.* Equal shares to all employees, equal percentages of year-to-date annualized pay, or perhaps a hybrid scheme like Mid-States uses (see main profile for more detail).

- *Determine the payout timing.* To avoid potential cash flow problems, Wilson says you should schedule payment no sooner than one-half of your average collection period. If the delay will be over twenty days, you should consider issuing a voucher to employees for the bonus, payable at a scheduled future date.

- *Test and announce the plan.* Before launching the plan, Wilson suggests having a select group of employee representatives review and walk through it. These beta testers can point out any potential problems and help clarify issues related to the plan. Supporters in this group can also help you get faster buy-in from the rest of your employees, "carrying the flag" in a sense for the value and the win-win nature of the plan.

quarterly or yearly results to be paid. "At that point we would set that bucket aside, and start on a new bucket," Wilson says. Each new bucket paid out a larger percentage to employees, so that buckets at the end of the year were worth more in bonus than buckets at the beginning.

The self-funding nature of the plan—employees only receive bonuses out of generated profit—limited Mid-States' financial risk while promising significant rewards to employees for helping profits grow. Payments were frequent, as many as ten a year, leaving little time to forget about the bonus plan.

Prior to the Bucket Bonus plan Mid-States had been dividing up its year-end profit fifty-fifty; half went to Mid-States' six shareholders, and half stayed with the company to reinvest in future growth. If profits were $320,000, shareholders and company would each receive $160,000.

But because the goal of the Bucket Bonus was to help all Mid-States' employees think and act more like business owners, management wanted to pay them more than a token bonus for profit results, perhaps 10 to 20 percent of their annual pay. "We figured we should pay them a share of the profits roughly equal to what the company owners got," Wilson says.

So with the onset of Bucket Bonus, that yearly profit of $320,000 would be split three ways instead of two—slightly less than $107,000 apiece to shareholders, the company, and the new participants, employees.

Mid-States was sensitive to the hit shareholders and the company would take in the new bonus split; Wilson compensated by increasing the annual profit goal by an ambitious 35 percent. Using the $320,000 target in the example, the profit goal was now $432,000. That meant the company could pay out as much as $112,000 to employees in bonus, and still leave $320,000—original targeted profit—to be divided between the owners and company.

Back to that original bucket figure of $75,000. Wilson helps clarify: "If we exceeded our new profit goal of $432,000 only slightly, we could fill six $75,000 buckets and pay out some pretty good bonuses without hurting either shareholders or the company," he says. "Filling up six buckets also would allow us to pay a bonus every couple months if we stayed on plan. And we believed frequent payouts were critical to keeping the profit goal and the bonuses at the top of everyone's mind."

The third step in Bucket Bonus plan creation—a critical one—is determining how much bonus to pay employees out of each bucket. For its first $75,000 bucket, for example, Mid-States decided to pay bonuses using 5 percent of the bucket, or $3,750. Later buckets paid much more "because if we made more profit we could afford to pay more in bonuses," Wilson says. The second bucket paid 7.5 percent, the third 10 percent, the fourth 12.5 percent, and so on up to buckets that paid 20 percent to employees.

To keep the staff from focusing too much on profitability at the expense of sales growth, Mid-States built a feature into the plan called the Sales Adder. If the company's sales were 25 percent higher than the prior year's sales whenever a bucket was filled, the amount in the bonus pool doubled.

"That's a tremendous incentive for people to work to fill up additional buckets, because the bonus pool gets so much bigger," Wilson says. "It's a big carrot to focus on generating more sales."

The introduction of the Bucket Bonus plan meant the end of commissions for Mid-States' sales force; a combination of higher base salaries and the Bucket

Bonus replaced those commission dollars. The Bucket Bonus also replaced discretionary year-end bonuses for all Mid-States' employees. "The plan made a big improvement organizationally," Wilson claims. "Maybe most important, replacing traditional commission structures freed up our salespeople to be more consultative sellers, and to focus as much on what happens after the sale as well as making the sale."

Divvying Up the Bonus Payments

Another important question was how to split up the bonus money among Mid-States' employees. Wilson sought a simple and fair method of distributing the funds. After some debate, management decided that 35 percent of each bonus pool would be distributed equally among all full-time staff employees with at least one year of service (part-time employees were ineligible for this part of the bonus). The decision reflected a belief "that every experienced staff employee, regardless of position or salary, contributes to the financial success of the company," Wilson says. The remaining 65 percent of the pool was distributed to employees based on their year-to-date gross wages at the date of the Bucket Bonus payment. (Contract employees were the only group not eligible for either bonus pool amount.)

The distribution choice had two interesting results. First, management discovered there was little resistance from veterans to immediately including Mid-States' new hires in the wage-share bonus (the 65 percent part). "We needed these new employees to achieve our sales growth targets," Wilson says. "Everyone helped train them—but if they weren't performing up to par from the get-go, they were encouraged to leave the company before becoming eligible to receive their equal share. Even established employees who we felt were underperforming were pressured to improve or leave. High-performing employees didn't want to dilute their equal-share bonus with others who weren't up to par."

Another notable outcome was that bonuses paid to management, although larger in gross dollars than those paid to rank-and-file employees, represented a smaller percentage of their total wages than of employees' wages. "We learned over time that some employees considered themselves to be more 'valuable' to the company than their managers, because their bonuses were a larger portion of their total income," Wilson says.

To ensure there would always be enough available cash to make bonus payments, Mid-States created an additional requirement. At the time a Bonus Bucket was filled, the company's current asset-to-liability ratio had to be 1.25 or better, or there would be no bonus. In other words, if Mid-States had payroll, tax, credit lines, and other current liabilities of $1 million, it had to have cash, receivables, and other current assets of at least $1.25 million, "or we couldn't afford to add the bonus amount to our liabilities," Wilson says.

Establishing the ratio served another purpose. Although cash management was the responsibility of the company's leaders, Mid-States wanted to educate front-line employees, as part of an open-book management campaign, about the importance of cash management in a growing company, and used the ratio to do so. "As it happened, we never experienced a problem with cash flow, and all earned bonuses were paid to employees," Wilson says.

One pleasant by-product of the cash management education program: Mid-States achieved an enviable collection rate on receivables, with receivable days consistently below twenty.

Effect on Company Performance

In 1993, Mid-States' goals as part of the incentive plan were $4 million in sales and $320,000 in profit. It exceeded both targets, and paid out approximately $86,000 in employee bonuses, with employees averaging 9 percent of their annual pay in bonus checks.

Performance numbers improved from there. By the end of 1996, sales had grown to nearly $9 million, with profit of 12 percent, and employees earned an average of 15.6 percent of their base pay in Bucket Bonus money. (In those years, the company's strategic goals included a 25 percent annual sales increase and pretax profit of 8 percent.)

Another telling statistic from that period is average increase in base pay. From 1991 to 1996, the average base pay of Mid-States' employees increased only 1 percent a year, or just 7 percent overall. A big reason, Wilson says, is that the bonus largely replaced annual base pay increases as a primary employee incentive.

Effect on Employee Performance

Wilson also believes the Bucket Bonus had several positive effects on the performance of Mid-States' workforce. One was that employees began watching financial reports more closely because they wanted to learn more about the "spigots" that determined how much wound up in the profit buckets, and how they might personally affect those numbers.

"You could walk into any office and see big buckets outlined on wall charts, along with the associated bonus amounts," Wilson says. Each week buckets were marked with highlighters indicating the latest profit levels. When a bucket was filled, a small celebration usually followed.

Another effect was that unlike many companies where sales, operations, and accounting often seem to be pulling their oars in different directions, functional groups at Mid-States began focusing on the same objectives as a result of the plan, and cross-departmental cooperation improved.

"Bonus plans by themselves don't drive better performance," Wilson says. "They can help improve performance, but only if employees know in what areas improvement is necessary, how their work can contribute to better results, and how they stand to gain personally if company performance really does improve."

Lessons Learned

A bucket bonus plan will affect accounting conventions.

Whenever Mid-States filled a symbolic bucket, it paid the bonus out to employees, then set that bucket aside, in a sense. The set-aside is a practice likely to raise the hackles of your company accountants, so you'll want to know how it works.

When you pay a bonus your finance folks will post the payment as a labor cost on your income statement. So if you paid $7,500 in bonuses on your first $75,000 in yearly profit (your first "bucket"), your posted profit would only be $67,500. Under the Bucket Bonus plan, now you'd have to earn an additional $82,500 in profit, according to the income statement, in order to reach the $150,000 profit level needed to fill the second bucket and trigger the second payout ($75,000 times 2).

Because Mid-States' management wanted to create the idea of setting the bucket aside to avoid that problem, the income statement was modified to, in effect, hide that bonus payment. Wilson says your accountants can suggest several ways to do this without invalidating your financial statements. "It's not necessary to do, but we thought it imposed a kind of mental penalty on employees when they earn a bonus," Wilson says, "Not doing it would have cost our employees at least one bucket bonus payment in the first year."

If, unlike Mid-States, you're going to stick with standard accounting practices in your bonus plan and deduct the bonus payments from future buckets, you should consider adjusting the bonus pool and buckets accordingly, Wilson suggests.

In addition, employer taxes such as social security, workers' compensation, and unemployment insurance are due on payment of a bonus, typically 10 to 15 percent of the bonus amount. These also will be posted as labor costs to income statements. Due to complications and penalties should a company incorrectly compute and pay those taxes, Mid-States decided to leave them on the income statement but simply charge them against the next bonus bucket.

"Doing it this way greatly simplified the computations and accounting without significantly affecting the bonus program," Wilson says.

Sometimes close enough is okay.

Because the plan wasn't tied to traditional quarterly or yearly financial reporting, the financial information used to determine bonuses was usually a close estimate, and not always 100 percent accurate. But close enough counts in the Bucket Bonus concept, Wilson says.

"The plan was run from estimated performance by design," he says, "and I advocate that. I would much rather use 97 percent accurate figures I can get earlier than 100 percent accurate numbers I have to wait much longer for. The faster you give people performance feedback and bonus dollars, the better the connection between performance and pay. I see companies use quarterly bonus plans based on numbers that aren't available until a month or more after the quarter ends, which means people are getting bonuses six or eight weeks after the three-month performance period is over. I think employees' memories are short that way, and there can be a real disconnect."

Consider using a portion of bonus payments
to give employees equity in the business.

Wilson suggests calling the National Center for Employee Ownership (510-272-9461) for ideas on how to use bonuses to provide employees with equity in the company. "If they can't help you find ways to provide equity, look for some ways yourself to make the bonus payments more of an 'extra,' so employees don't start perceiving them as regular income," he advises. "All too often bonus payments become part of an employee's regular spending, creating frustration and even hardship in the event there isn't a bonus payment in a given month or two."

You also might consider paying part of the bonus into employees' 401K plans, for instance, or distributing all or part of it in U.S. savings bonds. Or consider more creative options. Wilson knows a CEO who distributed a monthly bonus payment in the form of gold coins, "and he was pleasantly surprised to find that over 80 percent of employees hadn't spent their coins and still had them at the end of the year."

Tips on Bonus Bucket design.

- *Set the base critical-number performance goal at the lowest level that still ensures the company's financial security.* For example, if your company's annual objective is 25 percent sales growth, begin rewarding performance— paying bonuses—at the 15 percent or 20 percent growth level. This means, of course, that you may wind up paying a bonus for performance "below plan," but the initial bonuses in a bucket plan aren't designed to be large, and any downside is small compared to the excitement you can generate among workers by making the first payout easily attainable.

- *Start with small bonus payments and let them grow.* People change very slowly. So as they begin to improve performance, you want to give them small rewards to encourage ongoing improvement, and then provide bigger rewards for performance beyond planned objectives. For example, under Wilson's watch Mid-States regularly paid out nearly 50 percent of all excess (beyond plan) profits in employee bonus and benefits.

- *Frequent bonus payment keeps people involved, better tying pay to performance.* Between four and eight bonus payments a year is optimal, Wilson believes. "Annual bonus payments rarely have much effect on performance."

- *Do not pay a bonus if it isn't 100 percent earned.* This may seem obvious, but it can be tempting to lower the plan's standards, once objectives are set, just to pay the bonus and make people feel good. In one case at Mid-States, Wilson says, "the critical measure was so close to goal that we had to investigate the computer round-off of numbers to determine if the bonus had been earned. After that, we specified the exact decimal point calculation of all critical number goals."

AMERITECH INTERNAL AUDIT SERVICES

In this company's risky but effective plan, quarterly bonuses for self-directed team members depend not only on hitting team performance targets but also on reviews by their team peers.

An internal auditing group, with its unswerving devotion to rigid rules and standards, is an unexpected place to incubate unique human resource practices. But Ameritech's Internal Audit Services group has proven itself an innovator by introducing self-directed work teams and a merit compensation pool tied to how well those teams perform quarterly against predetermined goals.

The distaste for playing it safe extends to how those team payouts are apportioned as well. When the auditing teams hit their preannounced goals, pool payouts aren't simply split equally among team members; they're divided up using a relatively subjective but effective rating scale and feedback system designed to match payouts to the effort various team members put into achieving the goals.

Spread among three Chicago-area locations, the self-directed auditing teams serve the needs of Ameritech's diverse business units including local and long-distance telephone service, cable TV, paging, security monitoring, electronic commerce, wireless data communications, and more. Ameritech's consumer services group alone serves eleven million homes and one million businesses in five Midwestern states. The teams' charge: as an independent function, appraise and evaluate company controls, activities, operations, or transactions for conformance to practices, effectiveness, economy, and method of operation.

The auditing organization launched the self-directed concept in 1993, and by the next year pilot teams were reporting on their experiences to audit management. Pilot results in hand, management committed in 1995 to dismantling the existing hierarchical structure and breaking the entire unit into self-directed teams within three years. Eight such teams, each with seven to fourteen members, now operate in support of Ameritech's various operating units. All team members carry the equivalent title of senior auditor.

Why a need for self-directed teams in a hierarchical structure that showed no overt signs of distress?

General auditor Bruce Adamec, who played a leading role in the group's transformation, explains. "Self-directed teams are based on our belief that team members can make superior decisions resulting in better, more timely results than can individual auditors working in supervisory-directed environments," he says. "In the new model, auditors' actions are designed to be driven by principles and values, not by rigid departmental rules, supervisory discretion, or management edict."

Creating the teams meant eliminating supervisor, manager, and lead auditor titles in the group of sixty auditors; only Adamec's general auditor position and four directors' positions remain at the management level. Before self-direction, Ameritech had an auditor-to-manager ratio of four to one. Soon after teams were implemented, the ratio grew to eleven to one.

The remaining directors were given a new role—coach—with one coach assigned to one or two self-directed teams. Coaches retain ultimate responsibility for team results and are responsible for designing forward-looking organizational and administrative support processes, such as establishing new audit methods, setting salaries, promoting people, and monitoring people development, whereas the audit teams have responsibility for actual audit work and output, in addition to managing client relationships. Coaches and team members have a number of shared responsibilities—all clearly defined in the auditing group's new charter. The coaches' assigned duties like hiring or budgeting also receive plenty of input from the teams.

Indeed, the new model calls for shared leadership by team members, rather than the "thinly veiled hierarchical supervision that exists in many such team environments," says Adamec. Teams receive incoming audit work, decide among themselves who works on what, set deadlines, issue reports, and work through conflicts—all with minimal input from management. In this model, the onus is on the audit team, not the coach, to perform audit work to the satisfaction of clients, to ensure an impartial quality review of the audit work by a team peer, and to issue a signed summary report of the work.

The eight teams are designed to survive the frequent comings and goings of their individual members; each year about 30 to 50 percent of Ameritech internal auditors are promoted out of the teams into nonauditing management jobs elsewhere within Ameritech. Very few auditors remain in the department for more than three years.

"Bonus Pool" Team Incentive Plan

Members of audit teams are compensated not only for their individual performance but also for the performance of their teams as measured by predetermined quarterly goals. About 25 percent of an auditor's annual bonus is based on a review of individual performance, with 75 percent resting on the team performance.

Ameritech audit management determines the amount of the merit compensation pool for the teams each year, with that pool paid out quarterly depending on each team's performance as measured by a standard scorecard. Teams are ranked in one of four categories based on their scorecard performance: exceptional, successful, acceptable, or needing development. That ranking determines how much of the potential quarterly payout each team is eligible for.

The scorecard evaluates audit teams in five weighted areas:

- Productivity as measured by the number of targeted audits completed by the end of the quarter.

- Customer satisfaction as measured by client ratings following each audit on eight dimensions of quality, including professionalism, timeliness, and reasonableness of recommendations.

- The dollar value of efficiency recommendations provided by the audit team.

- Team-to-team cooperation is measured by the time each team invests in sharing best practices or advice with other teams to improve audit quality and efficiency in the overall unit. "This helps avoid the silo effect, or teams becoming disconnected from one other," says Adamec.

- Internal investments are measured by the time teams spend on forward-looking special projects or extracurricular initiatives within Ameritech. "We expect team members to participate in these project teams—some they create themselves, others management sets up—to help us develop new audit methodologies for the future," he says. Auditors are expected to spend about 5 percent of their work time on such projects, although many thoroughly enjoy this "visioning" part of their jobs and spend up to 10 percent of their time.

Only those teams falling in the "needs development" category don't qualify for the quarterly incentive; others receive a percentage of the bonus based on their ranking. Teams in the "exceptional" category, for instance, can receive in excess of the entire quarter's incentive—greater than 25 percent of the annual amount. Teams ranked a notch down at "successful" receive 10 to 25 percent of the possible annual bonus for that quarter, and those ranked "acceptable" receive 0 to 20 percent.

In the plan's original design, each team qualifying for a quarterly payout was asked to divide its earned pool money among team members based on each member's perceived contribution to the team goals. Management felt the alternative—splitting the incentive money equally among all team members—would demotivate a team's high performers and unfairly reward low performers, Adamec says.

That approach didn't last long, however. "Teams were beating themselves up in what was seen as highly subjective debate about perceived contributions to goals," he says.

Without a better alternative, management decided that future payouts would be split equally among team members. Yet it wasn't long before Adamec grew unhappy with that system, too. The equal splits contributed to a dramatic drop in the amount of critical or constructive feedback team members gave to each other—something Ameritech audit managers felt crucial to helping teams continually develop and reach their potential.

So back they went to splitting payouts based on each team member's perceived contribution—only this time with a twist. Team members would rank-order each other based on their value to the team, providing written feedback to support those rankings. The average of those rankings would determine how much of the quarterly team bonus each team member received.

Here's how it works:

If there are ten people on an audit team, each team member ranks—on a secret ballot—all of their teammates from 1 through 10 based on their perceived contribution to team goals that quarter. Team member Pete might rank Janice 1, himself 5, and Joe 10. Everyone includes written feedback to support their rankings. They're also asked to include suggestions in three categories for each teammate: "do more of/do less of/continue doing."

In addition to assigning teammates a numerical rank, team members also vote on a percentage of the quarterly payout they feel each of their teammates should receive. The only hard-and-fast rule: there must be at least a 10 percent differential between the person ranked first and the one ranked last. So if the #1 rank is voted 15 percent of the quarterly incentive pool, the #10 rank can receive no more than 5 percent of the pool. The remainder of the team receives percentage payouts that add up to 100 percent. So for a ten-person team, the payout percentages might be, hypothetically, 15 percent, 14 percent, 13 percent, 12 percent, 11 percent, 9 percent, 8 percent, 7 percent, 6 percent, 5 percent for team members ranked 1 through 10, respectively.

If people feel there are three or four equally strong performers on their team, they can vote to award each the same top percentage of the bonus. So the top three performers could each receive 15 percent of the quarterly pool, with the remainder divided among the other seven members on the team. But each team member must be given a separate numerical rank as a part of the process.

All teammate rankings and written feedback are forwarded to the manager-coach assigned to each team, who compiles the average numerical rankings, the average percentage payout votes, and the individual feedback reports for each team member. Then, in an all-team meeting, each member receives and opens an envelope with his or her rankings and feedback, converted into anonymous format by the coach so no auditor knows who provided what feedback to whom.

The coach then facilitates a teamwide discussion after everyone gets a look at rankings and feedback; team members open the envelopes simultaneously so no one is singled out for attention.

The quality of this facilitation makes or breaks the ranking and feedback process, believes Catherine Eckersall, an audit team member from 1996 to 1998 who now serves as an Ameritech design analyst. Good coaches remove feedback that is too vague or smacks of personal attacks and include only comments the recipient can put to use. They also provide each team member with a statistical distribution of their rankings so they know, for instance, how many of their teammates ranked them at 1, 4, 7, or 10. The aim is to make the all-team meeting an educational event rather than a finger-pointing exercise. "If it's facilitated in the right spirit, the session can be a productive and enlightening process," Eckersall says.

The best facilitators give teams ample time to peruse their feedback during the meeting, then travel around the room and ask each team member to offer up one piece of that feedback—choosing from any of their "do more of/do less of/keep doing" categories—that resonates with them and that they feel they can take action on. What, the facilitator asks, do you think you can or should do about it in the coming quarter? If the team member is at a loss, the facilitator opens the floor to the team's ideas. Facilitators then hold team members accountable for implementing some type of action plan for improvement in the next quarter.

Says Adamec: "Our ranking and feedback process makes the coaches' role very important here. Coaches have to become adept not only at separating inactionable from actionable feedback, but helping team members act on that feedback, and teach them how to give teammates appropriate and useful suggestions, part of which is being more attentive to what others are doing around them."

The process also requires thick skin. It's possible that someone ranked 5 on a high-performing team might rank 1 if placed on a lower-performing team; in other cases, the line between the 3 rank and the 7 on the same team can be very fine. "Someone always has to be ranked last on each team, and that can be demotivating," says Eckersall. "Even if everyone on a team might be motivated and high performing, someone will always have to rank in the lower quadrant. Even those who flesh out the middle aren't always happy. That's particularly difficult when people feel they're working hard and getting quality work done on time."

On the whole, however, Eckersall believes the ends justify the occasional pain. "It can be a tough process to go through, but when you have a team that's underperforming, I've seen it help get them to the next level," she says. "When the payouts were split equally, it was harder to hold your teammates accountable. With the forced rankings, that's not a problem."

One other modification enhanced this peer-to-peer feedback process. When teams assign audit work to their members, they often form smaller subteams of two to three auditors each to work together on the projects. Some of these subteams had trouble holding each other mutually accountable for the quality of their work, Adamec says, with certain assumptions made about lower performance levels on other subteams.

To counter that, a week before a team holds the quarterly feedback session just described, it holds another coach-facilitated session that allows subteams to personally review audit work and reports recently completed by other subteams. "It allows everyone to get a better feel for the quality of peers' work," Adamec says. "Although most team members believed other subteams were using the same processes and doing the same quality of work they were, they didn't know for sure, and this proved it to them. Teams also find these sessions to be good knowledge-sharing experiences. Of all the changes we've made, this is one of the best."

The Beat Goes On: Other Recognition Tactics

Adamec also keeps part of his reward strategy for the audit teams discretionary, relying heavily on spot recognition devices to encourage and highlight specific team behaviors. Stock options are a favorite tool. Adamec awarded five hundred options (vested at three years) to one team member he thought was best at holding teammates mutually accountable for results and to another who launched a special project team that resulted in introduction of more efficient, computer-aided auditing techniques to the entire auditing group. Another auditor proved adept at "asking the kinds of questions that kept his team from going down the road to Abilene," Adamec says, "so I gave him stock options for his ability to save his team those headaches."

How does this type of recognition, which on its face can appear quite subjective, play with the troops?

"There's been a fair amount of controversy, and some question why certain people receive awards and others don't, but I do it to send messages, and it's all based on behavior I observe myself," Adamec says. "I also work hard to spread it around. I've gotten a good amount of follow-up e-mail from auditors who say 'thanks for recognizing people—it gives us a better idea of the types of behavior you're looking for.'"

Peer-based recognition also is a key part of this strategy. Twice a year the eight self-directed teams can submit to a committee of their peers audits they feel represent their best work over the preceding six months. The review committee, using five published criteria, votes on what it considers the four best audits. In an Academy Award–style presentation at a biannual conference—with the envelopes opened by a glamorously dressed team member—members of all four finalist teams receive individual $500 American Express gift certificates, with the top team capturing a trophy.

Measuring Payback from Reward Practices

Adamec believes there's no better evidence of Ameritech's benefit from use of the merit compensation pool and recognition tactics than the new behaviors exhibited by his auditing teams.

"We'd been talking about the need for some of these behaviors for a while, but it wasn't until we implemented the incentive and recognition systems that people started paying serious attention," he says. "We see consistently better audit reports being written, a part of which we attribute to things like the Academy Award ceremony for the best audit reports. Even though it's the team bonus pool and stock options that first got everyone's attention, I think it's the public recognition for a job well done that the teams really enjoy."

Ameritech auditing is also a rare group that measures its success in part by a high turnover rate—that's right, a high, not low, rate. When auditors are regularly promoted into nonauditing management positions in Ameritech's business units, audit management knows it's doing its job. The goal is to achieve 35 percent "positive" turnover each year, and in 1997 and 1998 the group turnover rates were 50 percent and 70 percent respectively. "More than 90 percent of those who left in that two-year span were promoted within Ameritech," Adamec says. "The important thing for us is to develop people and build their teamwork skills while they're here, and the reward and recognition system contributes to that."

Lessons Learned

Consider a quarterly rather than annual bonus payout schedule.

Among the chief lessons Ameritech learned: use a quarterly rather than an annual merit pay plan for its self-directed teams. For starters, people are often promoted out of the audit teams at a regular clip during the year, and a shorter period to measure and reward team performance makes sense—the team is more likely to remain intact for a quarter, rather than a full year. "We not only have promotions out of teams, but we allow people to move from team to team if they show an interest in what another team is doing," Adamec says. "So a quarterly incentive system makes sense for that type of environment."

Equally important, the quarterly system helps keep behaviors and business goals tied to incentive pay at the top of team members' minds better than a more protracted yearly payout system would, he says.

Shorter measurement periods also aid the unique rating and feedback process Ameritech teams use to divide up merit payouts among team members. Observing and documenting teammates' behavior over three months is much easier—and provides more accurate, timely information—than having to compile that information over twelve months.

Coaches require as much attention as the teams they oversee.

Choosing the right people as coaches for self-directed teams, and continually developing their skills, has paid big dividends for Ameritech. Coaches not only play the critical role of counselor and confidant to teams, at Ameritech they're also expected to teach team members how to give constructive feedback to peers, and to weed out vague, unusable peer feedback from the kind teammates can easily take action on.

Coaches must shift their emphasis from making decisions to teaching the teams to make their own decisions, from assigning work to encouraging ownership, and from being the chief client contact to becoming more of a "barrier buster."

To help managers build these new coaching and facilitation skills, Ameritech auditing has hired external consultants familiar with the self-directed concept to observe and advise both coaches and the self-directed audit teams.

TEXAS GUARANTEED STUDENT LOAN CORPORATION

This nonprofit uses a mix of corporate-level and local "cash carrots" for its work groups to help strike a healthy balance between customer service and financial goals.

The Texas Guaranteed Student Loan Corporation (TG) is a lifeline for those who dream of attending college but have little of the funds to make it happen. TG, as it is known by employees, administers within Texas the largest student financial aid program in the United States, the Federal Family Education Loan Program—known in a former life as the Guaranteed Student Loan Program.

As a 501 (c)(3) not-for-profit organization chartered by the state, and with a board of directors appointed by the governor, TG doesn't face the same pressures to produce quarterly profits as its Wall Street–driven counterparts.

So why did TG turn to group-based cash incentives as a way to drive the organization's financial and customer service performance to new heights?

Let's just say TG is addicted to continuous improvement. Contrary to appearances, the Austin-based organization is *not* a state agency and thus receives no state funding. Most of TG's income is derived from fees paid by the federal government for administering a federal student loan program. Revenues include fees on: the student loans it guarantees, prevention of loan defaults, collections of defaulted student loans, and revenues for maintenance of outstanding loans. Under the student loan program, schools determine students' (and their parents') eligibility for loans, private lenders like banks and credit unions provide money for the loans, and TG then reviews loan applications and guarantees the loans, that is, guarantees that lenders will be repaid in the event a borrower dies, becomes permanently disabled, defaults, or has a loan discharged in bankruptcy.

Thus it's in TG's best interests to maintain a high level of service to clients like school financial aid offices and student loan note holders, and also to borrowers in good standing and defaulted borrowers, who usually could do without the contact, thank you very much, but who may need help in finding options to avoid credit problems. Although TG is not-for-profit, it must maintain financial strength to provide innovative solutions and tools to customers and give noteholders confidence in TG's ability to pay claims.

TG's Corporate Incentive Program is aggressive for a not-for-profit organization. James Patterson, TG's vice president and chief financial officer, says he and other managers had to involve board members early on to make a convincing case to the organization's ten-member board of directors to sign onto the plan. The board has become a big backer of the results-based, pay-for-performance plan.

"We'd always rewarded people only in the traditional way—with basic merit increases based on individual performance determined in annual performance appraisals," Patterson says. "We didn't want to abandon that, just scale it back a bit and create a new incentive for people to work together as team members over and above individual performance. We also felt the program would help our employees look at TG more as a business, and lift organizational performance to new levels."

By scaling back merit increases that affect base pay and adding incentive bonuses, TG was in effect saying, "We want to reward based on current performance, not past results."

TG's 475 team members operate not within a traditional hierarchical structure but in work groups designed around the organization's key internal work processes and subprocesses. Thus, there is an administration "process group"—not an administrative division—under whose umbrella are "subprocess" groups of accounting, human resources, training and organizational development, communications, and corporate services that work together as one team to provide administrative support to the organization. Other major process groups include operations, information technology, business development, customer focus, and policy and compliance, each with its own subprocess groups.

TG's corporate incentive program is designed around this structure and the deliverables within it. The plan, run as a "phantom" or pilot in 1997 (no payouts) to test the system, first went live in fiscal year 1998.

How the Plan Works

The plan has two key components:

- Incentives tied to how the organization as a whole performs annually on overarching corporate goals, particularly two key metrics: overall customer satisfaction and "surplus revenue over expenses" (remember, TG is a not-for-profit). Performance at this level determines if any award is paid out and if so, which of three multipliers is used to determine the award amount.

- Incentives tied to how individual units—both TG's process and sub-process groups—perform against their annual performance goals and measures (PGMs). Those PGMs are tied directly to overall corporate goals, and performance against them determines one of three multipliers in determining award amounts.

Corporate Goals and Incentives

Each year management sets four escalating performance targets at the corporate level for both the external customer satisfaction measure and the "surplus revenue" measure. The first target is called the budget level (B), with the escalating targets known as B + 1 (budget plus one), B + 2, and B + 3, stretching beyond expectations.

The targets get increasingly harder to achieve. The budget level—the baseline performance target each year—is assigned an 80 percent probability of achievement, B + 1 a 60 percent probability, B + 2 a 40 percent chance, and B + 3 20 percent. Financial performance at each level must result in no less than 65 percent of the incremental financial performance over the B level, remaining with TG after award distribution.

A minimum of B + 1 performance must be achieved each year at the corporate level in *both* customer service and financial performance to trigger the company-wide incentive bonus.

"We wanted to strike a healthy balance between customer service and financial results," says Patterson, "to avoid focusing too heavily on one at the expense of the other. We don't want to make our customers deliriously happy but go broke in the process. Conversely, we don't want to be so cost-conscious that we create dissatisfied customers. In other words, the plan keeps us focused on 'cost/benefit' when managing our business."

The corporate customer satisfaction measure is derived from the average of two semiannual surveys sent to external customers and tallied by an independent third party. Survey respondents typically are school financial aid administrators, student loan lenders, and student and parent borrowers. Customers are asked to rate TG's service performance in a variety of key areas using a rating scale of one to five, with five being best.

So in a typical year, for example, TG might set these four hypothetical performance targets for customer satisfaction survey scores:

Budget: Average score of 3.70 or above

B + 1: Score of 3.85

B + 2: Score of 4.00

B + 3: Score of 4.15

Keep in mind these scores include those from defaulted borrowers contacted by TG. The four targets for financial surplus (hypothetical, dollars in millions) might be the following:

Budget: $21.00

B + 1: $25.00

B + 2: $27.50

B + 3: $30.00

Award payouts to team members are designed to fall back to the lesser of the two corporate performance levels; in other words, if customer satisfaction hits the B + 2 level, and financial surplus B + 1, team member incentive pay would be calculated at the lower B + 1 payout level.

Plan designers built the program with the idea that TG would retain no less than 65 percent of incremental financial improvement from the plan, with the remainder going to team members in the form of incentive awards.

To participate in the plan, a team member must attain a minimum score on the performance expectations portion of the individual performance appraisal.

All regular (nontemporary) employees who achieve that score and work a minimum of twenty hours a week are eligible to participate. Awards to part-timers are prorated based on their hourly work schedules. For example, a regular part-time employee working twenty-hour weeks would be awarded 50 percent of the available bonus amount.

Those currently covered by other performance incentive plans in TG—like collectors of defaulted loans—are excluded from the corporate incentive plan.

How award incentives are calculated at all employee levels is described in the section Calculating Award Payouts.

Subprocess (Team) and Process (Organizational Unit) Incentives

Each subprocess in TG—the work groups that make up the broader process areas—agrees on a set of key performance goals and measures (PGMs) for its team each year; the measures are tied to process deliverables and signed off on by all subprocess team members and TG's CEO.

Goals are weighted for importance by the work group, and each deliverable is expected to have at least one "effectiveness" and one "efficiency" measure or component. The weighted aggregate percentage of goals attained at the end of the year determines a multiplier used in calculating subprocess team members' annual incentive pay.

Consider TG's default prevention unit as an example—a subprocess group under the broader "operations process" umbrella. Default prevention might target as one of its annual effectiveness measures "loan cure rate." The efficiency measure is cost per 100 cures; drilling down further, the specific target for the two measures might be to cure more than 85 percent of delinquent loans for less than 20 cents per 100 cures. Performance is documented and tracked in a way that can be easily audited.

Performance on both efficiency and effectiveness measures is tracked and posted monthly on public bulletin boards (and on TG's corporate intranet) within the accounting subprocess group, and performance against goals is rewarded on an annual basis.

The principal tool for measuring effectiveness in most goal areas is customer satisfaction surveys, which are administered by an independent third party. Customers may be internal or external.

One outcome of linking incentive pay to subprocess goals is greater awareness by the rank-and-file of their unit's annual goals, and how they might influence them on a daily basis—even if those goals are outside the scope of their primary job responsibilities. Says Tom Sharp, TG's manager of corporate training and organizational development: "If you ask any person in the organization what they're measured on and where their subprocess team stands on those measures for a given month, odds are pretty good they'll be able to tell you."

TG also put in place mechanisms that encourage cooperation between subprocess teams in pursuit of a larger goal: the success of an overall process area. The "owner" or top manager of each subprocess—usually a midlevel manager—has 20 percent of his or her incentive tied to how well the organization does in meeting corporate goals; 20 percent is tied to how well other subprocesses within their shared grouping perform against annual goals; the remaining 60 percent is tied to hitting goals in the manager's own subprocess area.

So, for example, 40 percent of a human resource manager's bonus would depend on how well the entire organization and administration process where that manager works—including accounting, communications, training and development, corporate services, and communications teams—performs against its annual targets.

"The 20 percent encourages teamwork and ownership in the success of the entire process, not just within the boundaries of the manager's own subprocess," Patterson says. One direct result is that subprocess groups often offer some of their resources to other groups to help out during those groups' peak work times or schedules, and managers are more motivated to share ideas to improve performance.

The teamwork incentive extends to "process owners"—TG vice presidents—as well. Approximately 50 percent of each VP's incentive is tied to how well the entire organization does in meeting annual goals.

"Again, it gives them a strong incentive to find ways to help out other process owners," Patterson says, "and ultimately helps everyone by increasing corporate success and corporate-level payouts. The better subprocesses do, the better processes do and ultimately the better the corporation performs as a whole."

To further encourage knowledge-sharing and team play within each process group, all subprocesses log onto TG's corporate intranet each month to update and publicly post their performance against monthly goals and measures. "Each subprocess's year-to-date performance is posted out there for all to see," Patterson says. "Since the work of one subprocess affects another in determining overall process performance and incentive pay, it allows groups to keep tabs on each other's progress so they can jump in and help if possible."

These monthly subprocess reports also are printed out and posted on bulletin board "scoreboards" in work areas, along with updates on corporate-level performance.

Calculating Award Payouts: What Team Members Reap

Incentive payouts to TG team members are calculated using three multipliers. First is the salary range midpoint for a team member's job position; second is a percentage based on the corporate performance level for customer satisfaction and financial surplus (B + 1, B + 2, or B + 3); and third is a weighted aggregate percentage of goals met for the subprocess, process, and corporate goals.

At the end of each fiscal year, an overall score is calculated for each subprocess and process area, based on a weighted aggregate percentage of each goal achieved. The score is then used as a multiplier and applied to the percentage of salary midpoint based on the corporate performance level achieved (B + 1, B + 2, or B + 3).

For example, if TG achieved an overall B + 1 performance level for the year on customer satisfaction and financial surplus, and the overall percentage of goals met for a particular subprocess was 90 percent, team members who work in that particular subprocess at pay grade seven would be awarded 7.2 percent (8 percent of the corporate performance multiplier for B + 1 performance times the 90 percent subprocess performance multiplier) of their salary midpoint as an incentive award.

For team member pay grades two through nine, established multipliers are 8 percent of their salary midpoints for B + 1 overall company performance, 13 percent for B + 2 performance, and 18 percent for B + 3 performance. For pay grades ten through thirteen, those midpoint multiplier percentages are 10 percent, 15 percent, and 20 percent.

So the payout formula might look like this:

Incentive award = percent of subprocess performance goals achieved × percent of salary midpoint determined by corporate performance level × the employee's salary midpoint

Team members at pay grades two through nine receive their bonus payment in one lump sum. But those at pay grades ten and above—essentially professional and management level—receive their bonuses distributed over three years (50 percent, 25 percent, 25 percent). Team members must be employed at TG at the end of each subsequent year to receive the deferred amount for that year.

Why the deferred payments for managers? "It's partly a retention device," Patterson says, "as well as our way to encourage team leaders to take the long view on performance. We don't want managers to focus only on current-year performance at the expense of long-term performance." In addition, the cost savings of the deferral keeps the award amount at a level that provides a strong incentive while satisfying the requirement that no less than 65 percent of the incremental financial improvement remain with the organization.

Let's compare how incentive payouts might look for a TG employee, John Smith, and a TG manager, Jane Doe, in two hypothetical scenarios. All bonus amounts are gross (before tax)

John Smith was employed as a pay grade seven team member in the human resources subprocess for the entire fiscal year. TG attained a 4.01 (B + 2) customer satisfaction score and achieved $31.78 (B + 3) in surplus revenue, resulting in an overall B + 2 award. That B + 2 gives John a 13 percent multiplier for overall corporate performance, based on established percentage of salary midpoint. The human resources subprocess had an aggregate score of 99 percent of goal targets on its weighted PGMs for the year. John's performance expectations score on his last performance appraisal exceeds the minimum needed to participate in the plan. John's annual lump sum bonus is thus $3,234 (13 percent × 0.99 × $25,127, the latter being his salary midpoint).

Jane Doe, our fictional manager, was employed as a pay grade ten team member in the human resource subprocess for another fiscal year. TG attained a 4.16 (B + 3) customer satisfaction score and achieved a $28.23 (B + 2) in surplus revenue, resulting in the B + 2 award. The combined weighted score of performance against corporate goals, administration process goals, and HR process goals was 109 percent of target for the fiscal year. Jane's performance expectations score on her last performance appraisal exceeded the minimum to participate in the plan. Thus, Jane's bonus award is $5,892 (15 percent × 1.09 × $36,037, her salary midpoint).

But rather than a lump sum, Jane's bonus distribution as a manager is as follows: current year: 50 percent of bonus, or $2,946; year two, if employed at TG on the last day of the fiscal year, 25 percent, or $1,473; year three, if employed at TG on the last day of the fiscal year, 25 percent, or $1,473. If performance goals are met in subsequent years, those bonus distributions will be layered on top of Jane's deferred award distributions (interest is not earned on the deferred awards).

All bonus payouts are distributed after year-end survey results are tabulated and the independent financial audit completed, typically around mid-December. If employees are promoted or their jobs reclassified sometime during the incentive plan period, their incentive pay is prorated based on the number of months they're in the pay grade. Employees also have the option of rolling their bonus payments into a 403(b) plan. (TG does not have a 401K.)

Setting Ambitious Yet Attainable Targets

The biggest challenge in year one of such plans often is setting appropriate performance goals tied to the incentives. The idea, of course, is to set targets that make team members stretch, but not so far that the plan frustrates more than it motivates. There's a fine line between goals that are too easy to hit and those so ambitious they negatively impact morale.

"In some cases we didn't have the baseline data we needed to set proper goals—particularly in the cost efficiency area—because the activity-based costing tool used to track and document cost performance was in its infancy," Patterson says. "So in a sense you're setting the stage in year one—gathering historical data and creating baselines to move into the future. With time, the goal-setting challenge becomes easier."

Goals must be as measurable as they are meaningful. Ask yourself: Are you choosing performance areas that can be objectively documented? If you do hire independent third parties to verify or tally data as part of the plan, will there be enough data available for those auditors to examine?

Goal-setting in TG's subprocess groups works like this: a subprocess team leader (middle manager) gathers all team members at the year's start to identify goals and assign a weight to each; the goals are tied to already-determined process deliverables. Those goals are forwarded to a process owner (senior manager) for review or challenge, and ultimately on to the CEO, who signs off on each subprocess and process incentive goal plan in the organization.

To help its subprocess and process groups set ambitious but realistic goals, TG created a Performance Goals and Measures Team, a cross-process group with planning and budgeting experience that consults with groups during their goal-setting stages.

Measuring Fruits of the Plan

In the plan's first fiscal year, TG hit the B + 2 corporate incentive level—two levels above budgeted performance, and a target assigned only a 40 percent probability of achievement. Strongest gains were seen in overall customer satisfaction scores. Prior to introduction of the incentive plan, the first survey of fiscal year 1997 scored 3.60 (on a scale of 5), whereas that survey score increased to 4.09 in fiscal year 1998.

On the financial side—surplus revenue over expenses—performance under the plan exceeded expectations in three key revenue areas. The rehabilitation of defaulted student loans increased by 82 percent over prior year performance, cures of delinquent loans (default prevention) improved by 20 percent, and actual collections of defaulted loans improved by 12 percent.

Equally important, according to TG's top management team, is that many process and subprocess managers reported heightened interest among frontline team members in how their own work groups, and the company as a whole, performed against targeted goals. "Those people who had blinders on are starting to take them off," Patterson says. "Rather than thinking only about success in their own jobs, they're beginning to think more about their teams, their entire process areas, and the company as a whole."

According to Milt Wright, TG president and CEO, the corporation's team members deserve credit for the improvements made to the student loan process in recent years. "Our team members are the reason for our financial success and high level of customer satisfaction," Wright says. "The incentive plan gives them a way to benefit from the meaningful contributions they make to TG's success."

TG had implemented similar team-based performance goals and measures in subprocess areas a few years prior, but without the accompanying dollar incentive. "It was more difficult to get people truly focused and energized around those group goals without the financial incentive," Patterson says. "It was much more about individual performance back then."

The plan also has helped TG managers approach budgeting with more of an eye toward cost control and the bottom line, not always a given in not-for-profit management settings. "In the past the only real incentive managers had was to meet budgeted revenues and expenses," Patterson says. "But in the incentive plan's first year, we've seen managers more conscious about reaching or exceeding revenue goals at a lower cost, stretching beyond expectations (i.e., budget). They knew every dollar saved would help in terms of the corporate performance part of the incentive plan. We've seen a lot more attention paid to activity-based costing reports as a tool to find cost efficiencies."

Lessons Learned

The plan can roll out before baseline data is in.

TG faced a choice: it could hold off the rollout of the incentive plan until it accumulated more historical, baseline data—particularly in the area of cost efficiencies—that would make it easier to set realistic goals linked to incentive pay. Yet without the carrot of an incentive plan, it would be more difficult to convince employees to do the extra work of gathering and documenting that kind of data on top of their normal job duties.

TG management opted for rolling out the plan first, knowing the appropriate data would soon follow. "It was a bit of a catch-22, but we decided to go ahead and roll the plan out and let the baseline data quickly catch up to it," says Patterson. "It's worked better than anticipated."

Simplify and communicate.

TG went to great lengths to ensure team members understood how the plan worked, how bonus calculations were made, and how employees' own actions could influence plan payouts. Prior to rollout, all TG employees were gathered in small groups for education and question-and-answer sessions about the plan, and both a Q&A paper and the full master plan were posted on TG's corporate intranet for employees to access anytime. In addition, a stuffer was included with award checks to explain payout calculations.

Despite all that, TG knows there's still work to do in making the plan easier for all to understand. "We'll continue to look for ways to simplify and streamline it, and to better communicate to employees how it works," Patterson says. "Ultimately, though, I think the main message is getting through—that the better employees' work groups do on their own performance goals and measures, the better off the corporation will be, and the better off they'll be in terms of understanding the business and having award checks in pocket."

Coach or root out team members who don't pull their own weight.

It's a problem common to use of team-based incentives: some team members don't pull their own weight, yet they receive the same incentive pay as their harder-working or more proficient teammates.

Although the problem didn't rear its head much in year one, Patterson says TG is positioned to respond in two ways. "One, of course, is to encourage peer pressure—we find that's been pretty effective," he says, in helping root out laggard team members or get them back on track.

Performance problems also are addressed through individual performance appraisals. Approximately 50 to 70 percent of employees' appraisals measure how they perform, on an individual basis, on their subprocess team's established PGMs (performance goals and measures) for the year, with more weight placed on PGMs over which they have the most control. For example, if an accounts payable clerk isn't performing well in the PGM area of processing checks, but the rest of his or her team shows a pattern of doing well in that area, the weighting of that performance area might be increased on the clerk's individual appraisal. By increasing the weight, in addition to some individual performance coaching and feedback, TG hopes to nudge the clerk toward better performance and team behaviors.

RR DONNELLEY & SONS

"Small games" tied to open-book management at this company spark teams' interest in cost-saving and productivity goals—and employees share in the spoils along the way.

The power of open-book management rests on one simple but paradigm-altering premise: give rank-and-file employees entry to the doors traditionally marked "management only," educate them about heretofore secret data and decision-making tools found therein—budgets, financial forecasts, and income statements—and they'll begin to feel and act more like business owners and less like bricks in the wall. The hoped-for result is a workforce more educated and concerned about the company's business as a whole, with a better understanding of how their daily actions contribute to—or undermine—bottom-line success.

But how to spark such engagement? It's one thing to open the books, quite another to get weary or disinterested frontliners to read them and put that knowledge to use. After all, it's just such a prospect—making weighty decisions based on interpreting often-complex data—that makes many shy away from management jobs in the first place.

In the Northeastern Division of RR Donnelley & Sons Company, playing what's called "small games" has proved to be one way to leap that hurdle and engage the rank and file in open-book practices. A small game, as open-book organizations use the term, is simply an initiative focused on immediate improvement in a given work area, unit, or work team, rather than an entire department, which would be a large game. Each game has a starting point, a set of rules, a goal, and a team reward for what constitutes winning. Those rewards typically aren't large—often things like $50 gift certificates, catered lunches, or days off with pay. The more enduring reward for game players is the challenge of setting a goal and finding a way to beat it, and learning more about teamwork and business management along the way.

For the company, returns from sponsoring games come in the form of a more educated and plugged-in workforce, and the gains in productivity, cost reductions, or profits that result directly from the small games.

In late 1998, nineteen such games were running in Donnelley's Northeastern Division, with three others in the development stage.

Getting Games Off the Ground

RR Donnelley is the largest commercial printer in the United States, and its Northeastern Division in Lancaster, Pennsylvania, consists of two plants—East and West—with some twenty-five hundred employees. The East plant cranks out millions of copies of products like *Reader's Digest, TV Guide,* and *New York Times Magazine,* and the West plant prints telephone directories and catalogs for companies like Bell Atlantic and Williams-Sonoma.

When Don Robb, the division's former manager of organization development, introduced open-book management to the company in 1995, he knew he'd need some quick wins to build support for what was viewed as a risky new strategy. Small games fit that bill.

Among Robb's first moves: creating a Small Game Advisory Council of management and frontline representatives from each divisional area. The council's role is to advise work units in the creation of games, evaluate and sign off on all games created, and ensure that rewards for those games are appropriate. The council laid out three broad guidelines and supporting criteria to help Donnelley teams create their games:

- Each game must teach Donnelley's business and include a plan for educating employees about the business, how the objectives of the game relate to the business, and how each person can influence the performance.

- The game must address a real business problem; games must be designed to "drive a weakness out of the business."

- The games should generate a "measurable and sustainable" improvement to Donnelley's business. After a game ends, Donnelley looks closely at whether the improvement continues, and players (employees) are expected to create mechanisms to track ongoing performance.

Other criteria: anyone in the plants—not just managers—can create a game; official scoreboards must be used to track and communicate results to game participants; the length of the game must be predetermined; payouts must be self-funding (typically 25 percent of the generated savings or revenues goes directly to game participants); and product quality and customer service must be maintained throughout the course of the game.

And one other thing: teams should have some fun playing these games.

Diary of Two Small Games: NASCAR and Derby Dash

A game created by Donnelley employees called NASCAR '98 illustrates the company's evolution in the use of the small game concept. Rather than being developed and handed down by management, the game was devised by a Donnelley press operator in collaboration with his frontline peers, all stock car racing fans. "A best-case scenario—those who'd be playing the game actually designing it," says Eric Bergstrom, the division's current manager of organizational development.

For the game, a "racing crew" consists of the eighteen- to twenty-person team working on an offset press. The game's purpose: to increase individual crew awareness of how its performance affects the overall performance of the module (a module encompasses two to three Donnelley departments) in which it works.

The NASCAR game targets one of a large printing company's greatest enemies: materials waste. Four waste-reduction goals were identified: "make-ready" waste, "run" waste, prepress waste, and also press-run delays (the last aimed at time savings). Game goals for the first half of 1998 were set as improvements on year-end 1997 performance; goals for the second half were tied to improving on first-half 1998 performance.

The overarching goal: at NASCAR's conclusion, "the press crews would have a better understanding of how their efforts to cut waste in the four identified areas contribute to the overall financial performance of the business," Bergstrom says.

"Pit crews"—usually one machinist and an electrician—also are involved in the game; the pit crews are assigned to individual presses to ensure they keep running in top condition, much the same way their namesakes do in real NASCAR competition. Pit crews share in any payout the team receives at the game's end.

Each press crew chooses a real NASCAR driver and a Matchbox car to represent it on a large racetrack scoreboard posted on the wall in the press area; Velcro on the cars attaches them to the Velcro track. Cars are positioned on the track based on how the press they represent is doing that month against its own waste-reduction goals. That self competition is a guiding principle, because Donnelley wants to guard against pitting press versus press. "NASCAR isn't based on competition between presses—we don't believe that's entirely healthy—but rather on presses competing against themselves, or the monthly goals they set for themselves," Bergstrom says. "We liken it to people who run marathons not to win, but simply to better their own personal best times."

A visitor to the Donnelley plant could walk into the press rooms and quickly determine how presses were performing that month simply by scanning the big NASCAR board. "There might be times you see a car skidding sideways on the track, and you know darn well something's gone wrong with that particular press," Bergstrom says.

Crews can gain or lose laps based on their press's performance for the month. Laps might be taken away for documented customer complaints, for instance (ten laps subtracted for the month the complaint arises), because one of the guidelines is to maintain a high level of service to customers through the course of the game. Conversely, if there is a documented conservation of printing paper—a cost savings—a crew would advance an additional lap.

A pace car on the scoreboard represents how the department as a whole is doing against its goals. For any month when the four departmental waste-reduction and speed goals are all met, the whole group (module) is treated to a celebratory catered meal or dinner out. That recognition is important, Bergstrom says, because the ultimate goal of small games is to improve departmental performance, which feeds gain-sharing plans.

NASCAR isn't completely free of competition. There is a winner each month: the press that performs best against its own goals, determined by number of laps run. Each winner receives an authentic NASCAR checkered flag (which many proud press operators hang from the front of their presses) and the winning team is featured in the Gallery of Winners photo display next to the NASCAR scoreboard for the entire year.

These monthly winners also receive $40 individual gift certificates that each team member can use at a local shopping mall. If other press crews beat all of their goals in a given month, but aren't the overall department winner, each crew member receives a $20 gift certificate to the mall. "Hitting those goals is quite an accomplishment, and we don't want it to go unrecognized for those presses that don't win the top prize," Bergstrom says.

A yearly NASCAR winner also is named—the team with the most points at the end of the twelve-race (twelve-month) season.

That small dose of competition has helped turn many a game skeptic into a participant, Bergstrom believes. "We've had people not really into playing the game at the start who, after their press wins for a month, climb up on the previous month's winning press to take down its checkered flag, and plant it with vigor on their own winning press."

Don Warner, a Donnelley process improvement specialist who participated in the NASCAR game, is among those who warmed to the value of the small game concept. "Early on there was some skepticism about NASCAR because crews didn't think they could achieve the new goals based on their past performance," he says. "But as the game wore on, there was growing interest, teamwork—and competitiveness. The game began as a drive toward process improvement, and ended up surprising us with the magnitude of dollar savings it generated."

Another small game, played in Donnelley's directory bindery department, was called Derby Dash. The game is directly linked to NASCAR and has much the same feel—a simulated horse racing track serves as the game's scoreboard—but uses different metrics. The goal of Derby Dash is for the plant's bindery teams to reduce the cost associated with "kill books" and increase "net good books per hour." In other words, the aim is to ship high-quality products with a smaller amount of waste. One goal for kill book reduction, for example: improve from the average of killed books over the last two years (a percentage of total books) to a smaller percentage in a coming measurement period. All calculations begin the first of the month at midnight and end the last of the month at midnight.

The open-book or learning piece of the game is to "increase the awareness of machine utilization by bindery members, and the role everyone plays working as a team to make the bindery more efficient," Bergstrom says.

Management explained the costs associated with Derby Dash's two key measures to all bindery employees at the game's start (using total costs from the prior two years as examples), as well as the hours the group could save if it met new bindery speed goals. That information is conveyed as well through banners and posters hung in crew areas. Similarly, other specific actions that bindery team members might take to help cut costs were amply explained at the game's start. For instance, hoist drivers could double-check loads coming off a palletizer for product mixes or misflagged loads, or employees could pull bad paper stock before it causes a machine to stop or is bound and becomes a costly "kill book."

Crew performance against goals is posted weekly on the Derby Dash scoreboard. All full-time bindery and shipping workers employed in the department during a month a Derby Dash goal is achieved (including hourly office employees) are eligible for the game's monthly reward, a $40 gift certificate to a nearby shopping mall. As with NASCAR, bindery teams are also rewarded for hitting overall departmental goals, often with a catered lunch or dinner out.

Bergstrom says a big benefit from Derby Dash is that it facilitates a higher level of cross-departmental communication and teamwork in the plant.

"This game is dependent upon the quality of printed product coming out of the NASCAR game," he says. "The better the quality coming out of the pressrooms, the more successful Derby Dash teams will be in hitting their goals." Derby Dash players understand this symbiosis—the NASCAR press that delivers to them the highest-quality product each month is treated to a free lunch.

In that sense Derby Dash also serves as a check on the NASCAR game running in another area; if NASCAR teams cut corners on product quality in order to meet their productivity goals, those problems will show up downstream in the Derby Dash game. "It's ultimately a safeguard for our customers against game players getting so zealous in meeting their game's productivity or cost-savings goals that, at times, quality might slip," Bergstrom says.

Adds Pat Waltz, a process improvement specialist who developed the Derby game: "Like NASCAR, some of the initial goals set in Derby Dash looked pretty daunting to the bindery teams, but most teams have regularly met or exceeded them. The game has helped us see that when we focus on a goal and really pull together as a team, we can accomplish things we didn't think possible."

The game also facilitates the swapping of best practices among bindery operators, Waltz says. "If one bindery line is doing exceptionally well, but another is doing poorly, together they might not meet their overall departmental goal—

both lines have to be doing well. That's led to more cooperation and sharing of tips and improvement ideas between high and low performers."

To the same end, monthly huddles Donnelley management holds for employees at each plant—a linchpin practice of open-book management—also help improve game performance. In the huddles, plant managers share with frontliners the previous month's financial information and other key operational numbers, and together the group forecasts the coming months' performance. The division controller, Jim Mead, facilitates the huddles and takes time throughout the meeting to provide lessons in business literacy. Huddles are in effect another opportunity for a shared learning experience.

"The huddles give employees a sense of how all our activities—small games and otherwise—are contributing to productivity or financial goals, and what actions or contingency plans might be needed if for any reason we're off course on a goal," Bergstrom says. The briefings also include a purposeful review of the division's latest customer satisfaction data. "Customer satisfaction drives bottom-line performance, and we stress to our teams that it's difficult to achieve financial goals without happy customers," he says.

Lessons Learned

Games and huddles improve employees' understanding of how they can influence the numbers.

Playing the small games, as well as attending the regular team huddles with management, has greatly improved the line of sight for the rank-and-file and first-line managers as to how they can affect divisional goals—and influence their own awards. Both groups report a new understanding of how decisions they make every day on the front lines contribute to the plant's overall performance—or lack thereof—and to their own gain-sharing payouts.

Performance on small games like NASCAR and Derby Dash feed plant gain-sharing, but they aren't the sole determinants of those payouts. "We've had hourly employees come up to supervisors and ask, 'How can we be doing so well in our NASCAR game and not see the same benefit in gain-sharing?'" Bergstrom says. "The answer, of course, is that gain-sharing measures many more metrics than just that one press's material yield. We teach employees that in the huddles. So employees can now say, 'If I do this as a member of my press team to improve our materials yield, it will not only help the press meet its goals and put us in good stead in the NASCAR game—it will aid everyone's chances at bigger gain-sharing payouts.'"

Create a new level of frontline engagement.

In past years, responsibility for setting and hitting productivity or cost-reduction goals rested solely in the hands of Donnelley management. Now, Bergstrom reports, "we see more front-line people who understand what their monthly or quarterly goals are for the specific piece of equipment they work on, and what the barriers and limitations are to achieving those goals. And rather than complaining about problems in the plant, we're seeing more of those complaints become constructive suggestions for improvement."

Other evidence of growing frontline engagement: most of the small games that ran in 1995 and 1996 were devised by Donnelley supervisors or managers; by 1998, however, some 75 percent of games were created and implemented by the plants' rank and file. Playing the games is highly contagious, Bergstrom says; he's watched more than one standoffish pressroom grudgingly recognize the value of a game being played in an adjacent pressroom, and then fashion a game like it for itself.

"When you talk about creating a company of businesspeople, you're not going to do it overnight," he stresses. "You're never going to have 100 percent engagement in these small games—some employees will always just want to punch in, do their jobs, and go home. But we're seeing a growing number of people who like having more responsibility and input for helping to run the business, and for driving out problems and inefficiencies."

**Small games aren't just about payouts—
they're about business literacy and lessons in teamwork.**

Bergstrom says playing the games has taught his workforce about Donnelley's business in ways classroom training never could. "You can't underestimate the value of these games in teaching our people," he says. "We could put them into classrooms for hours on end and not get the same learning benefit we get with NASCAR, Derby Dash, and the other games. Not only do the games give them stronger line of sight on strategic business goals, they're much more fun and engaging than classroom training."

The games are more about communication and the value of teamwork than about the size of rewards for hitting goals, Bergstrom believes. One award in a small game is a day off with pay, for example—a highly coveted but relatively low-cost reward. But in keeping with the spirit of open-book management, Donnelley wants to ensure the day off is taken by team members without disrupting the team's productivity. Thus, it's understood the team will have to work a bit harder to cover for missing teammates on their day away. "That's what open book is about, learning how to manage costs and boost productivity—we didn't want those teams to work overtime and incur extra costs to cover for that missing person," Bergstrom says. "So there is an open-book lesson there, too."

Some games fail.

Although the majority of small games at Donnelley have met or exceeded expectations—more than 95 percent have shown not only improvement but sustained improvement, say administrators—a handful haven't caught on. Why? Explains Bergstrom: "If a game does fail, it's usually because goals are set unrealistically high—accumulating historical data can help with that—or there are forces at work outside the control of people playing the game, or you may have a significant environmental problem. In our case, maybe it is a press or binding line that goes down for a period, causing us to produce in less than an efficient manner." But even with a failed game, the department and employees still often reap valuable educational lessons about the business. In that way there's no such thing as a failed game.

THE AMERICAN SOCIETY OF COMPOSERS, AUTHORS AND PUBLISHERS

Incentive plans tied to quarterly sales and service goals help self-managed teams at this organization focus on "need to do" over "nice to do."

Dismantling a hierarchical structure in favor of self-managing teams can be a mind-stretching experience for a workforce accustomed to working under a command-and-control charter. Yet that stretch pales compared to the leap required when management starts to pay those newly formed work units in part by how they perform as a team—particularly when most have never before depended on the efforts of coworkers for any type of monthly or quarterly pay.

It's a leap managers at the American Society of Composers, Authors and Publishers (ASCAP) were willing to take following a radical downsizing and restructuring of ASCAP's General Licensing area in 1995. ASCAP was founded to provide compensation to member songwriters, composers, and lyricists for the public performance of their music. The group's main function is to protect the rights of its approximately 80,000 members by licensing and paying royalties when their work is played on the radio or TV, or in bars, hotels, shopping malls, bowling alleys, restaurants, or concerts. The organization is the largest performing rights society in the world in terms of license-fee collections and royalty payments to writers and publishers.

ASCAP believed pushing more decision-making responsibility down to front-line work teams was a key to its future when it closed twenty-six district offices and reduced its workforce by 70 percent. As part of that plan, the remaining workers were placed in new self-managing work teams in the areas of licensing sales, account services, and administration.

The Incentive Design Process

Because the use of self-managing teams was new territory for the organization, Lynne Lummel, the director of organization development for ASCAP, knew providing teams with a strong operating charter was crucial. After examining what other companies had done and conducting an extensive literature search, Lummel designed a six-step performance management model for the new teams to use:

1. Develop strategic organizational goals.
2. Develop team goals linked to those organizational goals.
3. Develop individual performance goals and standards.
4. Create monitoring and reporting procedures to track team progress against goals.
5. Identify, from the preceding processes, gaps in team or individual knowledge and any process-related problems, and create training plans to address them.
6. Reward results of team and individual performance.

This last step—particularly team-based financial incentives and noncash recognition—was deemed critical to supporting ASCAP's new strategic goals. But before linking incentives to performance, self-managed teams needed to learn how to set proper goals: set them too high, and the difficulty of achievement (and lack of payouts) could doom the plan; set goals too low, and incentive payments might soon be seen as entitlements.

Training sessions stressed how team goals should incorporate at least one of four broad criteria: quantity, quality, time, and cost. Lummel emphasized the difference between performance *goals,* which require a measurable result (say, obtain payment on 95 percent of delinquent accounts by July 31) and performance *standards,* which require a measurable activity (make seventy-five calls a day with fifteen contacts per day).

To encourage ASCAP sales and service team members to work together efficiently to achieve team (and thus corporate) goals, each was provided with an organizational unit incentive plan (ASCAP calls it a variable pay plan) linked to hitting predetermined monthly, quarterly, or annual goals. A splashy new awards program, relying on the power of trophy value, also was introduced in support of the organizational unit incentive. That plan recognizes and celebrates teams, and individual performers on teams, who meet or exceed revenue and licensing, collections, and customer service goals each year.

ASCAP reworked its performance appraisal system to reflect the shift to self-managed teams. The revamped process places 80 percent weighting on individual performance and about 20 percent on peer ratings of how individuals perform as team members. The teamwork rating for account services employees, for instance, uses eleven team-related competencies—things like how team members facilitate team meetings, how they train peers, whether they cover for teammates when needed, and the like. Team members are rated annually by their peers on how they perform on these competencies.

The Plan for Account Service Teams

ASCAP has two account services teams eligible for a quarterly organizational unit incentive based on the team's performance against predetermined objectives. The account services teams are responsible for collections and customer service for approximately forty-five thousand of ASCAP's licensed accounts, mainly bars and restaurants. Some of the goals tied to incentive pay include account collections, revenue, and turnaround time on customer requests.

At the start of each quarter, an account services team submits to management a report showing results against team objectives and performance goals for the previous quarter, in addition to objectives and goals for the coming quarter. If quarterly performance goals are achieved, payouts are a percentage of each team member's base pay. If the team performs at goal, everyone on the team receives a percentage of their base pay—often 3 to 5 percent. Base pay varies, and so too do the individual dollar amounts of the checks. The pay is considered part of salary for purposes of calculating benefits (401K and so on) and reporting total earnings.

A quarterly goal and payout schedule for an account services team might look something like this: "Of the delinquent accounts on the January 23, 1998, list, we will make 100 percent contact. Our goal is to have 90 percent of those accounts no longer delinquent as of March 31. Predetermined payout for hitting that goal: 3 percent of base pay for each team member."

Later in the year, the same team might set this revenue target and payout schedule for the third quarter: "Hitting 100 percent of quarterly targeted revenue will mean 5 percent of base pay for each team member, hitting 95 percent to 99 percent of goal will result in 2 percent of base pay, and 94 percent or lower will result in no payout." Progress against goals is measured by automated daily cash receipts and monthly revenue reports.

Another quarterly goal might emphasize customer service: "We will have a two-week response time on incoming correspondence. Meeting goal means 5 percent of base pay for the quarter; progress toward goal will be monitored by weekly reports from team members."

How do members of the account services teams view the incentive plan? From Lummel's perspective, "The team is happy as long as it hits its top-level award in each measurement period—there are a number of award tiers for each goal. Early on, if they hit the lower or middle award tier, they started challenging the fairness of the system. But that's become less common now that we have four years of historical data built up—teams have a better idea of how they should be performing on collecting delinquent accounts in a month or quarter, or calls or contacts to be made each day."

Kevin Garrelts, an account services specialist at ASCAP for five years, serves as team leader for a twelve–person account collections team populated by collections managers of varying levels. Among the biggest benefits of the team-based monetary incentives, he believes, is helping to separate the need-to-do from nice-to-do on a daily basis.

"There are competing priorities on any job or within any team," Garrelts says, "and by identifying those goals that are ultimately of more importance to ASCAP, the incentive system focuses the energies of our team. When people arrive in the morning, they know what their key goals are for the day, in large part because of the incentive plan. And they get a sense of accomplishment at the end of a quarter when they hit a goal and get the extra incentive pay."

Garrelts says setting plan goals that were measurable as well as meaningful was a challenge in the early going, due mostly to the lack of historical data. Other performance areas eluded objective measurement. An initial goal for customer correspondence that required clear and concise letters appeared reasonable on its face, for example, but proved notoriously difficult to measure. "Who was going to check every outgoing letter—and by what uniform standard?" Garrelts asks.

In the absence of historical data, the team did some research outside ASCAP to help create reasonable goals for the plan. Team members called several well-known collection agencies in the Atlanta area, for example, to determine what a reasonable daily "talk time" might be for ASCAP's own collections agents. The consensus: four hours on the phone in any eight-hour day; ASCAP went with a like amount. "Talk time doesn't guarantee you'll get revenue results, but it's been identified as a path to success," Garrelts says. A similar process was used to determine how many promised payments ASCAP collectors might expect from delinquent customers in a given day.

The development of clear individual and team performance standards hastened the team's progress, Garrelts says. Each of his account services team members is appraised annually on three competencies—one being quality of teamwork—that determine their annual merit increases. Collections employees, for example, have 80 percent of their overall rating tied to individual performance in their key job function (collecting revenues owed ASCAP), 18 percent of the rating tied to their performance as a team member, and the remaining 2 percent tied to innovation, or generating new ideas to improve some facet of the team's work processes. That same 80-18-2 percent split is used for all team members.

The 80 percent for collections employees also includes things like customer service performance (customer letters must be responded to within five days, for example) and administration (every incoming letter must be appropriately documented).

The 18 percent team-member component is based on the entire twelve-person team's review of each member's performance in eleven identified competencies. Those competencies include helping with special projects outside the normal workload, facilitating at least one team meeting per year, taking on new

work when other team members are absent, training new team members in specific skills, and more. To receive a "completed with excellence" appraisal score
on the team measure, team members must score at least twelve of a possible
thirteen points, as rated by their team peers. Each of eleven competencies is
worth one point, with one measure—"reporting and discussing the impact of
your weekly team performance with other team members"—given a heavier
weight of two points, says Garrelts, because of the importance of good team
communication. "If someone's numbers were below goal in a given week, we
ask them to come to the weekly meeting prepared to explain why," he says. "If
someone just says 'I don't know' every time, they won't get a passing grade on
that competency. In order for the team to help that person, he or she has to effectively report how they're doing and what problems they might have. Without that information, it's difficult to help."

Another competency—training the team's new hires—is also important,
Garrelts says, because "it means a couple days of downtime for the trainer,
which takes time away from their own collection revenue goals. So we reward
people for doing the training by making it a competency worth points."

Scoring ten to eleven points on the team review earns a "completed" rating;
nine or less means "incomplete" performance on the team member component,
which accounts for 18 percent of the employee's overall annual performance
rating.

Team members are asked to document examples of their performance in
competency areas throughout the year, should any disputes arise in the end-of-
the-year peer appraisal process. One of the eleven competencies is purposely
deemed "other," Garrelts says, a catch-all for "anything a team member did over
the year they think they should be given credit for, something the rest of the
team didn't acknowledge in the other ten competency areas."

The last category, innovation, accounts for only 2 percent of each team
member's rating. To receive a "completed with excellence" here, team members are expected to generate two to three documented ideas each year to help
the team meet or exceed its goals. Creating just one such idea earns a "completed" rating, and zero triggers an incomplete. "We expect team members to
provide the team with at least one good idea for improving process or performance every year," Garrelts says. "It's about getting people to participate in
continuous improvement."

Tracking Performance Against Goals

Investments in new technologies have played an important role in the success of
the new team-based structures and organizational unit incentives. Early in the
teams' histories there were no automated information systems to monitor team
activity or progress against goals, and most tracking was done via inefficient
and time-consuming paper lists, or by requiring team members to monitor a

cumbersome mainframe database. A new electronic system in late 1996 allowed the account services team to monitor individual collection calls and incoming phone call activity, and made more data available—and easier to access—on customer payments and activities like number of phone contacts made, messages left, faxes sent, and more.

Organizational Unit Incentives for ASCAP Sales Teams

Organizational unit incentives are used with ASCAP's licensing sales teams as well as service teams. Each team consists of three to five field and telephone workers, charged with selling some one hundred different types of ASCAP "licenses" or contracts to potential clients around the United States. The twelve teams receive base pay plus an incentive tied to hitting predetermined monthly goals in overall revenue as a team. Unlike the account services' plan, sales team payouts are not a percentage of base pay but rather equal dollar amounts for each team member. For example, if a monthly sales target for a New York area team is $100,000, and the team bonus for hitting goal is 10 percent of that figure—$10,000—each person on a ten-member sales team would receive $1,000.

Individuals on sales teams also have their own revenue goals, in addition to targets for license contracts sold and sales prospects identified (a sample prospect being a restaurant playing live music, for instance), depending on their role on the team.

The Importance of a Companion Awards Program

Once that sales incentive plan was firmly ensconced, Lummel initiated a companion awards program to publicly recognize both high-achieving teams and individuals. Awards are presented during an elaborate conference each January at ASCAP General Licensing headquarters in Atlanta. A "Sales Team of the Year"—based on a weighted average of annual performance in overall revenue, licenses sold, and prospects identified—has its name engraved on a trophy displayed in sales licensing headquarters, and each team member receives a plaque and a highly coveted leather jacket featuring the ASCAP logo, with an approximate value of $300.

The winning team also gets to choose the location for its next team meeting, anywhere in the contiguous forty-eight states. The Atlanta ceremony isn't a winner-take-all proposition, though. All sales teams that exceed 100 percent of their annual goals (revenue, prospects, and licenses) also receive a plaque and a merchandise gift bearing the ASCAP logo, often a light jacket. Awards also are given to sales teams with the top quarterly and monthly performance for that year.

Says Lummel: "The ceremony and awards are a way to celebrate team accomplishments that otherwise wouldn't get much public recognition. The awards are not expensive to us; it's just very elaborate with high visibility among peers and management. And it's a real bonding experience for the teams."

ASCAP considers it vital to recognize individual performance on sales teams as well. Awards are given for the area (field) and telephone sales "licensing manager of the year" (ASCAP calls all team salespeople "managers") based on performance against annual individual goals, with winners having their names inscribed on a trophy kept at ASCAP headquarters, and also receiving smaller individual trophies and the leather ASCAP jacket to take home. Individual salespeople on teams who exceed 100 percent of their annual goals are recognized with an ASCAP merchandise gift.

"We think it's important to recognize high-performing individuals even if their sales team as a whole might not be doing as well," Lummel says.

The account services teams also are eligible for recognition awards, but as there are only two such teams, most of the awards are tied to individual performance—an account services "manager of the year" (all team members are called managers) and "manager of the quarter." Eligibility for manager of the year requires a minimum score on the last annual performance appraisal, with the winner chosen by vote of team peers and account services management, who vote using predetermined criteria. Account services winners receive awards similar to the sales teams.

Another Key Piece: Skill-Based Pay

Skill-based pay is another component of ASCAP's reward mix. Team members can increase base pay (and potential incentive payouts that are a percentage of salary for account services teams) through the company's "job knowledge promotion" system. If length of service and performance appraisal scores qualify them, employees are given a chance to take written and oral tests to advance to higher levels within their particular job category: level one or two or a senior level. Each level has three requirements to be met for promotion: core competencies, specific job knowledge, and general knowledge.

Use of Lotus Notes software makes the written testing both time and cost efficient. ASCAP employees eligible for the written test receive electronic mail with an embedded button; clicking the button downloads the test to their screens via Notes, and triggers a test timer—two hours is the typical time limit. Employees then complete the mostly fill-in-the-blank test relating to their specific jobs. (For instance: How well do sales team members understand copyright law or ASCAP's license agreements? How do they handle the ten most common objections by customers to a license agreement?) Employees hit "close" to stop the timer and "end" to send the completed test back on its electronic journey to Lummel or another test administrator. "We test people all around the country this way very cost-effectively," Lummel says.

The oral exams—conducted over the phone or in person—use actual business scenarios and an interview format to test employees' customer service, collections, or sales skills. If employees score a certain level on these tests, they receive the job level promotion in addition to a small percentage increase in base pay.

Measuring Payback from the Plans

A move to self-managing teams and accompanying organizational unit incentives comes with no shortage of skeptics. But nothing quiets the voices of discontent like early results.

On the sales side, the average value of an ASCAP license sold has increased substantially since the advent of team-based sales incentives, Lummel claims. Under the old system, sales reps' performance was weighted more heavily on the number of licenses brought in rather than the average value of each license to the organization. The average revenue individual ASCAP sales licensing managers generate also has increased significantly from pre-1995 levels.

Other anecdotal evidence of the incentive plans' influence continues to come in: by 1997, revenue per ASCAP employee had increased 72 percent and net revenue increased by 42 percent from levels before the reorganization and incentive plans, Lummel says.

ASCAP also measures the ROI from new team-based structures and incentive plans in part on lower turnover on account services and sales teams; high turnover, of course, means higher recruiting and training costs, not to mention some lost revenues. On the sales side, ASCAP has seen definite benefits—tangible as well as intangible—to having salespeople sell as part of a team rather than as the traditional "lone wolf," Lummel claims.

"The decreased turnover is partially a result of higher base pay and the incentive plans, but we believe it's also a result of the new team environment," she says. "This can be an awfully tough job, and as part of a team salespeople receive more empathy for what they're going through from fellow team members, and more sharing of ideas and strategies for improving sales. They're all in it together, so they motivate each other and depend on each other for success. It gets to a point where you don't want to let your teammates down. The same can be said for account services teams, where collections is a very challenging job and the team empathy and knowledge sharing really helps."

Lessons Learned

Deal with fairness issues of plan design and saboteurs.

The incentive plan for ASCAP sales teams initially stirred more rumblings of discontent than the account services plan. The latter was more readily embraced, Lummel believes, because designing payouts as a percentage of base pay was seen as more equitable (those with higher base pay receive a proportionally larger payout) than paying all team members equally based on the team's performance against goals, which the sales plan does.

With the sales plan, Lummel says, "the team splits an incentive payout equally—even if one team member brings in significantly more revenue than another. It's almost inevitable that the person bringing in more will start resenting the poor performer. A sales rep at 125 percent of goal will not be pleased with a team member at 75 percent of goal. In reality, 75 percent may be enough to keep a job—anything below that and a team member gets a performance warning—but it's not okay on a team where everyone else is at or above 100 percent."

ASCAP's answer wasn't to abandon the plan design or toss the baby out with the bathwater, Lummel says. Rather, she relied largely on the power of peer pressure to root out poor performance on sales teams; rarely is ASCAP management forced to intervene with team members who aren't pulling their weight. "One of two things tends to happen—either the performance improves, or the team members eventually leave on their own due to pressure from teammates," Lummel says. The challenge, of course, is to keep the focus of such peer-to-peer feedback on documented performance against agreed-on team goals, not personality issues, so as to avoid emotional battlefields.

The account services teams also experienced a few early problems surrounding perceived "uneven" performance levels. Some team members stayed late to make extra calls on accounts or take customer calls, but others left work early. In the initial team meetings, high performers accused low performers of being lazy, and low performers accused top performers of unrealistic expectations and perfectionism. What broke the deadlock? Says Lummel: "Again, the accumulation of historical data helped both sides set more realistic performance goals—the data gave them a better sense of what was realistic to accomplish in a given month or quarter."

If in the rare case peer pressure doesn't work to correct subpar performance on teams, management typically intervenes with some form of performance warning, Lummel says. "If substandard performers do linger on teams, you can't hesitate—you need to find another place for them, or let them go," she says.

That's what ASCAP did in 1998, installing a more rigorous selection process to replace, rather than learn to tolerate, those with a history of laggard performance on sales teams. The organization worked to hone team leaders' hiring skills, upgraded a training program for new sales team members, and added modestly to team members' base pay "to ensure we're attracting the right kind of people," Lummel says. "One of our biggest lessons has been how essential it is to get the right people on your teams from the beginning. If a team isn't achieving its goals and its incentive payouts, you'll lose your quality people and keep your mediocre performers."

Use recognition to support organizational unit incentive plans.

A noncash recognition awards program used in conjunction with an organizational unit monetary incentive can be a powerful way to boost the incentive's effect on strategic business goals. But Lummel suggests developing team-based awards before individual awards rather than simultaneously, unless the team output is the sum of the individual outputs.

That design sequence was key at ASCAP, she says, "because it allowed us first to get some control over team goals and rewards so we knew we were measuring the right things at the right level. Once you know the results a team can be expected to produce, you can better see where the individual pieces of the team puzzle fit in."

Thus, creating recognition awards for individuals trickled down from the creation of team goals, as did accountability for hitting those goals within the team structure. ASCAP teams usually meet each week to review each team member's performance against his or her individual performance goals, with the team leader keeping a chart of each teammate's results and sharing those results with the entire team.

Less is better: keep the size of geographically dispersed teams small.

When ASCAP launched its sales team concept in 1995, many teams were as large as nine members. That size created a problem, Lummel says, due to a resulting "team within a team" phenomenon. "If we have a five- or six-person sales team working under the same goal and same team incentive, because of our team structure we tended to get triads or smaller groups working within that team—and one of those groups-within-a-group could be doing poorly, the other quite well, but both getting the same umbrella dollar payout if they hit the overall team performance goal," she says. Smaller team sizes reduce that chance, foster greater familiarity and interdependence between members, and mean that team members are more likely to be working on the same licensing accounts.

ASCAP now believes its ideal sales team size is three to five people. That usually means two field salespeople to one phone salesperson, with the field people responsible for feeding the phone expert prospects to "close." Larger and more geographically dispersed teams faced other problems as well: greater difficulty in communicating, inefficient or slower problem solving and decision making, and increased chances of factions forming within the team.

ASCAP account services teams faced a related size dilemma. Data showed some team members were making more outgoing collections calls, and others were taking more incoming calls from customers, creating a conflict between collections and customer service priorities. To address the problem, an eight-person account services team was divided into four regional "subteams" of two members each, with one team member specializing in collections and the other customer service.

Strive to retain individual accountability.

As the ASCAP teams evolved, some team members no longer wanted to be appraised on individual performance at all—they only wanted to be measured by team goals. "These were mostly poor performers who wanted to get lost among the team," Lummel says. "We stressed to them that teams are the sum of their parts, and it's important to measure the parts as well as the whole. The individual is accountable to the team. The team is accountable to the organization."

Also, some sales team members initially weren't pleased that their individual as well as team performance would be publicly compared to other licensing salespeople. That attitude began to change, however, when ASCAP started awarding top performing salespeople (as well as teams) with the trophies and impressive leather jackets. "It wasn't long before people wanted a monthly list of how they stood against other salespeople—and we weren't offering them a dollar of money as an incentive for performance, just the noncash merchandise awards and trophies," Lummel says.

Patience is your friend.

As the process unfolded it was a challenge for teams to establish realistic performance goals due to a lack of good historical data. Without that frame of reference, sales teams were left wondering how many cold calls or contacts should be made in a day, and account services teams wondered how many delinquent accounts they should expect to collect on.

That uncertainty is why Lummel waited three years to create the companion awards recognition program linked to team and individual performance. The wait provided enough time to collect the performance data needed to set realistic award targets.

"If we had set up the awards program earlier, with goals set too high or too low, we would have shot ourselves in the foot and lost credibility," she says. "Until we had a good grasp of what a reasonable goal was, we'd have been awarding the wrong people for the wrong behaviors or results. Poor performers might have received awards by happenstance rather than for day-in, day-out strong performance. We had to make sure we'd closed all those loopholes before rolling the awards program out."

ORGANIZATIONAL UNIT INCENTIVES IN ACTION: CARS IV RESEARCH

One organization has studied the effects of organizational unit incentives in the "real world" since 1989. The Consortium for Alternative Reward Strategies, or CARS, has conducted four major studies of organizational unit incentives in the workplace since 1990. CARS is a nonprofit group funded by consortium members and research sponsors whose objective is to help organizations better design and implement performance reward plans for all levels of employees. It was founded by Jerry McAdams and Elizabeth Hawk, formerly of Monsanto and now with Sibson & Company. Initial funding was provided by the American Compensation Association, the Society for Human Resources Management, Ohio State University, Texas Instruments, Allied Signal, Federal Express, Monsanto, Maritz, The Travelers, and Motorola.

The first three CARS studies, conducted from 1989 to 1996, examined hundreds of organizational unit incentive plans in manufacturing and service firms, relying largely on surveys of management-level employees to gather information on the plans' effects on their organizations.

All three studies sought to answer a core question: Do gains from use of organizational unit incentives exceed payouts by a significant amount? The answers were consistent over the three studies:

- The majority of the plans studied spent the time to determine the gains. The plans paid for themselves twice over—a 200 percent gross return on payout.

- As organizations gain more experience with the plans, the issue becomes less about the size of the payouts and the returns to the company and more about creating a framework for employee engagement to affect the measures.

The fourth and latest study, dubbed CARS IV, took a different tack in its research-and-reporting work from 1996 to 1999. For this study, CARS researchers conducted in-depth case studies of organizational unit incentive plans in eleven plant locations in four separate organizations.

Rather than examining the incentive plans only through management's lens, this study gauged plan effectiveness from multiple points of view—the employee's perspective, management's perspective, and to the extent possible, objective financial results of the plan. In each of the eleven sites, CARS researchers interviewed top management, middle management, and human resources leaders, conducted surveys of frontline employees and managers with follow-up focus groups to clarify findings, and reviewed incentive plan documentation and design in a quantitative audit.

Organizational unit incentive plans in the CARS IV study had to meet the following criteria:

- Rewards are based on performance of an organizational unit (company, division, department, work group, or other unit).

- The plan is not exclusively for the executive or management level—it must include a broad group of employees, if not all.

- Goals and potential payouts are announced up front (in other words, "Do this, get that").

- Awards are based only on performance for the preestablished goals; there's no management discretion in the determination of awards for each employee (except for a performance rating affecting a total pool payout sum).

- Plans pay out in "real time" (versus mandatory deferral of awards to a savings or retirement account).

Goals typically targeted by work groups, divisions, departments, or entire organizations include financial measures (profit, return on capital, and so on), productivity, cost reduction, worker safety, and customer satisfaction indicators. Often there are combinations of measures at the corporate and local unit level. All plans used results-based, rather than activity-based, performance goals.

Most of these plans are considered to be self-funding—they pay out only when the improvement occurs and there is a reasonable value added by that improvement. Like all incentive plans, the payouts are not added to base pay and must be earned each time, which protects companies from adding to base pay levels or other overhead costs. In a few cases, companies choose to pay people slightly below competitive market labor costs and make up the difference—and often more—through the organizational unit incentive.

The remaining cases in this chapter are an overview of how organizational unit incentive plans worked in action at four different companies and their eleven sites in the CARS IV study. All companies have been given fictitious names to protect their confidentiality. The survey data, focus group comments, and perspective of both management and employees provide insight into what makes an organizational unit incentive successful in both its design and implementation phases. Because the "lessons learned" focus largely on process, not specific plan measures or content, they apply across industries. It is important to note that each of the four companies had a unique plan, designed to meet its needs. The plants (the organizational units) customized their company's plan by measuring performance at the plant level. Although the plan design is essentially the same for each plant within a company, the effectiveness was not. To the degree there are significant differences among plants' performance, it is an issue of how the plan is used, rather than how it is designed.

One note: CARS does not infer causality in the data. The statistical analyses support statements of relationships, not claims that one element directly causes another (for example, that introduction of an organizational unit incentive alone contributed to annual profitability growth). Many variables contribute to shifts in organizational performance, incentive plans for organizational units being just one.

Table 5.5 is an overview of the plans studied in CARS IV. The evaluations of the effectiveness of the plans came from an analysis of the performance data, management interviews, focus groups of middle managers and employees, and an all-employee survey. The ten categories for evaluation from management and employees included the following:

- **Objectives** has two elements: How well does the plan fit with our business objectives? (environmental) How well does the plan connect my work with the overall success of the plant? (personal)

- **Culture** has two elements: How much management support is there for the plan and how engaged is it in helping employees earn awards? (management support) How effective is the plan in creating teamwork, solving problems, and doing quality work?

- **Value** has two elements: How satisfied are employees with the payout amounts, considering what is necessary to earn them, and are they recognized for their contributions? (reward and recognition) To what degree does the plan influence employees' actions and commitment to the company? (individual outcomes)

- **Awareness** has one element: How top-of-mind is the plan as a driver of performance?

- **Performance-reward link** has two elements: How well do employees understand what actions are necessary for the plan to be successful? (contingency) How effective is the plan in relating employees' actions and the size of their awards? (sensitivity)

- **Overall:** How well do employees like the plan?

The results of the extensive employee survey were quantitative and statistically analyzed. The focus group and interviews were qualitative. Both results influenced the effectiveness evaluation of the plans.

TECHNOLOGY AND MANUFACTURING, INC.

Technology and Manufacturing, Inc., is a global Fortune 100 company organized into eleven strategic business units. T&M's organizational unit incentive was implemented in part to help drive two strategic business objectives: bringing more innovative, high-quality new products to market faster, and capitalizing on rapidly growing markets around the world (other than Europe) and lessening reliance on any one geographic region. Because T&M competes in world markets where supply almost always exceeds demand, it's critical that it remain a high-quality, low-cost producer, and the three-year-old incentive plan serves

Table 5.5. Design Overview of Organizational Units Studied in CARS IV.

	Technology and Manufacturing, Inc. (T&M)	Acme, Inc.	Materials Processing, Inc. (MP)	Food Processing and Packaging, Inc. (FPP)
Number of Plant Sites	3	3	2	3
Number of Employees per Site	120–680	30–250	120–250	325–450
Union Presence at All Sites	Yes	No	Yes	Yes
Years with Group Incentive Plan	3	12	3	6
Participation	All site employees	All site employees	All site employees	Hourly employees
Payout Structure	Equal value to all participants in a given plant (noncash)	% varies by level	Equal percentage of base to all participants in a given plant	Equal pay opportunity for each hour worked for all participants in a given plant
Measures	• On-time delivery • Productivity • Safety • Yield • Cost of poor quality	• Profit • Return on assets (one plant only) • Quality • Diversification (one plant only)	• Cost per unit • Spoilage • Quality • Safety	• Productivity
Payout Cap (target payouts are lower)	$750 award value	10 to 18% of base, depending on level	5% of base	None
Payout Frequency	Quarterly	Quarterly	Quarterly	Semiannual

that goal. T&M management has indicated its desire for a challenging "six sigma" standard for product quality, which means a given factory can have a defect rate of only 3.4 parts per million. As a comparison, manufacturing facilities in the United States average about 180,000 defective parts per million.

Three T&M sites, each with anywhere from 120 to 680 employees, were studied in the CARS IV research. Of the four companies in the study, T&M as a whole had the highest effectiveness ratings in seven of the ten categories measured.

The incentive plan, entering its third year of operation during the study, gives equal weight to five measures at all three sites:

- Cost of poor quality (rework, off-spec material, failure of equipment, downtime, product waste, and redo)
- Rolled throughput yield (the percent of raw material that goes into each step that is "done right the first time")
- Safety performance (number of reportable injuries by OSHA standards)
- On-time deliveries as a measure of customer satisfaction (percent of deliveries that arrive at promised time)
- Capacity productivity (individual products are "weighted" together to make up the plantwide metric, which is based on overall revenue. More credit, or weight, is given to products that generate the most sales.)

To develop quarterly and annual goals for each of the five metrics, T&M used baseline performance figures from the prior year. When goals are achieved, all plan participants in each plant receive a noncash award of equal value. Performance is measured monthly, quarterly, or whenever the goal is met. It depends on the measurement. Quarterly awards are in the form of merchandise or company stock and potential payouts are capped at $750 per employee in award value.

T&M uses six earning levels, each based on the number of "green lights" that told everyone they hit a goal. Eight so-called green light awards are needed to qualify for a minimum level one award, and forty-four such green lights are needed to qualify for the top level six award. The range of noncash award choices is extensive. The number of green light awards required for specific merchandise range from eight green lights for a golf bag, twelve for a twenty-inch TV, seventeen for a weekend trip, twenty-two for a camcorder, to forty-four for twenty shares of T&M stock. Employees can cash in their "lights" whenever they earn them or they can save them up for a bigger award.

To add another layer or recognition and celebration, some of the plants also created team-based recognition awards to complement the organizational unit incentive. At one plant, for instance, a quarterly Vision award recognizes team (and individual) performance and productivity improvement, often spotlighting a team member who has acquired an important new job-related skill or a team that has had exceptional results with a significant project or special assignment. Award recipients are recognized by a supervisor or team leader with a "certificate of achievement" and their choice of a $100 gift certificate, or combination of $50 restaurant certificate and $50 certificate to be used for company merchandise.

The same plant also gives a quarterly Ideas award that recognizes work teams or individuals for achievement in three areas: product quality improvement, significant cost reduction, or exemplary customer service. Award recipients receive a company jacket and a certificate of achievement, and are honored at an annual off-site recognition dinner (spouses included), where each team delivers a short presentation on its accomplishments. In addition, a Saf-T award recognizes work teams or departments that show the greatest improvement in safety performance each quarter.

Results and Feedback

During the time of the study, T&M expanded the plan to all ten plants and 5,700 employees. The payouts in noncash awards averaged $500 per employee, for a total cost of $7.1 million over twenty-seven months. The plans contributed significantly to the total performance improvement valued at $157 million during the same period.

In addition to looking at the financial aspects of the plan, CARS looked for feedback from employees and managers at the three study sites for their perceptions of the plan's effectiveness.

Echoing a common finding in the CARS IV data, the opinions about plan effectiveness vary by level of employee. Sixty-four percent of plant management felt that the plan had a positive effect, whereas 55 percent of team leaders and only 26 percent of shift or section leaders agreed. Interestingly, about 55 percent of the team members (most of the employees) felt the plan had a positive effect. This disconnect between shift leaders and employees is probably a result of the way the plan was implemented. Almost everyone found out about it at one time (the plant managers were briefed in advance). The communications were driven by corporate managers. The first-line managers probably felt bypassed, which can only reduce their commitment to making the plan work to its fullest potential.

Corporate leaders also specified the measurements to be used, although what constitutes performance improvement was customized to the plant. It was essentially a top-down process. The plant managers surveyed wanted some changes: more flexibility in selecting plan measures to make them more meaningful at the plant level; more timely and effective communication about the plan from the corporate level; and increased "motivational value" for employees from the plan.

One plant manager conceded the difficulty of getting all employees to buy into the plan. "My intent is to get as many people actively involved as possible—if that means 70 percent of people want to help, I get them to help," he said in a focus group interview. "The other 30 percent I can live without."

Among things the employees cited for improvement: the plan was a "good benefit," but it wasn't appreciably driving their day-to-day behavior; goal setting was too rigid and removed; employees wanted more input into goal setting; and plan administration needed to be improved.

In one T&M plant, only 29 percent of employees felt increasing their individual performance would result in a higher award, and 60 percent felt the size of their award was determined by too many things beyond their control, like production line shutdowns, broken parts due to reduction of inventory, and measures set unrealistically high. Commented one employee: "It might help if we were part of setting goals . . . we want to know where they came from and why."

Managers joined employees in their belief that it was difficult to influence two plan measures—the "cost of poor quality" and "on-time delivery"—because recurring problems with machinery prevented the plant from meeting its ambitious goals.

At another plant, communication was cited as a problem. Only 24 percent of employees said their manager regularly talks about the incentive plan and how it fits into the overall objectives of the organization. Fifty-two percent of employees there viewed the incentive plan as "special recognition" as opposed to regular compensation, suggesting a reasonably good awareness of the plan and its objectives. Forty-eight percent, however, felt the plan was easily confused with other plant plans and corporate human resource initiatives. It is easy for corporate managers to forget that all reward plans have to be presented in a coordinated fashion, demonstrating an alignment with overall objectives and with each other.

Generally, employees appeared pleased with the plan. Said one in a focus group: "The plan recognizes us for doing a good job. A lot of times supervisors are too caught up in what they're doing to think about recognition for us. With an established plan, it's never forgotten."

The research also suggests management needs to stand ready to address employee concern and not shrink into the woodwork should a plan not produce anticipated payouts. One plant did not meet as many of its goals as in the previous year, and thus didn't receive as many green light awards. Ever since, according to the CARS surveys, plant employees have thought this was due to plan goals being set unrealistically high by management. That may or may not be true, but the perception of an incentive plan is what counts.

Improvements to the Plan

T&M has an ongoing task force to review the plans and make the changes that make the most business sense. The following improvements were made for fiscal year 1999:

Give Plants More Control in Choosing and Tailoring Plan Metrics. Plants can now tailor their own plan goals from a menu of five broad categories that cascade from the corporate level: productivity, product quality, safety and environment, customer satisfaction, and a financial metric. Plants must select at least one metric from each category to use in their local incentive plans. But creating their own metrics should give both managers and workers better "line of sight," or sense of control, over performance that can influence measures and the size of payouts. To ensure consistency across business units, a T&M vice president signs off on all incentive plan goals.

Encourage Employees to Get Involved in Creating Goals. Giving employees a bigger say in setting goals tied to payouts has multiple benefits. They gain a better understanding of the business objectives of the plan, feel more connected to the organization, and gain new understanding of how their individual efforts can affect plan success (or failure) and increase (or decrease) awards.

In a survey conducted two years earlier, less than half of T&M employees felt the amount of awards paid was fair relative to the amount of work needed to earn them, and some of the perceived unfairness was attributed to the difficulty of achieving established goals. Said one employee: "How the aggressive stretch goals are set is often questioned. Plant morale is low because it seems like no matter what we do or how hard we work, we barely miss receiving a green light award."

Getting employees more involved in goal creation will help establish goals that still require an appropriate performance stretch but will be more realistic.

Shift the Burden of Plan Communication from the Corporate Level to the Plants. When T&M reorganized from three sectors to eleven business units, new "plan champions" were identified at each plant site. The primary role of these champions is to provide more effective monthly and quarterly updates to employees about progress against incentive plan goals, largely moving that responsibility from corporate to local level. In past surveys, a majority of employees in two of T&M's plants indicated uncertainty about whether they were on track for specific awards at any given time in a plan's progress. The change is designed to keep the employees in the loop and the plan more at the top of the mind for all involved. It doesn't mean, however, that corporate will stop communicating about the plan, only that other voices nearer the action will help reinforce the plan message.

Of all the CARS IV companies, T&M has the strongest and most energetic corporate support in driving communications and promotion of the plan. The shift from primarily corporate to site communications is viewed with some concern, but it was the consensus that although the site may not be as creative it will be better received as "their own."

A plant manager echoed the general consensus: "The (incentive) plan not only contributes to performance but also to the whole team concept, of which the plan is only a piece. . . . It's a very good tool for making the link between performance and plant objectives. It also helps align the goals of the plant with the goals of the department."

ACME, INC.

The experience of Acme, Inc., a progressively managed company with an aggressive employee stock ownership plan, highlights how important proper plan execution and a preexisting culture of management-employee trust are to the ultimate success of organizational unit incentives.

Acme is in a tough business. Capital improvements and technology do not make a great deal of difference. It is a people-intensive manufacturing operation, often subject to market influences that affect the bottom line and seem beyond the control of the employees. Essentially all of the plan's measures are based on the bottom line, life or death to small operations. Acme has staked its success on making employees business literate. The challenge is translating that literacy into action.

Acme's mission statement emphasizes employee engagement and customer success, and backs up those words up with an open-book management philosophy that lays bare the company's profit-and-loss statements. The company teaches nonmanagement employees how to interpret and use the numbers to improve company performance—and their own potential payouts from the incentive plan.

Acme management sees organizational unit incentives as a natural extension of the open-book policy of allowing frontliners to see numbers and participate in decisions. They believe that it makes sense to make everyone accountable for success and for them to share in the gain.

Results and Challenges

Despite its strong philosophy of employee participation, Acme found some challenges in plan implementation. Of the four companies in the CARS IV study, Acme's plan had the highest effectiveness ratings in only three of ten overall categories measured. One very successful plant and two rather poor performers heavily influenced those ratings. (The three high ratings were on how employees' work fit into the overall success of the plant, improved teamwork as a critical factor in success, and the degree to which individual actions affect plan outcomes.)

One problem was that the corporate culture of employee involvement hadn't trickled down and gained a foothold in two of the plants; there were significant differences in business environments and management styles at each of the three Acme plants examined.

The earning potential from the incentive plan is the highest of all the CARS IV plants, capped at 10 to 18 percent of base pay, depending on job and salary level. Incentive payouts are based on a percentage of base pay, depending on employees' job level. The payouts are paid out quarterly in cash.

Although the incentive plan design and measures were similar at all plants, results and effectiveness differed greatly due to plan cultural and operational issues at the three sites.

The largest determinants of incentive plan success at Acme appear to be the level of trust hourly employees have in management, and the communication from plant management to employees regarding plan specifics such as measures chosen, payout calculations, and specific actions employees could take to influence payout levels.

All three plants, with a range of 30 to 250 employees, primarily use a profit-before-tax measure as the key driver of incentive plan payouts. Plan measures (baselines) are adjusted annually.

Although there is some opportunity in all plants for employees to participate in shaping plan measures, currently only one Acme site—plant 1—openly solicits such feedback from employees prior to plan rollout. (There the general manager asks for employee feedback on plan design prior to making any adjustments to plan measures used.) As a result, a feeling of "noncontrol" over plan measures showed up consistently in surveys from hourly employees at the two plants where such feedback isn't formally solicited.

One Site's Successful Experience. Plant 1 clearly experienced the most success with the incentive plan, measured in terms of financial payout, business literacy training, and employee engagement. The plant ranked first or second in all categories for all four companies studied. Both plant management and employees gave the plan strong marks and considered it an important component in "driving process improvement and tracking performance against plant goals." This alignment of management and employee perception is a good barometer of health and acceptance of a plan. At the other two Acme plants, salaried managers and hourly employees had more divergent views about the motivating value, fairness, and payback to the organization of the incentive plan.

The data spotlight another important reason for success at plant 1: management doesn't vanish in tough times. According to employee surveys, plant managers continue to communicate about the plan whether or not goals are being achieved and payouts made. In times of success, management stresses reasons for the gains—specific actions and decisions that contributed to achieving unit objectives—and uses individual recognition for employees. In bleaker times, when targets are missed and payouts are meager or nonexistent, management doesn't crawl into a bunker, but rather openly communicates with employees about possible reasons for underperformance—apparently without laying the blame on one group or another.

On average, 73 percent of plant 1 employees said plant management talks often about the plan and how it fits into the organization's overall objectives, and 81 percent said it is very clear to them and their coworkers what it takes to earn a bonus. Management continually communicates which profit and loss line items drive bonus payouts. After a management-employee meeting, follow-up sheets are distributed to employees so they can ask questions not addressed in the meeting. Over 75 percent of employees said they know at any given time if they're on track for earning a bonus, and how big it might be.

Another 80 percent said the bonus plan helps keep key plant goals at the top of everyone's mind, reminding them of what they need to do each day to make the plant successful. Commented one employee: "I can take a look at the board (showing monthly progress against goals) and quickly know how we are doing. If we meet or exceed their projections, we're making money. We have meetings every week and go through the numbers. I know the things I do that might create extra costs. We are not kept in the dark."

Said another: "Productivity would go down if they took the plan away. The plant would still be successful, but it would be harder (to meet goals). The plan helps motivation."

On the management side, the plant's general manager said she was "very satisfied" with what the company receives from the plan compared to payouts made to employees.

Few successes are unqualified. Some 70 percent of hourly employees believe the size of their bonus is still determined by too many things outside their control. "I can make my numbers and others may not—the individuality is difficult to control," said one focus group attendee. Echoed another: "My work is based on productivity and the work of others in my plant on different things like sales. If everyone in my immediate area improves performance, it doesn't necessarily mean a higher bonus because sales may not go as well."

A manager at plant 1 had a different concern: "The incentive system is not based on product quality. Employees don't get rewarded for what customers find valuable; it's not directly related to the quality of the product. The bonus is based on overall performance, and quality is one part of that, but not the first element."

Two Sites with Greater Challenges. A different story from that of Acme's plant 1 unfolded at Acme plants 2 and 3, where bleak spots outnumbered the bright in the data. In particular, employees in both plants largely viewed financial plant measures as beyond their control. More troubling was that many in plant 2 had a general distrust in the accuracy of numbers that determined their payouts. When asked to agree or disagree with the statement, "When management says something about the plan you can believe it's true," not one employee at plant 2 who returned the survey agreed.

Not surprisingly, the effect of the plan's operation on performance at the two plants didn't come close to approaching results at plant 1.

According to CARS researchers, one immediate way both plants could improve is by communicating more regularly about progress toward goals—say, weekly—even in those times when a bonus may not be forthcoming. These meetings can be used to share financial information with employees on a line-by-line basis, and explain to employees the line items they can—and can't—affect. Management also could solicit more employee questions about the measures and how payouts are calculated, to improve line of sight and a sense of trust from employees.

Unlike plant 1, plants 2 and 3 show little congruency in employee and management perception of the plan. Whereas hourly employees hold management responsible for the lack of success of the incentive plan, management insists hourly workers "fail to understand the complexities and big picture factors of the business impacting the reward plan."

Although 83 percent of managers at plant 2 said they were satisfied with the plan, none—0 percent—of the employees said they were satisfied with it. Some 84 percent of managers at that plant said they were able to track performance measures used to calculate the bonus payout, but only 14 percent of hourly employees felt they could do so. Also, 71 percent of employees reported that too many things outside of their control determined the size of their bonus.

Commented one hourly employee at plant 2: "It wouldn't make a difference if they eliminate it (the bonus plan). It would almost be better because it's frustrating to see how we never get it."

More than 70 percent of hourly employees at plant 2 reported that they didn't know at any given time if they were on track for receiving a bonus; only 24 percent said, on average, that everyone where they work seemed to know how the plan worked. Said one disenchanted hourly worker: "We've been asking for the numbers since January and we don't get them. There is something they don't want us to see. In February we had two meetings and we were supposed to have four."

Echoed another: "The bonus plan is a requirement but in reality it doesn't really exist. Management can make it happen or not. We can have an outstanding year and still not get the bonus. Their projections determine the bonus, and those projections may not be on target. Too many unreasonable goals and projections. And they are always changing them from one month to another."

One plant 2 manager did report he's working much harder to help his direct reports understand the plan, breaking down profit-before-tax figures into smaller elements and emphasizing better tracking and explanation of things like overhead absorption, labor performance, and material usage.

Perhaps the general manager at plant 2 sums up the communication and employee education problem best: "When we're doing well, I think about the plan once a week," he says. "When we're not, I just worry about getting through the month without losing money."

The CARS IV study was conducted at plant 3 just after the plant had missed a year of quarterly plan payouts for the first time in the plan's twelve years of operation, and reaction to that naturally spilled over into survey responses. In addition, a change in plan design had added product performance under warranty as a new metric—something many employees didn't think they had adequate control over. Said one plant worker: "A lot of the bonus is now based on warranties and current inventory, and a lot of people don't feel they have control over the availability of parts or orders, or if we can sell enough to cover what we've purchased."

Because the bonus was achieved so many years in succession, it also tended to be seen as an entitlement and as part of regular compensation, so its power as a motivator had decreased. Miss a payout, however, and people will be up in arms. The general manager at plant 3 put his finger on this problem: "One of the biggest risks you have with these bonuses is that people will set their lifestyle based on bonus levels achieved in the past. It's the same with overtime. But I don't know how we could have warned them not to count on them."

All of Acme's measures are financial. Their experience suggests that even in small operations, using only financial measures of performance can create too long a line of sight, even with an active business literacy effort. Trust and an engaged workforce seem to make the difference.

MATERIALS PROCESSING, INC.

The two plants studied at Materials Processing, Inc., a metal processing company, again illustrate how the same incentive plan design can have widely disparate results at different locations. The variance in plan effectiveness and payback is largely a function of environment, culture, employee-management trust, and communication levels, not of the size of reward payouts.

The two plants have 120 and 250 employees, with a union presence at each site. Under the three-year-old incentive plan, all participating employees earn an equal percentage of base pay for hitting plan goals, with a payout cap of 5 percent of base pay per employee. Quarterly awards are given in cash.

Responses to the same survey questions varied greatly at the two plants, with one reporting an average of 25 percent more favorable responses than the other.

Response to the plan was more favorable at plant A1, largely because of a perceived strong culture and high employee trust of management; 76 percent of employees said they were satisfied with the incentive plan overall.

Most employees also reported they were "very aware" of plan design mechanics and how their own actions might influence plan success or failure.

At plant A2, which experienced a management transition during the research period, there was no similar sense of a supportive culture or trust of management. Employee responses indicate the organizational unit incentive plan did not help strengthen plant performance, but rather was a lever in continuing distrust of management.

The plants used quarterly performance against the following metrics to determine award payout levels:

- Cost ("employee-influenced manufacturing costs" or EIMC)
- Productivity (largely a spoilage measure)
- Quality (the two plants used distinct product quality measures)
- Worker safety (used by just one plant)

Plan Results

Table 5.6 shows how the organizational unit incentive plans correlate with value added to the plants over the two years studied. (Note: because of other variables, the numbers do not indicate causality, but do infer a relationship between the incentive plan and plant results.)

As Table 5.6 shows, plant A2 did not experience the same level of financial payback as plant A1, although few companies would ignore a $2.40 gain for $1 spent. The CARS study suggests applying plant A1's plan design to plant A2, which was recently purchased from another company. A2 had experienced a

Table 5.6. Payout and Value Added by Materials Processing Plants (Two Years).

Plant	Average Payout per Employee per Year	Number of Quarters Payout Earned (of 8)	Average Payout per Quarter (when there was a payout)	Total Payout (8 quarters)	Estimated Value Added	Value Added as Percentage of Payout
A1	$1400	7	$407	$350,000	$2,000,000	570%
A2	$540	3	$360	$270,000	$660,000	240%

transition in management as well as culture, in addition to adapting to new accounting systems and encountering some engineering problems. There was apparent misalignment between MP's corporate goals and the operational goals of the newly acquired plant, and the organizational unit incentive plan just reinforced that misalignment. Plant A2 managers indicated in surveys and focus groups they wanted to customize the design handed down from the corporate level to accommodate their unique situation.

Employee surveys showed a prevalent perception that plan payout sums were "out of the control" of plant employees. Seventy-five percent of employees at plant A2 also said the payout formula was too complex.

Another large group of employees felt corporate managers didn't understand what realistic goal targets were for plant A2. Said one focus group participant: "I don't think there is a perfect (organizational unit incentive) formula, but I don't think the current formula was designed with employees in mind. It was designed as a carrot but sometimes we can't even smell it (the incentive)." Less than 20 percent of plant A2 employees said the payouts are fair compared to the effort needed to achieve them. (Remember that the payouts are capped at 5 percent of pay.)

Said a plant A2 manager: "If we're really looking for improvements in operations, we have to be willing to stand back and give these people the opportunity to make more mistakes, but I don't see patience in our management groups. Something new gets introduced and they want to see a benchmark [reached] immediately."

Some 70 percent of respondents at plant A2 disagreed when asked if "an increase in performance will lead to an increase in plan payout." Less than 30 percent believe the organizational unit incentive plan helps give their work group a sense of ownership in solving plant problems or improving the way the group works.

The bottom line for employees at plant A2: the plan hasn't been successful in helping employees better understand their own roles in plant success, nor in mobilizing them to improve plant performance. Added another manager: "The percentage pay isn't enough to motivate workers. The hourly workforce will protest more if they lose their free coffee than their organizational unit incentive plan." And another: "The theory is great but the execution is a bomb."

Yet the experience of plant A1 suggests that one of the biggest benefits of these plans is that—when well implemented and monitored—they can keep key strategic goals at the top of most employees' minds. At plant A1, 71 percent of survey respondents indicated the bonus plan reminds them what they need to do each day to help meet plant goals.

Said a plant A1 employee, referring to safety performance in a focus group discussion: "The plan is a tool for employees to become more aware of accidents and how to avoid them." A plant manager said, "It's just good business management to keep your employees informed, and to share responsibility with hourly and salaried employees."

Common Problems, Varying Remedies

Give Employees a Greater Sense of Control. The data suggest that employees at both plants do not believe they have as much influence over plan measures, and thus payouts, as they should.

MP's plant A1 operational measures do not have the intrinsic problem of a long line of sight that Acme's purely financial measures have. But not many measures can be insulated from outside influences and still reflect the organizational unit's performance. Plant A1 has customized reasonable line of sight measures. Employees will generally want measures they can directly control, but in this case that would require changing the level of measurement from plantwide down to the smaller unit level. If A1 was larger, say 500 or more employees, that might be a good approach, but with 125 employees it doesn't make much sense. The teamwork the plan has helped to create would be threatened. Management should ratchet up the frequency of communication and education about the measures, regularly updating employees about progress against goals, and actively engaging employees to address performance if off track.

Plant A2 has the same problems as other companies that have been acquired. It takes time and lots of hard work to integrate the existing culture and objectives with that of the new owner. Most of the time companies must just work through it, but when the process affects employee incentives—even if there were no incentives before the acquisition—people feel "put upon." Incentive plans are an opportunity to create a framework for teamwork and meeting the organization's needs, but if the management team doesn't feel it is their plan, they will not use it as effectively as they could. The CARS IV team suggested a redesign of the plan by a cross-functional team of plant A2 employees and managers, under the guidelines set up by corporate management. If plant A2 really does need a different plan, the team will be able to make a compelling case and gain the sense of ownership they require for the plan.

Consider Removing Existing Caps on Payout Levels. Survey results from both hourly and management employees in plant A1 suggests the existing cap on payouts was a demotivator, given the plant's pattern of success in reaching or exceeding plan goals. Managers as well as frontliners wondered if the cap— 5 percent of base pay—couldn't be increased as plant performance escalates to certain levels beyond targeted goals. In other words, if the performance goes up, the reward size also needs to rise, considering that the incentive is self-funding. Said one employee: "If we are constantly bumping up against the cap, why can't they release [raise] it?" Added a plant manager: "The incentive plan has been in effect for three years, and the payout cap is the only problem we've encountered." And finally, another MP manager: "If you go four or five years with the same payout, I have to believe the plan loses strength and impact."

It is not clear if raising the cap in plant A2 would help or hurt the situation. They only hit the cap twice in eight quarters, and considering the problems with the plan's design and operation, the lack of performance and payout may have been due solely to influences other than the plan. Raising the cap might be an option to be considered in the plan redesign, but only if it is determined there is a solid business reason to do so.

Ensure That Corporate Plan Goals Align with Plant Goals, and Scale Back Total Number of Goals. Using fewer measures to calculate organizational unit incentive payouts might improve employees' focus. With four measures, the plan is on the high side. People can't focus on a lot of measures, particularly if they need a good deal of education on what the measures mean and what they need to do to affect them. The real problem with four measures is the 5 percent cap. The amount riding on each measure is small, which results in people feeling a lack of connection between their contribution and the reward.

FOOD PROCESSING AND PACKAGING, INC. (FPP)

The three plants studied at Food Processing and Packaging, Inc., illustrate the challenge of implementing an organizational unit incentive plan in environments where there is low employee-management trust.

An organizational unit incentive plan was introduced to hourly employees at FPP as part of a broader initiative to increase employee involvement and productivity. CARS IV data indicate the largest obstacle to the plan's success is the existence of conflicting goals: employees and managers across the plants are rewarded based on different measures that are sometimes at cross-purposes.

The organizational unit incentive for hourly employees is based solely on productivity, generally defined as the amount of product (output) made during each hour worked by an employee (input). At FPP, the incentive is calculated using this formula: the actual packaged pounds for each product are multiplied by a standard "worker-hours per pound" multiple. These standard hours are compared to the "actual total hours paid" to determine the hours "gained." Fifty percent of that gain goes into an award pool for employee organizational unit incentives, with the remaining 50 percent going to plant profit. The employee pool is divided by the total hours worked in the plant to determine the payout per hour. Finally, each employee's actual hours worked are multiplied by the payout per hour to calculate an individual payout. Those payments are made twice each calendar year, in July and in December. This is a classic gain-sharing formula, developed by industrial engineers in the 1970s and still used in hundreds of manufacturing plants in North America.

The bonus for the plants' top management team is tied to overall profitability of the company. Middle management has a profit-sharing plan tied to bottom-line performance of the entire division (of which the three plants in the study are a part). Hourly employees (including team leaders) have the organizational unit incentive plan based on plant productivity.

Profit in the food business is directly affected by the cost of the food as raw material. All levels of management are reinforced to focus on reducing direct cost as the most immediate way to improve profit. Productivity at FPP takes only labor cost into account, so a productivity goal encourages reducing or maintaining labor cost while increasing production. Although profit and productivity should be aligned and complementary, in this case the hourly employees see them as conflicting objectives.

Adding to this, or perhaps because of it, is a history of employee-management mistrust in the plants. The CARS IV surveys showed a strong perception among hourly employees that management manipulates the plan numbers and intentionally makes decisions that reduce the total incentive payout for organizational units to increase short-term profit and, in turn, increase their own pay under the management bonus plan.

Consider the timely repair of faulty machinery. Some hourly employees indicated their payouts under the organizational unit incentive plan are low because management is not spending money to fix the machinery, which keeps costs down (favoring manager bonuses) but inhibits higher productivity (negatively influencing organizational unit incentive payouts).

In addition, according to employee survey data, plant management is often hesitant to share with hourly employees important financial data that might help the employees better understand how their actions contribute to plant profit or loss. Employees think this is because management believes front-liners are incapable of understanding the data and the calculations for organizational unit incentives. Surveys, especially at the two poorer performing plants, suggest hourly employees feel management is intentionally not educating them and makes little effort to engage them in improving performance through teamwork.

Hourly employees are paid overtime and it is the most direct way to increase personal income. Overtime is a management decision that is driven by staffing and demand for product. But because overtime has a negative effect on the way productivity is calculated at FPP, a management call for overtime sends a message that conflicts with the organizational unit incentive plan.

Table 5.7 gives results from organizational unit incentive plans at FPP's three plants over four years.

Table 5.7. Organizational Unit Incentive Plan Performance at Food Processing and Packaging.

Plant	Average Payout per Employee per Year	Number of Years Payout Earned (of 4)	Average Payout per Year (when there was a payout)	Total Payout (4 years)	Estimated Value Added	Value Added as Percentage of Payout
Red	$850[a]	4	$850	$1,243,000	$2,486,000	200%[d]
Blue	$350	2	$680	$270,000	$540,000[b]	200%[d]
Green	$50	2	$100[c]	$182,000	$364,000	200%[d]

[a]At the Red plant, a large error in calculating an organizational unit incentive payout in the last of the four years—a six-figure miscalculation—also didn't do much to increase employees' trust of management. The explanation was that the calculation was never properly audited. Said one employee in a focus group: "Twice since we've had the organizational unit incentive plan, management said it made a 'mistake' and took more than the promised half of the total payout (for company profit)." For three years, the payout was about $1000. The fourth it dropped to $225.

[b] The Blue plant calculated a productivity gain for the first two years, with a payout of about $700 per employee. The last two years there was a loss in productivity and no payouts.

[c] The Green plant improved productivity in the first and fourth years, but modestly. The payouts were $145 and $68, respectively. At that level, the payouts tend to be more insulting than anything. The plan showed a significant loss of productivity in the middle two years and, of course, there were no payouts.

[d] Due to plan design: 50-50 split of gains with employees.

Making Improvements

The company has made attempts to improve communication about the plan by establishing organizational unit incentive committees at each plant. The committees, which have both management and hourly members, are charged with explaining the details of the plan to employees—why measures were chosen, how payout calculations are made, and progress against goals. Although some committees have voiced a desire to help employees discover ways to improve their plan numbers, management prefers they confine their role to explaining the details of the existing plans.

Only 47 percent of employees at the Red plant (the most successful plan user of the three) felt their organizational unit incentive plan fit in well with the way they work in the organization. Because the plan emphasizes volume, many employees also felt product quality was sacrificed in the process. The concerns focused on business issues rather than trust, at least until the calculation change was made.

Management had indicated its goal at the Red plant was to communicate details and progress against incentive plan metrics every quarter. In reality, say surveys, those meetings occur only twice a year. That limited communication is reflected in the survey responses: only one-third of plant employees said they fully understood how the plan works, and only 36 percent said they know at any given time if they are on track for earning an award, and how large it might be. Commented one hourly employee: "Employees here in general need more communication and education. If employees don't ask questions, they're left in the dark."

Said one Red plant manager: "The intention is for each person to be able to see the direct connection between his or her own work and reaching the plan objectives, and to have an awareness of a common work connection. I'd love to have both, but I think both are low right now. Many do not see the big picture."

In the Blue plant only 24 percent of hourly employees said their manager helps them "do what it takes" to earn an award, and less than a third (32 percent) feel the amount of the reward they're eligible for is fair compared to the amounts managers can earn. Only 25 percent reported understanding how the organizational unit incentive calculation actually works.

Said one Blue manager: "The organizational unit incentive plan isn't understood by hourly employees, and as a salaried employee, I don't understand it well enough myself to explain it. There is too little communication about the plan."

An hourly employee at Blue echoed the comments: "Few employees have a clue about how many product cases were packaged and if a goal was met. They don't know how they're performing on a day-to-day basis against goals; therefore they can't understand organizational unit incentive." Only 39 percent of plant management and 33 percent of hourly employees said they think the organization does a good job of communicating the ongoing status of the plan.

At the Green plant, trust was an equally large issue. So too was finding time in increasingly busy schedules to spend on the incentive plan. Convincing employees fatigued from repeated overtime shifts to summon the energy and interest to learn about line items on a profit-and-loss statement, or how to calculate complex incentive payouts, can be difficult.

In all FPP plants, the common issue seems to stem from a lack of alignment between manager and employee incentive plans. This is compounded by the employee plan's use of only one measure, productivity; by the complex calculations for that measure; and by a lack of trust, engagement, and effective communications, making for tough sledding. Considering the history, consideration should be given to a more balanced set of measures with clearer calculations as a fresh start. Recognizing this, FPP has begun an in-depth review of its plans and how to make them more effective.

MAJOR FINDINGS FROM THE CARS IV DATA

Up to this point the discussion has centered on specific plants and their experience. As part of the case studies, CARS researchers also reviewed incentive plan documents, communication materials, employee payout levels, and to the extent possible, the financial effect of the plans on the respective organizations and plants. Analysis of the CARS IV data, interviews, and surveys yields these key lessons:

- Good implementation can overcome slightly flawed design. In the cases studied, the differences in local plant implementation and support drove incentive plan effectiveness twice as much as differences in plan design.

- Contrary to popular belief, the size of payouts did not unduly influence employees' overall satisfaction with the plans.

- The strongest driver of a culture that supports incentive plan effectiveness is the plant manager, and through that manager's example, the direct supervisors of people. Likewise, a key indicator of plan success is the level of trust hourly employees have in management regarding the plan design, fairness in setting measures, and payout opportunities. Not surprisingly, plants where a high level of trust and a supportive, communicative culture was evident outperformed plants where a more antagonistic culture was present.

- Organizational unit incentive plans are a complement to, not a replacement for, a well-thought-out and articulated business strategy. Particularly in smaller organizations, there's a risk that an organizational unit incentive plan can become a substitute for active strategic management.

- One element that separates effective from ineffective plans is how well employees understand the measurements, and what they can do each day to influence them.

- Organizational unit incentives are a reward *and* recognition mechanism. Most employees don't believe they work harder as a result of the plan, but they do appreciate the recognition for a job well done.

- Cost control in plans is important, but extremely tightly controlled incentive plans tend to evolve into cost control exercises, not a management tool designed to educate and reward employees for their contributions to boosting company performance.

- In successful incentive plans, managers keep communicating about the plan regardless of good or bad times. In good times, employees need to understand that incentive payouts aren't a given or an entitlement, and that they must continuously improve performance to ensure payouts. In times of poor performance resulting in small or no payouts, companies need to resist a natural urge to stop communicating about the plan. Instead, this should be used as an opportunity to reinforce what it takes to be successful, to be honest about any factors outside of employees' control that may have influenced plan results, and to use concrete examples of what employees might do to help get the plan get back on track. Also, incentive plans should be reassessed annually to ensure they still reward the objectives needed for organizational success and that measures provide an appropriate line of sight for employees.

- Organizational unit incentive plans, by design, do not reward individual performance. Where it is possible and desirable to measure individual performance within plans, companies can combine organizational unit incentive plans with individual rewards. This allows managers to reward for team effort while differentiating individual performance.

- How much employees think about the plan is a key indicator of its effectiveness. Is it at the top of their mind in their daily or weekly responsibilities, for instance? Or do they only think about it at the end of the month or quarter when results are posted?

- It may go without saying, but most plant employees are not interested in incentive opportunities at the expense of their base salaries.

- Organizational unit incentive plans must be aligned with other human resource systems and the messages they send—most critically, the performance management or appraisal process—to ensure that the pay-for-performance message inherent in organizational unit incentives is reinforced by other systems. Employees must be held accountable in annual performance reviews for how they perform as part of a work team or unit as well as how they do individually. If you stress teamwork but measure and pay people based solely on individual accomplishment, your systems are at dangerous cross-purposes.

- If there's a silver bullet, it's this: Use good design principles and communicate, educate, engage, and celebrate! Continually "work" the plan as you would any key business strategy. Operating a plan on autopilot usually invites employees to put it on their own back burners.

CHAPTER SIX

What We've Learned: Lessons from the Trenches

W hat have we learned? This chapter summarizes how you can best utilize project, recognition, and group incentive plans to improve teamwork and organizational performance.

CUSTOMIZE THE PLAN

Any reward and recognition plan must be customized to the organization in question. What worked at OMI probably wouldn't have worked at Chase. Rockwell's business objectives and culture are as different from Mid-States as Ameritech's is from that of Donnelley. Focus on the best principles to meet your company's needs, not on the so-called best practices some experts say you should impress on your organization.

Plans that reward and recognize teamwork depend on a variety of factors. So trying to use anyone else's plan intact in your organization would be unlikely to work. But there are ways to design new plans or revise old ones.

In the CARS IV research, Materials Processing's plant A2, newly acquired from another company, installed the plan that worked just fine with plant A1. It was significantly less effective because it was not customized to the unique culture and desired objectives of A2. Consideration should always be given to customizing a plan to the organizational unit (see the box on the next page for examples). The area of the country, type of employee and management team, history, operating

---

CUSTOMIZATION

The need for customization is true even for project incentive plans to reward cost reduction and revenue enhancement. These plans typically use the same tried and true formula for a variety of industries. Examples are UtiliCorp and Community Health Care. They are in different industries with very different employees, yet the formula and process for their plan look very much the same: teams come up with ideas, do the research, propose the changes, and get rewarded for the results. Both use noncash awards.

However, each company has customized this formula. For example, their performance-reward schedules differ. UtiliCorp uses a catalog of merchandise, and CHC awards a debit card to be used with a wide range of stores and national merchandise catalogs. One company awards teams for approved ideas, and the other pays half the award on approval and the other half on implementation. The communication, promotion, and idea-processing systems are also customized for each organization.

---

norms, and what a site needs to accomplish for success are often different. Sometimes it can be handled by the way performance is measured—different sites have different baselines—and often different measures are necessary.

Let's go back to Susan Vitale and the BIZCOM scenario and see how what we've learned from the cases applies to her situation. Recall that she did customize her plan to the organization. Here's a quick review of her reward and recognition plan.

Susan made no major changes in the organization's base pay and benefits plan where they attempt to remain competitive in their labor market while monitoring turnover rates and recruitment efforts. They continue to reinforce their capabilities through development programs. They also provide a limited number of individual incentives tailored to special needs such as signing bonuses for hard-to-attract people.

Key changes began with the elimination of the employee of the month, quarter, and year, and the Chairman's awards. They were replaced with a spot bonus plan that allows supervisors and managers to recognize team players and teams that make a contribution. Peer nominations, run through their supervisor or manager, are also encouraged. The spot bonus plan is facilitated by a cross-functional, multilevel team with a rotating membership. Susan serves as the team's champion.

Susan gave managers a set of guidelines for a project team award. However, she wants the award given judiciously and only for projects that make a major contribution to the success of their organizational unit or the company.

Susan's biggest intervention is an organization unit incentive. Her design team developed a plan that makes all employees eligible for incentives based on how well the organization does on two levels: total organization revenue growth, and department level cycle time and a customized departmental measure. Measurements are recorded monthly with payouts made annually.

ALIGN PLANS WITH BUSINESS OBJECTIVES

Successful plans supplement and reinforce the practical objectives of the organization. A plan should not be merely a nice thing to do for the employees. It may well be nice, but it will not survive as a strategy for business improvement unless it constantly reinforces business objectives.

In some cases, you need to be specific. The traditional financial measures of performance are alive and well as the primary focus of reward plans, but they are being complemented by a scorecard that reflects internal operational and customer-oriented measures. Rockwell Automation uses local measures to reflect performance from the bottom up and then modifies the incentive payout based on how well the overall organization does on operating return on sales—a critical financial measure. The scorecard is being used in most unit incentive plans, with changes in measures that reflect the demands of the business and the market. Great Plains Software customizes each of its project team incentives and recognition to the need at hand. Whether the company is driving to a new software release date or coming up with new and innovative approaches to a highly competitive market, the plan always fits the business need.

In other cases you can be general. Bayer's reinforcement of continuous improvement reflects a belief that investing in people and recognizing their contributions pays off financially, although the linkage between the plans and the financial gains is not a direct one. Quality is the watchword at OMI and it recognizes a wide range of contributions, including community involvement. Chase has learned that the general objectives of being the employer and investor of choice requires allowing the employees to decide what behavior and contribution is worthy of recognition.

Specific or general, however, plans must be aligned. Most of the case studies in this book are of companies that have more than one plan, often supporting organizational unit incentives with recognition plans. They combine the specific with the general. Project and organizational unit incentive plans offer the opportunity for specific return on incentive investments. Recognition plans are a pure investment in creating an environment where the contributions of people are appreciated and celebrated. They have a common focus on what makes the business perform better, and that is the keystone for success through teamwork.

Susan has kept her eye on the mark. She has aligned the organizational unit incentive plan with the organization's business objectives while bringing it closer to the employees' line of sight with department measures. The "combo platter" group incentive that includes two levels of measures—overall organizational revenue growth with two department-specific measures—is a creative intervention. It meets the goal of being simultaneously general and specific.

SEND THE RIGHT MESSAGE

Recognition plans and their cultural messages are intertwined. Both can support an effective culture of teamwork or, inadvertently, work against it. There seems to be a basic conflict between making sure outstanding performers are treated they way they deserve—special rewards, publicity, special assignments—and trying to get everyone working together as a team. It is easy to create winners—the few—and losers—everyone who is not a winner.

Organizations want it both ways: reinforce teamwork *and* outstanding contributors. Continual reinforcement of teamwork is a business strategy. It is much more difficult and time-consuming to the organization than picking and rewarding a few outstanding contributors. One of the many valuable learnings of these cases is the creativity they use to address this issue.

Create Many Winners, Few Losers

Competition is healthy is the marketplace, but it can be destructive and often demotivating in the workplace. Most companies in this book have done away with the "winner-take-all" award plan model. Some select the best or winning team, but they recognize many others who participated and thus contributed to the success of the company. The rule of thumb in regard to recognizing teams and individuals is, the more the merrier.

ASCAP's variable pay plan allows all account services teams that hit their targets to receive payouts that represent a percentage of each member's base pay. Even their Sales Team of the Year plan isn't a winner-take-all award. All teams that exceed their goals are invited to the awards ceremony and receive a plaque along with company merchandise.

Ralston Purina Company's centerpiece recognition plan, Best of Breed, selects a winning team but also acknowledges the runners-up with cash and commemorative items. In addition, the Top Dog, Great Dane, and Bulldog plans are other ways for more people to be recognized.

Bayer's highly coveted PAA plan also provides various forms of recognition to all teams that submit award applications. The recognition continues through the many stages of the total process that culminates with ten finalists.

Chase's Service Star is perhaps the most inclusive of recognition plans. It focuses on the core values the company needs to be the employer of choice and investor of choice: teamwork, customer focus, initiative, respect, quality, and professionalism. All employees are able to recognize their peers for contributing to the core values. For other awards fewer people are selected, but the plan's foundation is broad and open to all.

Involve Employees in the Selection Process

Many companies in our sample have found that a peer voting process increases the impact of the plan. When employees have say in the selection of teams for awards, they see the plan as open, honest, and fair.

A joint nonmanagement and management committee at every level drives the selection process at Bayer. Then, in a rather unique twist, the winning team is selected by a vote of the other nine finalists based on clear criteria and documentation of their work.

In Merck's recognition plan any team or individual can nominate any other team or person in the plant for a variety of reasons. They have to provide the reasons for the award, but are free to give them out as they see fit. The plan uses rotating teams of employees to serve on the steering committee to sift through the nominations for the team bonus of stock options, but after selecting the finalists, the teams themselves make the final selection.

CARS IV's Technology and Manufacturing found that their employees wanted to be more involved in setting the measures and goals. It creates ownership where it belongs—in the eyes of both management and the core employees. For those suspicious management teams that think this is just a way to give the store away by setting low goals on less important measures, it is rarely the case. Employees are very responsible when given the opportunity to become involved. They often set more meaningful and tougher goals on more appropriate measures than the top management team. After all, the employees know what works and what doesn't. They are closer to the day-to-day work.

Markem found it necessary to avoid a "bake-sale" voting process by asking a steering committee to select the team finalists for the European trip. Then they turn it over to the people. After reviewing displays of each team's accomplishments, all the people in the plant vote in a secret ballot for their choice. Carefully considered but limited choices got the focus off of personalities and onto the value of the team's contributions.

Trust the Folks

It is too bad that management has to be reminded that employees are adults. Too often policies, communications, efforts to educate, and reward plans reflect adults talking to children. Treat employees like adults and they will act like adults.

Acme's Plant 1 has the highest ratings of any plant in the CARS IV study with essentially the same measures in Plans 2 and 3 that had some of the lowest. The difference seems to be engagement, with which comes open two-way communications and trust.

Susan eliminated "beauty contests" such as employee of the month that created a small happy pool of winners and a large group of disgruntled losers. Her empowerment of the managers and supervisors to give out spot awards, supported by an employee-based team that monitors the plan, is positive. As Susan's plan also allows employees to nominate individual team players and teams, they have the best of both worlds. Susan has involved employees in the process but she has also acknowledged the importance of the role of managers and supervisors in the reward and recognition process.

In almost every case, particularly Donnelley, Chase, Markem, Ralston Purina Company, and Bayer, the message "we trust you" is reinforced by management allowing and then relying on the employees themselves to nominate, select, and celebrate those who make significant contributions. This cultural message is an essential element for true teamwork.

USE NONCASH AS WELL AS CASH AWARDS

Many of our case organizations use noncash awards because of their staying power. Everyone loves money, but cash payments can lose their motivational impact over time. However, noncash awards carry trophy value that has great staying power because each time you look at that television set or plaque you are reminded of what you or your team did to earn it. Each of the plans encourages awards that are coveted by the recipients and, therefore, will be memorable.

If you ask employees what they want, they will invariably say cash. But providing it can be difficult if the budget is small or the targeted earnings in an incentive plan are modest. If you pay out more often than annually and take taxes out, the net amount may look pretty small, even cheap. Noncash awards tend to be more dependent on their symbolic value than their financial value.

Noncash awards come in all forms: a simple thank-you, a letter of congratulations, time off with pay, a trophy, company merchandise, a plaque, gift certificates, special services, a dinner for two, a free lunch, a credit to a card issued by the company for purchases at local stores, specific items or merchandise, merchandise from an extensive catalogue, travel for business or a vacation with the family, and stock options. Only the creativity and imagination of the plan creators limit the choices.

Noncash Awards Are Not Limited to Recognition Plans

Plans that focus on ideas for cost reduction and revenue enhancement generally pay out in cash, based on a straight percentage of savings. Successful project incentive plans at UtiliCorp and CHC, however, reward with points for merchandise, ranging in value from a few dollars to $5,000 per idea. The use of significant noncash awards makes the plans even more powerful because the team member's family often chooses the awards. The recognition value is present both at work and at home.

Three of the eleven plans at Technology and Manufacturing operations, covered in the CARS IV research, use noncash awards in organizational unit incentive plans. The recognition value of these awards reinforces the message of the plans and the performance of the people by increasing their awareness.

Perhaps the most memorable noncash award is Markem's team trip to Europe. For most of the recipients it is the trip of a lifetime. And they not only remember it for years; they share their stories with others in the plant. The purpose is business and the reinforcement is very personal.

Bayer's President's Achievement Awards is a companywide plan that recognizes teams at various stages in a multilevel selection process with the ten finalists attending a lavish three-day celebration at company headquarters. Recognition for teams that do not make it to the finals means an award and the publication of their names and accomplishments in a company publication. Chase also uses a gala trip to New York to reward its SuperStars, plus a $5,000 cash award. Each SuperStar can bring a guest on the trip, making it an even more memorable event.

Great Plains mixes the types of awards within the same plans. It knows that some things need a cash award—such as completing a tough project under difficult deadlines—and that some just need a sincere thank-you. They know that the Friends List is critical for those who support a project team and the Pioneer Days event fills the need to celebrate their heritage and give people the opportunity to share their ideas. Great Plains has found that kind of recognition as powerful as any tangible award.

Give a Few Big Awards and Lots of Small Ones

The currency of recognition plans is lots of smaller awards. Although a thank-you honestly given is often enough, sometimes small tangible awards leave a more lasting impression. They need to be given close to the event or contribution. Waiting for days or weeks after the team does its work is just too late. Immediacy is critical and, surprisingly, not as expensive. An award worth $100 given right after the contribution is more powerful than an award of many times that amount given several months later.

Merck's Reasons to Celebrate Recognition Plan distributes certificates to team members for noncash items such as one video rental a week for a year, courtesy time off, or a new set of tires. The Tag You Win plan at OMI issues Quality Bucks that are redeemable for OMI merchandise at the company store, a lunch or dinner, movie tickets, gift certificates at a local store, and many other possibilities. Award givers are encouraged to tailor the award to the recipients. Donnelley uses gift certificates to reward for their myriad of games.

Ameritech's merit plan for self-directed teams is tied to a quarterly payout system. This is especially useful in a culture that includes lots of movement in and out of teams, but the organization finds that it also provides an incentive that supports desired behaviors.

Similarly, ASCAP's variable pay for teams is paid quarterly, but an awards plan that selects monthly, quarterly, and annual winners among sales teams supplements it. Progress toward their goals are measured by automated daily cash receipts and monthly revenue reports. As a result, team members are acutely aware of how close they are to accomplishing their goals for the quarter.

Donnelley's games result in annual winners but each month teams that perform best against their goals also receive an award. In addition, any team that beats its monthly goal, regardless of whether it wins or not, is rewarded.

Pay the Taxes on Noncash Awards

Employees expect to pay taxes on their base pay. They are often surprised, however, when they are taxed on a special or spot bonus in cash. Employees expect their cash bonus to be $1,000 as announced, and are surprised when the check is $720. It takes the punch away. They resent being taxed on noncash awards, although the IRS requires it to be reported as regular income. The answer is a common practice: grossing up. A 28 percent federal tax, plus state and local taxes, are added to the fair market value (or cost) of the award and reported as such on W-2 statements. The company pays the tax as part of the cost of the award. This additional cost is simply part of the investment in awards to reinforce employees for the contributions they make.

You do not have to have tangible awards alone. There is a lot to be said for pride of accomplishment through teamwork. Lotus says that bonus money is important, but primarily a satisfier. It was the experience of working as a team to successfully complete an extremely difficult project that kept all of the team members on board when it may have been easy to jump ship for more pay elsewhere.

Susan Vitale's spot award plan calls for awards up to $500 to be either in cash or merchandise from a catalogue. Susan might want to consider making all *awards under $500 paid in merchandise from a catalog. Given the organization described in the scenario, $500 in cash will probably have little impact on an individual and less if it is distributed to a team. However, the symbolic value of a noncash award will have long-term meaning for the recipient and, perhaps, for his or her family as well.*

COMMUNICATE, COMMUNICATE, COMMUNICATE

Every case study interview reinforced the importance of communication. Communication in rewarding and recognizing teamwork has a number of components:

- Education—how the measures work and what they can do to contribute to improving performance
- Performance feedback—telling people how they are doing
- Rewarding frequently—performance feedback is more powerful when attached to an award
- Message reinforcement—"these are our cultural values and this is how we make them real"
- Role modeling—showing how people contributed

Never Assume People Understand

Ask and educate. Employees are very resourceful and intelligent, but they are rarely well informed on business issues. If an organization assumes people know what profit is and how it can be influenced, it is probably wrong. Open-book management (often applied as "The Great Game of Business") has grown as a methodology based on improving business literacy in all employees, regardless of their role. The success of Donnelley and one of the three Acme plants in the CARS IV research reflect the power of giving everyone the opportunity to learn and understand.

Even something as seemingly obvious as the core value of teamwork may not be clearly understood. What is it? Working harder to contribute to the team's performance? What is the team? The work group? The company? The task force? How do I contribute? Do I share what I know and how do I modify my style so other team members will hear what I say? It is not as simple as the plan designers may think.

Not that employees are children who need to be reeducated. You don't want to spend a great deal of time educating in areas they already understand. So once you decide what to reinforce—values, specific measures, or general areas of contribution—check out what the employees understand and what they don't. Recognition, project incentive, and organizational unit incentive plans provide an opportunity to educate everyone about what can make a difference in the organization.

Donnelley makes sure that every game has a plan for educating employees about the business, how the objectives of the game relate to the business, and how they can influence the performance. The performance influence element focuses on the problems or obstacles to improvement—making a classic continuous improvement strategy very real to everyone participating in the game.

Mid-States' employees understand how to influence results for a number of reasons. It is a relatively small company and the line of sight to profit is direct. The company's owners are willing to share information so people can understand how the numbers are kept and what they mean. Finally, they allow employees to share in the decision-making process, including welcoming and training new employees, even though it may reduce their share of the profit "bucket." The present employees understand how new people can increase their sales performance and are quick to make sure they know how to contribute. As you would expect, they are also quick to act when they think the new person is a drag on performance, rather than a contributor.

Tell People How They Are Doing—All the Time

Participants in project and organizational unit incentive plans need and want to know how they're doing. It is a continual process, limited only by how available the data is. If you wait until the end of the quarter or year to tell people how the incentive plan is doing, they will not know where to direct their efforts. A Web site that is constantly updated with performance measures is being introduced in organizations with intranets and technology will soon allow the Internet to be used in a secure environment. A big scoreboard in the cafeteria that reports on progress adds to the excitement of the plan and motivates team members to keep going. It also adds to the fun. Companies in this book and in every case in the CARS IV data find that with feedback of performance comes the opportunity to continually educate and align people's efforts.

Donnelley's two games—the Derby Dash and NASCAR '98—both have a large scoreboard posted in the work area that reports on how each group is doing against its predetermined goals.

Texas Guaranteed Student Loan Corporation does the same thing on a monthly basis. It is more than a formal reporting process. Managers take on personal accountability to make sure everyone understands how the groups are doing and what they can do to improve. This manager-employee dialogue is an integral part of all the cases. The highest level of employee trust is in the immediate manager. Texas Guaranteed makes sure management owns the plan as an opportunity to improve performance through processes and subprocesses (organizational units) and individuals.

Merck's pay for performance plan makes a one-time payment to employees for hitting annual plant goals. In an effort to maintain motivation and improve line of sight, Merck holds regular meetings with employees throughout the year to explain the measures and report results.

Reinforce the Messages

The feedback of performance is pretty straightforward. Putting it into context and adding things to think about is a discipline many organizations don't have. Those that do are leveraging their investment in communications.

Chase makes sure that every time an employee recognizes a peer it is for demonstrating its core values. They want to make sure the employee writes on the nomination exactly which values they are recognizing. The process reinforces the message to both the nominator and the nominee.

Rockwell Automation focuses its CSMIP plan on very specific measures, but reinforces the message of teamwork and cooperation with a continual stream of communications through their plan champions.

Ameritech Audit found that it not only had to reinforce the message of teamwork and the individual contributions to team performance to their employees, but to the managers of the teams as well. We often take management ownership and support for granted and that is a mistake. They need reminders and reinforcement. Texas Guaranteed made sure the support is there by creating a management incentive based on how well organizational units work together.

CARS IV's Acme spends a good deal of time and energy on educating employees about how the business works and about finance. Its challenge is reinforcing the message while engaging the workforce to take action. It takes more than education to make a difference through teamwork. That does not negate the power of educating people through open-book management, but unless people feel they are making a contribution and management uses the plan as an active feedback and reinforcement tool, it will not be as effective as it could be.

Susan should not assume that the employees "get it." She should not assume they understand and have absorbed the intent of the rewards and recognition programs. It will be easy for her to make this assumption because the workforce is primarily scientific and technical people with advanced degrees. They may be smart, but they are not necessarily educated in business, organizational objectives, and measurements. Susan should take this as a great opportunity to educate as well as reward.

Role Modeling Works

There are a number of reasons for role modeling. First, we want other teams to know what type of performance is valued so it may serve as an incentive to them. Second, we want to share learning throughout the organizations so that others can benefit from their work. Third, we want the reasons behind the decision to be open so that everyone will see the rewards plan as fair. Finally, the publicity for the award is another form of recognition for the teams. Just about all of the organizations in our sample include stories about the awards in their internal company newspaper, some have innovative ways of publicly recognizing team accomplishments.

A word of caution: some individuals are embarrassed to be publicly recognized. Understand the difference between secrecy and respect for privacy. Ask for permission if you want to publicize an individual's contribution. If she doesn't want publicity, you can talk about the contribution without attribution. That's not secretiveness—just respect for an individual's wishes.

Each team award finalist at Markem creates two storyboards that describe their project. One is on display in the company cafeteria and the other travels to all departments, where it stays for several days at a time.

Donnelley creates large team game scoreboards on performance to date that are posted in the work area for everyone to see.

Bayer teams create their own three- to four-minute video highlighting the work of the team awards finalists. The videos, a welcome alternative to the twenty-page written summary, are made available to units throughout the company.

To implement its goal of sharing team best practices, Ralston prepares a booklet that describes the accomplishments of all recognized teams. However, the company takes it one step further by publishing quarterly Recognition News Notes highlighting associates who have been recognized, giving their phone numbers so others can contact them for more information.

ASCAP uses its annual conference in Atlanta to both reward and role-model high-performing sales and account service teams.

CREATE A SMORGASBORD OF PLANS

Organizations with a significant commitment to rewards and recognition use a variety of plans to achieve their goals. They realize that organizational unit incentives that pay out annually need to be supported by team accomplishments. They understand that some team contributions require an immediate acknowledgment that goes beyond a thank-you or a $50 gift certificate. In other words, a team-based organization needs a rewards and recognition basket that contains diverse options.

Our case studies make sure there is alignment between their plans and their business objectives or values. One plan cannot do it all. It often takes a combination to touch most, if not all, of the bases. Make sure that objectives and messages of your plans are not in conflict with each other or your business objectives.

Merck, for example, has a major organizational unit incentive that provides payouts for hitting annual plantwide targets. It is buttressed by a very active peer-based recognition plan that acknowledges important team contributions with noncash awards throughout the year and a quarterly stock option reward plan for exemplary teamwork.

OMI has a multitiered recognition plan that provides people with a variety of options. It starts with the Tag You Win plan that is designed to acknowledge all the great things that teams and team players do every day, including the Soaring Eagle, an award reserved for extraordinary team accomplishments; the Golden Apple, given to teams who participate in volunteer community service projects; and Partners in Performance, a unit incentive that pays bonuses to everyone in a facility for hitting specific business goals.

Ralston Purina Company has a wide variety of recognition plans at the regional level, such as Best of Breed for individuals and sales teams, the Top Dog award that allows team members to recognize teammates, the Great Dane award that goes to one sales team in the region for achieving superior results, and the Bulldog award for a team member who demonstrates tenacity in overcoming a major obstacle. Thank-you notes also allow individuals to recognize each other for going that extra mile. All focus on the business objectives of sales team results and business process improvement.

Susan needs to make sure that the spot awards are given for contributions to departmental or organizational objectives. The message is not "thanks for doing a good job" but "thanks for reducing the time it takes to bring a new product to the market." For example, an award given to the CONPRO team might state it was for a plan for eliminating three redundant steps from the development process resulting in a reduction in time to market of sixty days.

BUDGET FOR RECOGNITION ACTIVITIES

Many organizations pay for team recognition activities from general operating expenses. There is no line item in the budget for team rewards and recognition. However, as they see the importance and value of a regular plan of team awards, they see the need for a designated pot of money in the budget. Progressive organizations send a clear message that they expect these funds to be spent.

At Merck, each business unit and support group has a recognition budget for the Reasons to Celebrate Plan. The only complaints come from people who feel some units do not spend enough of their recognition allocation.

Ralston Purina Company's regionwide recognition plans are funded with a specific budgeted amount. The amount has grown over the years as the number of employees in the region has increased.

Each organizational unit at OMI has a reward and recognition budget for the various plans administered at that level. Each unit spends about 2 percent of its labor costs on recognition.

Susan wants to budget for recognition at the highest organizational level, rather than at the deparment level. Good idea. Some managers may see their department budget not being spent at the end of the year and give it out just to get the money for the next year. Some managers have the idea they are saving the company money by not giving out awards. Both are wrong. The goal is to get people to spend the money and do it regularly. The payoff from a recognition plan only comes by using it.

KEEP ADMINISTRATION IN MIND

Make sure you can administer the project and organizational unit incentive plans you design. Administration sounds like a detail, but it can derail the best of plans. It covers a number of areas. The ability to collect, process, and feed back performance data is perhaps the most important. Most business data is developed for reasons other than measuring performance. It is used for financial purposes, planning, process development, and general management reporting. It is often not in the right form for communicating back to employees how they are doing. Quite often you will discover that measures relied upon for years are not accurate enough for performance measurement purposes. There is a unique emphasis on measures reflecting what is really happening in the workplace when rewards are contingent upon them.

Quick turnaround of performance data is also important. Few things are more useless that information based on sixty-day-old data. You should try to feed back performance within five to ten working days after the end of the measured period.

Finally, keeping track of what project teams are doing, the nominations for recognition, and performance for incentives requires close monitoring. If you have a smaller organization, sophisticated tracking systems are not necessary. But a large organization, depending on the type of plans, can present some real issues that need to be thought out during the design phase.

Chase felt it was necessary to use an outside vendor to provide software and a database to handle the reward fulfillment, tracking, and reporting requirements. The existing local systems were incompatible with one another. Global management of the information was not just an efficient way to handle things, but critical to the success of the plan.

UtiliCorp and CHC also use special software and custom-designed administration systems to deal with the progress of thousands of ideas, each with supporting documentation, evaluation, approval (or nonapproval), implementation, and award issuance. They found it helpful to also track the evaluation committee processing to identify bottlenecks and smooth out the system.

Food Processing and Packaging, Inc., in the CARS IV study, decided during the operation of its most successful plans that it had not been accurate in calculating the value of the productivity increases, and payouts plummeted. Right or wrong, the sent message was "we made a mistake for years," but the message received was "management will make more money on its profit-based plan if we recalculate productivity to reduce payouts." A lot of good will and trust can be lost for a long time by changing the rules and the calculations during the plan's payout periods.

The good news is that investment in these systems creates an opportunity to refine plans as the demands of business change.

PAYOFFS ARE IN THE EYE OF THE BEHOLDER

The CARS IV research has investigated the return on the investments in organizational unit incentive plans since 1989. The very structure of these plans demands specific measures of performance improvement and it seems reasonable to calculate the value of the gains and compare them to the costs of the plan. For those who could provide the data (slightly less than half), the median return was $2.22 for every $1 of cost.

In the CARS IV study, the Materials Processing plants and Food Processing and Packaging reported from 200 to 540 percent gross return on their payouts. Technology and Manufacturing, Inc., management said its plans had contributed significantly to meeting the $157 million performance improvement objective. Acme pays out on meeting and beating financial targets.

Impressive, but it misses the point. Organizations can certainly make money from these plans, but it is surprising how difficult they find putting a dollar value to improvements in quality, productivity, customer satisfaction, cycle time, and the like. Even measures based on accepted financial procedures are challenged as being affected by influences other than employee-contributed improvement. The CARS IV findings confirm what our intuition and experience have told us for years. These plans are less about making a return on payout than they are about creating a framework for teamwork, employee engagement, education, and contribution.

In the majority of the case studies, the management team and employees felt the concept of the plans are good for them and good for the organization. Perhaps Great Plains comes closest to demonstrating the effect of proactive plans that attempt to touch all their employees in meaningful ways. The software business is rampant with turnover problems and Great Plains has dropped to an all-time low of 3.5 percent. Low turnover can be attributed to a lot of things, but the company believes its plans demonstrate the value placed on intellectual capital enough to constantly invest in it. That has a profound effect on turnover and, in turn, on the company's performance.

Project incentive plans contribute whatever management decides the project is worth. Most projects are to solve problems or develop products or services. These projects are considered important enough to invest people's time and energy. The cost of incentives is usually the least of the costs. They provide the process for engagement and contribution.

Employee-driven project teams that focus on cost and revenue are different. These cases and those reported in previous works have shown millions of dollars saved and earned for an acceptable cost in employee awards, communication, and administration. Teamwork is the hallmark of these plans.

Recognition plans are a clear investment in organizational values, outstanding teams (and individuals), a culture of cooperation and appreciation, and heightened awareness that the organization believes that its employees are critical to success. These plans take work and constant energizing and all our cases claim their organizations are better for them.

Susan needs to keep her eye on the ball. She has to remember the objective: create and support teamwork and collaboration. The fact that the plan requires specific measures and provides the possibility of a return on their investment is good and probably a business necessity. These are dynamic business strategies, requiring regular assessments for effectiveness. Performance data, employee surveys, and focus groups can be used to see if objectives are being met.

HOW PLANS ARE INTRODUCED AND OPERATED IS PARAMOUNT

Introduction and operation are twice as important as design. A well-introduced, well-operated incentive plan of average design will always do better than a poorly introduced, poorly operated one with a great design. The CARS IV backs this up. Although there were complaints about the line of sight being too long and complexity of design, the overwhelming issues focused on introduction and operation. That translates to management support and its ownership of the plan as a business strategy. Education, communication, feedback, and, most important, employee engagement drive success.

The incentive award itself is more a recognition of the importance of people to an organization's success than its size. It has to be large enough not to be insulting—at least 2 to 3 percent of base pay—and considered fair in relationship to the improved performance—payouts running from about 3 to 20 percent, depending on the level of the employee. Noncash awards in incentive plans run less, often under $1000. The real issue is how the plan is used.

Incentive plans should be introduced through the natural management chain. The objective is to create ownership in the plan by all levels of the organization. Effective implementation follows some basic rules:

- *Roll out the plan down through the normal management and supervisory chain.* The most important level of trust exists between a manager and his or her direct reports. That manager must be able to explain the plan and engage people in working together to improve upon the measures for it to be effective. If she doesn't understand it, she can't explain it. If he can't explain it, he can't own it. If managers don't own it, they will not be able to use it to everyone's advantage. The immediate managers should introduce the plan to their direct reports.

- *Keep it simple.* This does not mean make the plan simple. Plans may need to be somewhat complex to be effective. But when introducing a plan, simplicity is important. Answer the most basic questions: How does the plan work? What can you earn? What can you do, with others in the team or organization, to affect the measures? How can management help? All the details and intricacies of the calculations can wait. The messages need to be clear and people need time to absorb them.

- *Allow people to become engaged.* Employees can make a significant contribution if given the chance. Part of any plan is deciding how to get involved, both within their specific jobs and as members of the greater organization. Barriers to engagement ("You're just too critical to this job to give you any time to work on the cost reduction team") are counterproductive.

- *Communicate the plan again and again and again.* Successful plans are continually reintroduced though written communications, newsletters, and meetings. In addition, education in business literacy, progress on the plan's measures, and examples of what people are doing to make a contribution constitutes the backbone of a communications plan.

- *Get feedback on how's it going.* Employee surveys, focus groups, management interviews, and data reviews should happen regularly. They tell you what needs to be emphasized, where your successes are, and where you need to put in additional effort. If you wait until the end of the plan period, it is too late.

- *Do a formal evaluation that determines each plan's future.* Entitlements are expensive and they are created when plans are not doing their job. Plans should be evaluated for effectiveness and decisions to continue, adjust, or terminate are made based on that evaluation. The evaluation process should be announced when the plan is announced, so everyone knows it is a business strategy that must be adjusted with the needs of the organization.

There are no silver bullets. There is good will, faith in the value of employee contributions, good business judgment, and a willingness to act on a strategy of teamwork reinforced by rewards and recognition plans. We've learned how to manage financial, fiscal, and customer capital. Leveraging human capital is the challenge for the next century. Reward and recognition plans designed to encourage teams and teamwork is one way to meet that challenge.

BIBLIOGRAPHY

Belcher, J. G. *Results-Oriented Variable Pay System.* New York: AMACOM, 1995.

Case, J. *Open-Book Management: The Coming Business Revolution.* New York: Harper-Collins, 1995.

Case, J. *The Open-Book Experience: Lessons from Over 100 Companies Who Successfully Transformed Themselves.* Reading, Mass.: Addison-Wesley, 1998.

Handy, C. *The Age of Unreason.* Cambridge, Mass.: Harvard Business School Press, 1989.

Hargrove, R. *Masterful Coaching.* San Francisco: Jossey-Bass, 1995.

Kerr, S. *Ultimate Rewards: What Really Motivates People to Achieve.* Boston: Harvard Business School Press, 1997.

Lawler, E. E. *Strategic Pay: Aligning Organizational Strategies and Pay Systems.* San Francisco: Jossey-Bass, 1990.

McAdams, J. L. *The Reward Plan Advantage: A Manager's Guide to Improving Business Performance Through People.* San Francisco: Jossey-Bass, 1996.

McAdams, J. L., and Hawk, E. *Organizational Performance and Rewards: 663 Experiences in Making the Link.* St. Louis: CARS, 1997 (314-454-1776).

Milkovich, G., and Newman, T. *Compensation.* Chicago: Irwin, 1996.

Nelson, B. *1000 Ways to Reward Employees.* New York: Workman, 1994.

Parker, G. M. *Cross-Functional Teams: Working with Allies, Enemies, and Other Strangers.* San Francisco: Jossey-Bass, 1994.

Parker, G. M. *Team Building Workshop Facilitator's Guide.* Tuxedo, N.Y.: Xicom, 1997.

Parker, G., and Kropp, R. P., Jr. *50 Activities for Team Building.* Amherst, Mass.: HRD Press, 1994.

Scholtes, P. R., and others. *The Team Handbook.* Madison, Wis.: Joiner Associates, 1988.

Stack, J. *The Great Game of Business.* New York: Doubleday, 1992.

Stewart, T. A. *Intellectual Capital: The New Wealth of Organizations.* New York: Doubleday, 1997.

Tuckman, B. W. "Developmental Sequence in Small Groups." *Psychological Bulletin,* 1965, *63*(6), 384–399.

Wilson, T. B. *Rewards That Drive High Performance: Success Stories from Leading Organizations.* New York: AMACOM, 1999.

INDEX